Alexander Werth (1901–1969) was a Russian-born British writer and war journalist. He was the BBC's correspondent in the Soviet Union from 1941 to 1945, and the *Guardian*'s correspondent in Moscow from 1946 to 1949. He was one of the first outsiders to be allowed into Stalingrad after the battle and wrote several books describing his experiences.

'Alexander Werth was one of the greatest war correspondents of World War II and his descriptions of Leningrad under siege are as powerful today as when they were first published.'

–Antony Beevor

'Werth was the best outside observer of wartime Russia. Astute, independent-minded, a superb writer and not least a native Russian-speaker, he saw through the propaganda to the heart of the country like no other.'

–Anna Reid

LENINGRAD 1943

INSIDE A CITY UNDER SIEGE

ALEXANDER WERTH

Introduction by Nicolas Werth

Published in 2015 by I.B.Tauris & Co. Ltd
6 Salem Road, London W2 4BU
175 Fifth Avenue, New York, NY 10010
www.ibtauris.com

Distributed in the United States and Canada Exclusively by Palgrave Macmillan
175 Fifth Avenue, New York, NY 10010

ISBN: 978 1 78076 872 4
eISBN: 978 0 85773 502 7

A full CIP record for this book is available from the British Library
A full CIP record is available from the Library of Congress

Library of Congress Catalog Card Number: available

Printed and bound in Sweden by ScandBook AB

Contents

List of Illustrations

Preface

This book was originally intended to be merely a chapter in a much longer book on the war in Russia but many months may elapse before this longer book is completed and I felt, even before Leningrad was finally liberated in January, that the story of that city should be told by itself.

Leningrad holds a peculiar place in the Russian war. Its story can scarcely be regarded as a cross section of the war as a whole. It had during those 29 months of the blockade and semi-blockade a mass of military, organisational and human problems peculiar to itself. On the other hand, there were numerous aspects of the war in Russia not to be found in Leningrad. It is not without significance that during the blockade, and even after the blockade was partly broken, people in Leningrad should have continued to distinguish between 'Leningrad' and the 'mainland.'

When I was in Leningrad in September 1943, many people foretold that Leningrad would be liberated by a drive of the Red Army to the Baltic from Nevel or Vitebsk. They said so with a touch of regret and apology. One understood their feelings. And today one feels that there is a great poetic justice in the fact that Leningrad should have been liberated not from outside but by its own troops, the troops of the Leningrad front.

Leningrad has a large share in Russia's glory, but it has also a human greatness peculiarly its own. In Leningrad soldiers and civilians – and by civilians I mean men, women and children – were more completely united in their struggle and their fate than anywhere else, with the possible exception of Sebastopol.

Two things encouraged me to write this book. I am the only British correspondent to have been in Leningrad during the blockade, and the greater part of this book is a record of all I saw and heard in Leningrad during my visit last autumn. That visit will remain to me one of my three or four most memorable wartime experiences. A few pages are added on my more recent visit in February 1944. Secondly, Leningrad (though it was then called St. Petersburg) is my native city. I lived there till the age of sixteen – those early days are described in the preface to my book *Moscow '41* – but even now, after an absence of more than 25 years, I knew every street corner, and the stones of Leningrad had more meaning to me than those of any other town except perhaps London and Paris.

In this book I have recorded in detail what I saw and heard, but refrained from drawing too many conclusions. Let the details in their cumulative effect speak for themselves.

In conclusion I would like to record my gratitude to Mr. Molotov for having authorised my September visit to Leningrad, to Sir Archibald Clark Kerr, H.M. Ambassador in Moscow, for his encouragement and help, to the Press Department of the Foreign Affairs Commissariat for having arranged the visit, to my friend Dangulov and Lieutenant-Colonel Studyonov for their hard work and their good company during those days, and finally to all the people in Leningrad who in difficult conditions gave me so generously their time and their hospitality. The names of most of them will be found in the narrative that follows.

Outside Russia I wish to thank the Editor of the *Sunday Times* for kind permission to reproduce here some of the material previously published in that journal, and my warmest thanks go to my friend Leonard Russell for having agreed in my absence to see the book through the press.

A. W.

Moscow, February 1944

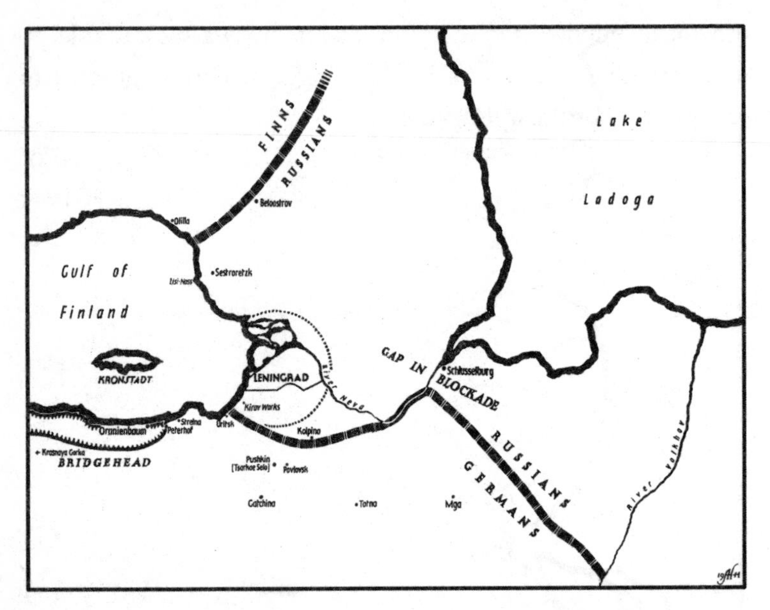

Map of Leningrad and surrounding region, 1943

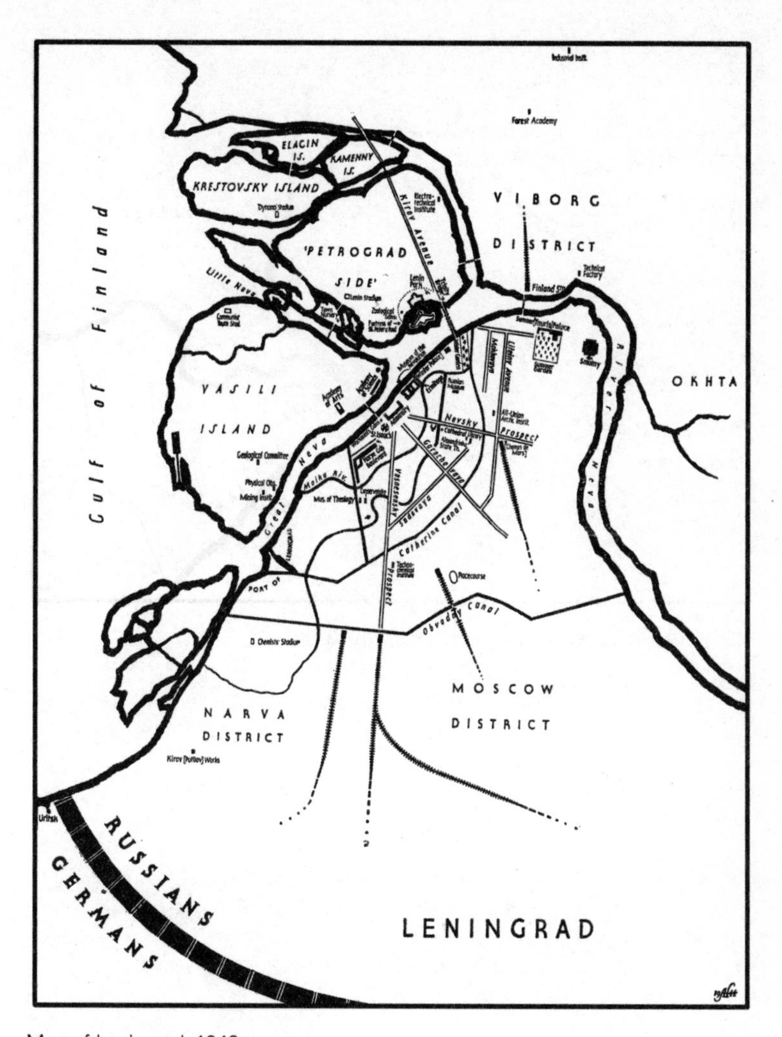

Map of Leningrad, 1943

Introduction

by Nicolas Werth

On 24 November 1942, His Britannic Majesty's Ambassador, Sir Archibald Clark Kerr, put the following request to Vyacheslav Molotov, the People's Commissar for Foreign Affairs: 'authorise the British war correspondent Alexander Werth to come to Leningrad to compose a piece on the city and its heroic defenders, which would be of global significance.' A few days later, Molotov replied in the negative: 'At present, we cannot authorise Alexander Werth to visit Leningrad. We are trying to keep the sufferings endured by the inhabitants of Leningrad from becoming too widely known. Until now, these sufferings have only been portrayed in a very biased fashion in the press and in newsreels.'

Alexander Werth was thus obliged to wait almost a year before, in September 1943, he finally received authorisation to come to Leningrad. Beginning in January 1943, a successful Red Army counter-offensive had finally broken the stranglehold the *Wehrmacht* had had on the city since September 1941. Nevertheless, when Werth arrived in Leningrad the German lines were still only 3 kilometres from the Kirov factories in the suburbs south of the city. The devastating aerial bombardments had ceased, but

Leningrad remained a city on the front line, regularly pounded by the German artillery. The worst was over, however, for starvation was – by and large – no longer killing the inhabitants of the besieged city. Werth was the first foreign correspondent (and the first Westerner) to record what remains one of the great urban tragedies of World War II: the longest siege ever endured by a modern city, during which nearly 700,000 civilians starved to death.

In *Leningrad 1943*, first published as *Leningrad* in London in July 1944, Alexander Werth writes modestly: 'There I reported in detail what I had seen and heard, choosing to avoid drawing any general conclusions. It seems to me that the facts reported speak for themselves.' And what facts they are! Despite the restricted nature of his visit, he was able not only to 'draw out' his interviewees, but also to directly address most of the major questions which would go on to be studied by historians of the Leningrad siege – the famine, first and foremost; the survival tactics used by Leningrad's citizens during the blockade; the blunders, difficulties and successes of the operations to evacuate the civilian population; the attitude of the inhabitants, whether heroism, stoicism, resignation or despair; propaganda and methods of population control; and the relations between the military and civil populations in a city on the front line.

Twenty years later, Werth would return at length to the tragedy of Leningrad, this time with a historian's detachment, in his seminal work *Russia at War, 1941–1945*, the first complete history of war on the Eastern Front, which was published in 1964.[1] *Leningrad 1943* remains first and foremost an eyewitness account. Werth tries to come to an understanding of why and how the people of Leningrad held fast, to 'explain, beyond words like solidarity, patriotism, self-sacrifice [...] the epic of Leningrad'. However, for Werth, this visit to the battered, steadfast city was also an emotional reunion with his place of birth, abandoned 26 years earlier, in 1917, on the eve of the October Revolution, as well as a chance to rid himself of the spectre of St Petersburg. At the end of his first day in the city, having searched in vain for his childhood home, he insightfully observes that 'Leningrad stood before me. As for Petrograd, St Petersburg [. . .] that was now only history and literature – and nothing more.'

Alexander Werth was born into a well-off family of industrialists of German origin who had lived in St. Petersburg for several generations. His father, Adolf Werth, was both a captain of industry and a senior official in the Ministry of Communications, one of those businessmen convinced of the need for state intervention to kick-start the economy of a country which, although rich in resources, still lagged behind in development. Intimately connected in the political circles of the Constitutional Democratic Party, he had the good sense to leave the country a few weeks before the Bolsheviks seized power in October 1917, setting up home in Glasgow, where his son attended university. After receiving a degree in journalism, Alexander Werth started work at the *Manchester Guardian*, becoming its Paris correspondent in the 1930s. From there, he monitored French politics closely, wrote many notable pieces predicting a serious crisis of French democracy in the face of the rise of Nazism, and became involved in the anti-Munich Agreement faction.

He was still posted in Paris when war broke out, witnessing the French defeat in May–June 1940, which he recorded and analysed in a short book published in London – having escaped at the last moment by boat via Bordeaux – under the title *The Last Days of Paris: A Journalist's Diary*.[2] A well-regarded journalist with fluent Russian, Werth immediately emerged as the obvious candidate to cover the war in the East following the German invasion of the Soviet Union on 22 June 1941. On 1 July, as a correspondent for the BBC and the *Sunday Times*, he set off in a plane taking members of the British military mission to Moscow, led by General MacFarlane. After a 16-hour flight via the Shetland Islands, he landed at Arkhangelsk. From there, the British delegation was taken by plane – this time, a Soviet one – onward to Moscow. Werth would remain in the USSR as a correspondent for nearly seven years, until May 1948. Like all foreigners posted to Moscow, except diplomats, he was based at the Hotel Metropol. It was right next door to the Kremlin, yet from the start he was frustrated by the dearth of information about what was happening at the front and by the restrictions placed on the movement of foreign journalists.

Thanks to his perseverance and easy manner, however, he managed to gain access to the front several times: to the region of Smolensk in September 1941 where, for the first time since 22 June, Soviet troops had managed to contain the lightning advance of the Wehrmacht; to Stalingrad in January–February 1943; and, in September 1943, to Leningrad. In March 1944, he covered the Soviet advance into Ukraine; at the start of August 1944, he was the first Western war correspondent to enter the Nazi extermination camp at Majdanek, discovered ten days before by a Red Army unit on 23 July 1944. At once, he sent off a long report to the BBC in which he described the gas chambers and the methods of mass extermination of the Jews. The BBC refused to broadcast his first-hand account. 'Not credible. A Soviet propaganda operation, a set-up. You have been tricked,' was the response of the BBC directors. They began to grow openly suspicious that their correspondent, who since 1942 had proven a tireless advocate of the opening of a second Western Front, and thus a supporter of the Soviets' chief demand, was too 'Russianised', even 'Sovietised'. In spite of this, Werth's weekly programme, *Russian Commentary*, which was broadcast on the BBC at nine o'clock in the evening on Sundays after the news, and was the only regular programme concerning the Eastern Front, was a huge success.

To better contextualise and illuminate Werth's remarkable account of September 1943, I think it opportune to briefly go over a few points regarding the history of the siege of Leningrad. In what circumstances was the town ensnared at the end of the summer of 1941? What do we now know about the dreadful famine which, during the winter of 1941–1942, decimated the population of the city? What have we learnt from recent studies – and there have been many since the opening up of state archives which followed the collapse of the Soviet regime – concerning the everyday life of the people of Leningrad during the siege, their strategies for survival, the way in which the local authorities handled the crisis, the state of mind of the population, the 'hidden' (and sometimes extraordinarily bleak) face of the siege of Leningrad?

Operation Barbarossa, developed by the Wehrmacht General Staff, dictated that four army groups would lead the Blitzkrieg against the USSR and force the Red Army to capitulate before the winter of 1941. The Finnish group, commanded by General Dietl and the Finnish Marshal Mannerheim, was to take Murmansk and the White Sea coast. The Northern group, commanded by General von Leeb, was to advance on Leningrad. The Central group, the most significant, led by General von Bock, was to march on Moscow. Lastly, the Southern group, directed by General von Rundstedt, was assigned to occupy Ukraine. As it had done elsewhere, the German advance on Leningrad moved with lightning speed. In two weeks the Soviet armies of the 'north-west axis', commanded by Marshal Voroshilov, a member of the Politburo and one of Stalin's intimates, were routed in the Baltics.

On 8 July, the German forces occupied Pskov, 200 kilometres from Leningrad, whilst the Finns advanced at a slower pace through the north-west, towards Petrozavodsk, on Lake Onega. In an attempt to slow the German advance on Leningrad, the authorities organised a mass levy of civilians. It must be said that, more than in any other Soviet town, tens of thousands of Leningrad's inhabitants – men (those ineligible for military service), women and youths – voluntarily came to the defence of their city, from the very first days of the conflict. Some of them formed auxiliary battalions, assembled in haste and soon despatched to the front, where they were decimated in their first engagements with German forces. The majority of the volunteers, however, were assigned to dig trenches and anti-tank ditches, to plant barbed wire, and to build fortifications and bunkers. By August, more than half a million citizens of Leningrad were busying themselves constructing three lines of defence, two of them directly outside the city.

When the German troops launched their 'final offensive' on Leningrad, on 10 August, the situation became catastrophic, and within a few weeks the city was surrounded. To the south-west, the first line of defence on the Luga River was quickly broken. On 21 August, the rail line between Moscow and Leningrad was severed when the Germans took the town of Chudovo. One week later, they took Mga and thus the final rail link between Leningrad and the rest of the country was cut off. To the south the situation was no less desperate for the Soviets, who managed nonetheless to retain a foothold at Oranienbaum once the Germans reached the Gulf of Finland. At the same time, further to the east, the German troops had arrived as far as the southern bank of Lake Ladoga and taken Schlüsselburg. At the end of August 1941, the Germans could therefore reasonably expect to launch an attack on Leningrad soon.

It was in this context of extreme peril that Voroshilov, Zhdanov, the Communist Party secretary of Leningrad, and Popkov, the president of the City Soviet, issued their famous call to the people of Leningrad, often referred to in Werth's account. This call on the people to defend the city alerted the citizens – who, like the rest of the Soviet population, had received no information concerning the scale of the defeat of the Red Army – to the gravity of the situation. By now it was too late to leave the city, which had been the target of German air raids since 4 September. The raids on 8, 9 and 10 September had been particularly violent and had sparked many fires, most notably striking the fuel and resupply depots near the port. At this critical juncture, the authorities briefly considered abandoning the entire city south of the Neva and concentrating the resistance in the northern districts. On 13 September, Merkulov, the NKVD (secret police) second-in-command, arrived from Moscow bearing a top-secret mandate from the State Defence Committee instructing the Leningrad authorities to blow up bridges, factories and public buildings deemed strategic in the event that the enemy should break through the final line of defence in the southern suburbs of the city.

Two days later, General Zhukov had been put in charge of the Leningrad front. Replacing the hapless Voroshilov, against the odds he succeeded in securing the front line a few kilometres south of the city, which nonetheless remained cut off from the rest of the country, except for the hypothetical possibility of communication via Lake Ladoga. It appears that, by this point, Hitler and the German high command had already decided not to attempt to take the city by force, but to starve it out. As General Jodl acknowledged at the Nuremberg Trials, the Germans had no intention of occupying the town, much less of feeding the survivors. Leningrad, the cradle of Bolshevism, must simply be razed to the ground, and its inhabitants perish of hunger.[3]

Hitler's plans did not come to fruition, but nearly one in three of Leningrad's remaining inhabitants would die of hunger during the winter of 1941–2. At the beginning of September, when the city was first surrounded and all rail links cut off, the supply situation was already dire. The speed of the German advance had caught out the authorities, who had not instituted a ration card system until 18 July, 27 days into the war. Besides this, other catastrophic mistakes had been made in the panic of the first weeks of war; namely, thousands of tons of supplies from the Baltic states invaded by the Germans had been evacuated by the Soviets to the East and not towards Leningrad. The city's provisions barely stretched to 35 days' worth of wheat and flour, 30 days of meat and 45 of fat. To try to conserve these meagre reserves, daily rations were reduced on three occasions between 2 September and 13 November 1941. For those included in the 'first category' (labourers, factory workers, engineers), the daily bread ration went from 600 to 300 grams per day. For white-collar workers and other professionals (second category), it went from 400 to 150 grams; for 'inactive adults' (third category) and children under 12, from 300 to 150 grams. These rations, meagre though they were, could not stretch the provisions out for very long.

Ersatz products were widely used – bread was padded with cellulose, specially treated cotton paste, and soya. Other unappealing substitutes were dreamt up, such as the 2,000 tons of sheep's entrails discovered by chance in the port district and transformed into a jelly intended to replace meat. Trying to relieve the pressure, the authorities arranged – with some hesitation, after the fiasco of a preliminary evacuation of children, who in July were sent to areas south-west of Leningrad which were then promptly occupied by the Germans – for the evacuation of some 'priority' citizens: skilled workers from strategically important armament factories, the scientific and intellectual elite, and relatives of the *nomenklatura*.

During the autumn of 1941, 70,000–80,000 people were evacuated (barely 3 per cent of the 2.5 million citizens caught in the siege), half by plane, and the rest by boat across Lake Ladoga. The lake became the 'Road of Life', also used to bring in some paltry supplies to the besieged city. At Osinovets, a small port was hastily constructed which, by the end of September 1941, could receive a dozen supply boats per day. This line of communication, however, was constantly under threat of attack by German aeroplanes based around 40 kilometres south of the lake. In reality, the quantities of provisions brought across this route were absurdly insufficient for the requirements of the population – in two months, the besieged city received a mere 24,000 tons of flour and cereals and 1,100 tons of meat and dairy products, which added up to 20 days of starvation rations. The early onset of winter prevented navigation on the lake from the beginning of November.

The only remaining mode of communication with the outside world was by air; however, resupplying by this method quickly proved inefficient and even fewer provisions reached the city. From 22 November, though, the lake was again traversable due to the thick layer of ice which had formed upon it. The only difficulty presented by the 'Ice Road' was bringing the supplies over terrible roads from the Vologda–Leningrad railway line, which passes around 20 kilometres south of the lake, up to the lake's edge, and from there across the frozen and snow-covered lake to Osinovets, linked by rail to Leningrad. But on 9 November, the Germans seized Tikhvin, severing the Vologda–Leningrad line. For a month, until the Soviet troops retook Tikhvin, the 'Road of Life' was cut off. On 20 November, the ration allowances were reduced for the fifth time: 250 grams of bread for those in the 'first category', 125 grams for everyone else. Other ration coupons – for meat, dairy products, fats and sugar, at the rate of a few dozen grams per day – were honoured only rarely, and after long hours of waiting, beginning in the night, outside empty shops.

From the second half of November, the number of deaths caused by 'nutritional dystrophy' – a euphemism used by the administration to refer to death by starvation – skyrocketed. For the last decade, the deadly famine which struck the inhabitants of Leningrad during the blockade has been the subject of several studies, by both Russian and Western historians.[4] Amongst the questions addressed, that of the number and social status of victims of the blockade looms large, and various differing estimates have been offered since the 1960s.[5] This task is made particularly difficult for several reasons: for one, the administrative divisions upon which the census was based in the 1930s do not entirely correspond to the borders of the city during the siege; for another, the military and civilian statistics are difficult to differentiate – in the besieged city, administrative bodies tended to become enmeshed, counting both civilian and military victims. Nevertheless, certain sources have proved to be invaluable, notably the ration cards which were distributed to all residents during the latter half of July 1941, and thus offer a relatively exact estimate of the total population of the encircled city. The 'card statistics' should, however, be approached with caution. Not all the cards were distributed by the same organisation, meaning there are likely to be duplicates, as well as numerous instances of fraud involving the cards of dead or evacuated people whose death or departure had not been duly registered (30,000 wrongfully used cards were confiscated during the winter of 1941–1942). The most reliable source, in all likelihood, remains the civil records which the authorities continued to maintain, often in the places with the highest concentration of deaths, such as hospitals. Nonetheless, a number of deaths – experts estimate between 10 and 15 per cent – went unreported.

Comparing all of these sources, today historians estimate the number of Leningrad residents who died during the most intense period of the siege, between September 1941 and July 1942, to be around 650,000–700,000 (a mortality rate 15 times the peacetime average). Close to one in three of the city's inhabitants caught in the blockade died, the vast majority from hunger and exhaustion, with victims of artillery strikes and bombing raids representing only 2 or 3 per cent of total civilian losses. The worst months were the winter months, particularly vicious that year (with temperatures dipping below 20°C for several weeks in a row in December and January). In December 1941, 54,000 deaths were recorded (that is, 13 times more than during a normal winter month), 127,000 in January, 123,000 in February, 98,000 in March, 66,000 in April. The torture of hunger was compounded by the cold. The only form of fuel was wood gathered by teams of woodcutters (the majority of them women), whom the city authorities tasked to cut down trees in the city's parks (with the notable exception of the famous Summer Garden, as Alexander Werth noted). Frugally parcelled out by block committees, the wood supply was still quickly exhausted. As to the distribution of electricity and gas, the supply was shut off from mid-November for private citizens. The city was plunged into darkness. Only a few official buildings, centres of civil defence and a limited number of administrative buildings, continued to be illuminated for a few hours per day.

The cold snap which took hold at the beginning of December caused pipes to burst in some unheated buildings, depriving residents of drinking water. As captured by Mikhail Trakhman in his gripping photographs, in the city centre citizens were reduced to boring holes in frozen canals or the Neva to extract murky water. From mid-December onwards the power shortage meant that even the city's most important firms, such as the Kirov factories, were forced to slow and even halt production. The city's chief mode of public transport, the tram system, ceased to operate, obliging the city's inhabitants to walk miles on foot to get to work or to the few-and-far-between bread distribution points, where endless queues numbering hundreds began to form from four o'clock in the morning. With a fuel shortage forcing almost all motor traffic to a halt, the sledge became the principal mode of transport for those unable to walk, pulled by those who still had the strength. Sledges were used to bring sufferers of 'dystrophy' to hospital, but also to take cadavers to cemeteries. Any hope of an end to this desperate situation rested in three possible solutions: break the siege with a counter-offensive; evacuate as many civilians as possible; or get more supplies and raw materials into the city.

In mid-December 1941, an attempt at the first of these solutions failed for want of troops, the chief priority of the Red Army high command at that moment being to drive the Germans as far from Moscow as possible. The second proposed solution took some time to implement. After a botched attempt at the start of December, when the authorities seemed convinced that the siege would soon be lifted in the wake of a Red Army counter-strike, a large-scale evacuation of children, pensioners, the 'idle', and mothers began during the second half of January 1942. Between 22 January and 15 April, more than 450,000 people were evacuated in motorised convoys across the frozen Lake Ladoga. The losses sustained were not inconsiderable – German planes bombarded the convoys, claiming many lives – and even amongst those who survived the crossing, some were so weakened that they would perish shortly after reaching Vologda, the first stop out of Leningrad.

A second wave of evacuations, this time conducted by boat, started up in mid-May 1942 after several weeks of forced inaction caused by the thawing of Lake Ladoga. During that summer, more than 500,000 additional civilians were evacuated, most of them women, children and the elderly or infirm, relieving some of the pressure on those left behind. By September, only 800,000 people remained, less than a third of the population at the beginning of the siege a year before. The city's evacuation committee had fulfilled its objective to 'turn Leningrad into a front-line city with only a core population of productive and economically independent citizens'. The third priority in order to hold out and save the civilian population was to bring in food and raw materials.

After Tikhvin was retaken by the Red Army on 9 December 1941, it took several more weeks to repair the railways, which had been damaged by the Germans, to the point where supply convoys could approach the besieged city by train. They went as far as Voibokalo, and from there were taken in trucks over bad roads and the frozen river as far as Osinovets, and from there to Leningrad. Uncertain and dangerous though it was, the 'Road of Life' allowed for a small but vital supply of food to reach the civilian population. On Christmas Eve 1941, after five successive reductions of rations, the authorities introduced the first increase – those in the first category saw their bread ration rise from 250 to 350 grams, while all other categories went from 125 to 200 grams. A month later the ration allowance rose again slightly, to 400 grams and 250 grams respectively.

Fifty additional grams per day could not hope to reverse their physical deterioration, and so the effect of the increased allowance was largely on the morale of the besieged citizens. In reality, however, during these ferocious winter months only ration stamps for bread (although this ought to be placed in inverted commas, so common were *ersatz* substitutes) were being honoured, and only after long hours of queuing at distribution points. Distribution of other foodstuffs theoretically included in the ration allowances remained irregular and sporadic until at least March 1942. Even though January and February saw a third increase of the food allowance (on 11 February, daily bread rations went up by 50 to 100 grams depending on category), the death rate reached its peak in these months. Several recent studies have shown that during the winter, death stalked the male population in particular, regardless of age. The deaths were often caused by sudden cardiac arrest, striking down victims in the street (police records show that nearly 5,000 corpses were picked up in January and February alone), at work or at home. Many of those that Alexander Werth spoke to mentioned this type of death.

Beginning in the spring this tendency reversed, and women – who during the wintertime had seemed to fare better – began dying in greater numbers, although the overall death rate fell sharply from April–May onwards (43,000 deaths were reported in May, 25,000 in June, 15,000 in July and 7,500 in August) as the decline in population led to increased availability of food for those still alive.[6]

Alexander Werth's book sheds light on the numerous survival strategies adopted during the siege, not only by ordinary people, but also by heads of industry and even the municipal authorities. In a short space such as this – for to do the subject justice would mean citing whole chunks of the wrenching private journals kept by many residents trapped by the blockade – how can one possibly convey what the great Leningrad poet Olga Bergholz called the 'tactics of micro-existence'?

> The tactics of micro-existence are what keep us alive – drawing a bucket of water on Gorokhovaya Street, then counting each step our cotton-clad legs climb to get home, then warming a dishwater stew over a bundle of sticks, then sucking on our crust of bread for as long as possible – behold all there is to distract us and save us from our thoughts, our feelings and, for many of us, keep us from insanity.[7]

Leaving the private domain to discuss survival strategies in a more objective sense, the most immediately obvious one is the decision to turn all of the city's green spaces and industrial wasteland into farmland. From the spring of 1942 onwards, they became vast vegetable gardens. The distribution of the plots was the cause of much frenzied haggling, which prioritised the most needy (hospitals, orphanages, nursery schools) but was also open to exploitation through the system of connections and privileges established before the war, meaning that large, strategically significant firms were left far better off than smaller companies deemed less important.

Under the blockade the collectives – whatever form they took – generally provided an invaluable support network. As long as a citizen could manage to get to school, to work or to their institution or factory, he or she could hope to gain some small advantages (even if this meant nothing more than a little heating, some medicine or a pale imitation of a collective canteen) from membership in the right work group, institution or organisation. Naturally, some support networks were more effective – when it came to the famine, some citizens of Leningrad were more equal than others.

As we have previously seen, individual entitlements were divided into categories. It should be remembered that this system was put into action in the 1930s, when the catastrophe of forced collectivisation of farmland and the eradication of private enterprise left the government with no choice but to introduce ration books (which remained in use until 1935), assigned according to a complex 'hierarchy of consumption'.[8] Those who contributed directly to production, whether labourers, manufacturing workers, supervisors or engineers, were better provided for than those working in offices or in administration. Other, less publicised factors also came into play, however, meaning that members of the *nomenklatura* and political, economic, scientific and intellectual elites benefitted from numerous unofficial privileges, including supplementary food parcels, private dining halls and otherwise inaccessible luxury goods.

Even now we know relatively little about how this privilege system functioned under the blockade. What is clear, however, is that certain employers could offer their workers a better chance of survival. It is hardly surprising to note that employees of the Baltika factory, which provided the city with bread, had a mortality rate three times lower than that of the general population, or that almost everyone employed by the factory which produced margarine survived the siege.

In both cases, the remarkable rates of survival can be attributed to smuggling – on both a small and large scale – and surreptitious siphoning off of supplies.[9] In general, despite working 11-hour days when the factories were operating at full capacity, factory work offered several advantages in addition to automatic placement in the 'first category' of rationing allowance. Many factories had access to supplies of raw materials which could be eaten in these extreme circumstances, such as industrial casein, albumin and dextrin. The most important and strategically significant firms, those contracted to work for the Ministry of Defence, could also make use of their close connections in the military to secure some of the prioritised provisions destined for the army. They also boasted their own fully equipped dormitories close to the factory sites (sparing workers the burden of commutes on foot), infirmaries and canteens where a bowl of hot stew could always be procured to accompany the bread ration, which – another not inconsiderable advantage – was distributed in the factory, rather than after long hours of queuing in the street in the freezing cold.

The famished citizens of Leningrad also had recourse to other methods, illegal but overlooked by the authorities – specifically, the black market. The famous Sennaya Square returned to its roots as a marketplace, becoming the hub of illegal traffic. Anything could be parted with for a little food, according to an exchange rate that rose and fell in accordance with current shortages. In the winter of 1941–1942, a fur coat could be exchanged for a pound of bread, a Persian carpet for two 25-gram bars of chocolate, and a gold watch for five or six potatoes. Whilst tens of thousands of the city's inhabitants were dying of hunger, a small minority were making a killing.

'Not All Were Brave' – this was the title given by Harrison Salisbury to one of the chapters of his monumental study of the siege of Leningrad, published in 1969.[10] Since then, several studies have explored a hidden side to the epic of Leningrad, one that is murky and sometimes appalling. The most notable of these is probably Nikita Lomagin's *Neizvestnaïa Blokada* (*The Unknown Blockade*),[11] using information gleaned largely from top-secret Leningrad NKVD reports, which were forwarded every week to Communist Party top brass and the Moscow NKVD. These reports presented an analysis of the general mood of the city's residents, but also contain precise details regarding supplies, the fluctuating death rate, crime levels, 'hostile demonstrations and anti-revolutionary actions' and any abnormal behaviour, most particularly concerning necrophagy and cannibalism.

In the isolated city, the secret police continued to maintain its surveillance network and keep a tight grip on the population, through its agents (of whom there were more than 1,200 at the end of 1942), but especially thanks to some 10,000 'political block representatives', who were selected by the local Party and the NKVD and were authorised to carry out document inspections and searches of anyone in their block at any time of the day or night. In addition, a network of thousands of informers kept the NKVD abreast of general morale in the city, carefully noting and passing on any subversive remarks they heard uttered. The postal service was also monitored, and any letter found to include 'negative information' of any kind was immediately confiscated.

According to police sources, the state of mind among the populace – which had been distinguished by a sincere patriotic spirit during the first weeks of the war – began to degenerate quickly from the second half of August 1941 onwards. A growing number of citizens questioned the lack of readiness for the

German invasion and the political and strategic blunder Stalin had committed by allying himself with Hitler in August 1939.

Even worse was the widespread circulation of rumours to the effect that 'the Germans are all right, they only have it in for Jews and Communists', 'if the Germans take Leningrad, it won't be any worse than being under the Communists!', 'the Germans are too strong and our soldiers don't fight back – what do they have to fight for? The Communists have ruined our people and robbed them of everything', etc. These 'defeatist rumours' only increased over the weeks that followed, according to the NKVD files, as everyday life became harder, rationing became more severe and the German advance proved unstoppable. It was in those long queues of housewives in front of empty shops that the NKVD informers gleaned most of their examples of 'defeatist and anti-revolutionary remarks'. The theme was always similar: 'What's the point of defending the city? We are going to starve to death. If the Germans come, perhaps they will feed us. We ought to open up the city.' But to what extent are these comments representative of the population?

Any evaluation of the statistics is fraught with difficulty. A critical analysis of police records – and especially of the numbers they cite – gives the impression that these negative sentiments were very much the minority. The number of 'defeatist and anti-Soviet remarks' reported on a day-to-day basis by the NKVD's informers was, by their own admission, estimated at a few hundred (fewer than 200 at the close of September 1941, between 300 and 400 two months later). As for the proportion of letters containing 'negative information' and seized by the censors, it wavered between 2 and 6 per cent. A few dozen handwritten 'tracts' pasted around the city ('Down with the war! Down with Communism!', 'Bread and peace!'); a call for a demonstration before the Hermitage (the former Winter Palace) demanding bread on the anniversary of the huge demonstration of workers on

9 (22[12]) January 1905 that sparked off the 1905 Revolution; and three or four instances of refusal to work extra hours (involving only a few dozen female factory workers) – excluding 'defeatist and anti-Soviet sentiments and rumours', this was the grand sum of the subversive activity reported by the Leningrad NKVC during the first months of the siege. Yet, repressive measures were extreme, as shown by a report, dated 25 October 1941, listing 3,375 'anti-revolutionary elements' who had been arrested since the start of the war. Unfortunately, there is no information on the nature of the crimes committed by these 'elements', but Paragraph 1, Article 58 of the penal code ('anti-revolutionary agitation and propaganda') allowed for a very wide interpretation of 'anti-revolutionary remarks'.

The worsening situation in the besieged city and the desperate lack of food were 'deeply scarring' the population, the NKVD reported in January–February 1942, as it continued to monitor 'several defeatist remarks' ('What good is there in defending the city? We're all going to starve to death') and 'anti-Party' sentiments ('those Party and NKVD big shots aren't queuing at four o'clock in the morning – they get served hot meals in their private canteens'). By this point, however, the NKVD's priority was economic crime, violence, food theft, ration fraud and the smuggling and black markets that flourished as shortages took a tighter hold.

The judicial records speak for themselves: over 17,000 thefts were brought to court during the blockade, and over 5,000 instances of gang violence and armed robbery. And the penalties were severe – including both 'anti-revolutionary' and common law crimes, between the summer of 1941 and the summer of 1943, more than 5,000 death sentences were issued. One particularly terrible aspect of this 'dark side' of life in the besieged and famished city, which was mentioned in every report sent to Moscow by the NKVD regional chief, Kubatkin, was cannibalism and necrophagy. The first cases surfaced in December 1941. In six months, police arrested nearly 2,000 people who had eaten human flesh, hundreds of whom had first murdered their victim for this purpose. Police uncovered gangs, composed of criminals and grave diggers, who trafficked in human flesh. Instances of cannibalism were severely punished, and a third of those convicted were shot, the rest sentenced to long stretches in prison camps. Remarkably, all of those convicted of cannibalism were recent arrivals in the city, peasant men and women who had fled forced collectivisation and marginalised drifters living on the outskirts of the city. This new proletariat, the hidden face of the USSR's second city, emerged out of a decade of extreme economic and social turbulence which had defined the 1930s.

Alexander Werth, forcibly sheltered as he was during his short stay in Leningrad, obviously had no way of witnessing the dreadful reality of life under the siege. In his account, he tried first and foremost to depict the heroic resistance of the defenders of Leningrad and the unflagging patriotism of civilians as well as soldiers, and to explain why and how the citizens had 'held out', despite their desperate conditions: the cold and a food crisis which far outstripped that suffered by Londoners or Parisians. Published in London in 1944, whilst the war still raged and Nazi Germany was still far from collapse, Werth's book was intended primarily to enlighten the British – who were proud to have stood alone against the Nazis for so long, little aware of what was happening in the East – as to the courage and tenacity of their Soviet allies.

In *Russia at War, 1941–1945*, written 20 years later, Werth undertook a deeper and more refined analysis of the 'spirit of resistance' unique to Leningrad. It had arisen, he suggested, from both a 'profound attachment to their city, beloved for its great history and, to intellectuals, for its remarkable literary pedigree' and 'the great revolutionary and proletarian legacy to which the city's workers remained particularly attached'.[13] Without trying to whitewash the most horrific elements of the tragedy endured by the inhabitants of Leningrad during the siege of their city, many modern researchers studying the Leningrad blockade have come to much the same conclusions.[14]

1

Moscow to Leningrad

This time it was really definite. The Narkowindel rang me up on Thursday night, September 23rd, and told me to be at the airport at 2 p.m. the next day. They said that Dangulov would accompany me and would pick me up in his car at the Metropole.

At the airport we were joined by Colonel Studyonov, our frequent guide on front trips. Little Dangulov who had never been in Leningrad before was as excited as I was about this trip, and it was something of an anticlimax to the 'great adventure' to see him emerge a few minutes later from the airport booking office holding in his hand three Moscow–Leningrad tickets, complete with their return halves! Then after a while an airport official said 'Passengers for plane number so-and-so, come this way.' That was our plane. There were several officers travelling; a young woman with a white coat and red beret, possibly an actress, and a middle-aged woman with a little boy. It seemed a healthy sign that children should be taken to Leningrad. Shortly before the plane took off – it was a comfortable twenty-seater Douglas – there was a heated discussion between the child's mother and an airport official who charged her with taking more luggage than was allowed, and accused her of 'cheating the State.' I don't know how the discussion ended. The cargo, apart from the passengers' luggage, contained numerous packing cases and the matrix of the

Moscow Pravda, which, no doubt, was going to be printed a day late in Leningrad. All this felt surprisingly normal.

And then we took off. The idea of going to Leningrad – after nearly 26 years – was hard to take in, and since I had been told nothing about the programme, I made no attempt to visualise anything lying ahead. There is a peculiar pleasure in abandoning oneself completely to the *imprévu.* We were flying north, leaving Moscow behind us almost at once. To the left I could see, among the autumn trees, the white sugar-cake pavilion of the Khimki bathing beach. There was a cold nip of autumn in the air, and I remembered regretfully how in this cold and rainy summer I had gone to bathe at Khimki only three or four times. Now the beach was quite deserted. Then we passed over a wooded belt of *datchas,* with an electric suburban train running along some railway. Moscow was now far behind us. And as we flew out of the immediate neighbourhood of Moscow into the great spaces of the northern forests – an ocean of dark-green fir trees with here and there a patch of fluffy bright yellow birches – I remembered the same scenery the day when I flew north out of Moscow in October 1941, when the fate of Moscow and of Russia was in the balance. The Germans were already at Viasma then. Then, as now, we flew under a ceiling of heavy leaden clouds, driven on by a cold north wind, and below there was the same vast expanse of dark-green fir trees with patches of fluffy yellow birches. But what a difference! Then, this country was in mortal danger, today it was in its hour of triumph.

The girl with the white coat and the red beret was dozing, at the back of the plane the middle-aged woman was playing with her two children – another one had turned up from somewhere – and in the front seats were three men with caps, two of them with Orders of the Red Banner, who looked like engineers or factory executives. The worst of air travel is that you never get to know your fellow travellers. Dangulov, sitting beside me, was talking excitedly about the trip, and also said that 'next time we must try to go to the Caucasus together.' He is a stocky little dark-skinned Circassian, with a passion for his native Caucasus, full of Caucasian stories, and altogether very good company. One day he told me the story of his family. It belonged to one of the few hundred Moslem families who, during the Russian conquest of the Caucasus, embraced the Orthodox religion, came down from the mountains, and founded the town of Armavir in the Kuban Steppes, as a result of which they acquired Cossack privileges. Armavir was burned down by the retreating Germans early in 1943. Dangulov had been a war correspondent of the *Red Star* until earlier this year, when he was ordered to return to his old job at the Foreign Office.

It was nearly four o'clock. We were over the great forest area, somewhere east of Kalinin. The sun had come out, and over us was a blue, almost cloudless sky. The country was a greenish-brown, and in this marshland the fir trees were small and meagre. Then we flew over a string of dazzlingly blue little lakes; and then over many more miles of forest. There had been few villages on our route, but here was one at least – a large village of log huts by the side of a large blue lake, and a big white church with golden crosses glittering in the sun. By the side of the lake a herd of cows was grazing. But how thinly populated this area is between the two capitals of Russia! And small wonder, when you look at these vast expanses of marshes and forests, stretching as far as the horizon, that there should be in existence whole partisan regions in northern Russia, almost inaccessible to the enemy for lack of roads. And how depressing these endless forests of northern Russia must have been to the German invader!

Another half-hour or so, and then we flew along a wide blue river, with reedy banks, winding its way through the marshes and forests. On these marshy banks were several little log-hut villages, undamaged by war. And then we flew over the still blue waters of another lake in which were reflected the autumn tints of the red and golden trees. We were flying towards Tikhvin.

Somewhere not far from Tikhvin we stopped for half an hour at an aerodrome that looked from the air like an ordinary field. The soil was sandy, and around the airfield were tall slender pine trees. It was still sunny, but cold, much colder than in Moscow. 'Beautiful air,' I said, breathing the cold scent, of the pines. 'Rubbish,' said Colonel Studyonov, 'you're in the Leningrad Province now, and Leningrad is notorious for its foul air and filthy weather.' He was an incorrigible Muscovite, and provided the first example that day of the old rivalry between the two capitals. Three sturdy youngsters, attached in some capacity to the airfield, came up and scrounged a few cigarettes from us. 'Miserable trees,' said the colonel.

There was something pleasantly leisurely about that flight to Leningrad. We walked among the pine trees for half an hour; then we were told to take our seats on the plane, but the girl with the red beret had disappeared behind the trees and we had to wait for a few minutes till she turned up, looking slightly embarrassed. Then we took off and again flew low over miles of forest. At one point we crossed a railway – was this the Tikhvin–Vologda line? Forests, marshes, little lakes. It was from this soil – 'from the darkness of the forests, from the soft watery marshes' as Pushkin wrote – that St. Petersburg rose, 'proud and luxuriant.'

At sunset we landed at another airfield. It also looked like an ordinary field, without hangars, and with only foliage-covered netting forming camouflaged sheds for the aircraft. Around was the real north Russian scenery, with a very muddy road fringed by small fir trees and yellow birches, and a few *izbas*, some of which had been destroyed by bombs and other badly damaged. 'Where's the buffet?' said the colonel. A bearded old man pointed to a dilapidated *izba* on the other side of the road. Here, at several rough wooden tables, some people were drinking tea. We sat down at the same table as a podgy little man with a high starched collar, a tie and a tie-pin, and a little Hitler moustache. The hut must have been newly repaired. The walls of the large room were covered not with wallpaper, but with newspapers of May 1943 – the *Front Paper,* the *Red Star,* and *Pravda,* the last containing pictures of the speakers at the All-Slav meeting in Moscow – among them the Metropolitan Nikelai and Wanda Wassiliewska. This was a sort of air force canteen, but passengers of the Leningrad plane – who were all more or less privileged persons – were allowed in. And what an introduction to Leningrad – hungry, half-starved Leningrad, as some still imagined it to be! The *devushka* always bright and cheerful like all canteen *devushkas,* brought us three big mugs of very sweet tea, and with it three large slices of very black and damp rye bread, and three enormous pats of butter, nearly the size of the hunks of bread, nearly a quarter of a pound each. It was a case of eating butter and bread rather than bread and butter. No doubt this was a privileged air force canteen – but still, things couldn't be very desperate at this rate. The ceiling of the hut was made of new plywood, and on top of the newspapers pasted on the walls a poster had been pinned with a Russian soldier trampling on a swastika, beside which also lay a dead and particularly loathsome-looking Hun. Through the only glass pane in the window – the rest had been replaced by plywood – we could see the crimson sunset with the fir trees silhouetted against it. 'Pleasant evening' observed the podgy man with the tie-pin, wiping his penknife on the bread and closing it, and abandoning half his butter in the unequal struggle.

The sun had nearly set as we took off for the third time – this time for our non-stop flight to Leningrad. Again we flew over miles of dark-brown bogs and forests that now looked black in the last rays of the setting sun, and when they had faded to a faint glimmer on the horizon in front of us, everything turned dark grey, the land and the sky. We were flying very low now. Since our last landing a machine-gunner was stationed in the centre of the plane and was now looking round into the grey sky in all directions. The earth was black now, and the sky dark-grey; down below there were a few lights, and outside one house a bonfire was burning. 'We sometimes fly this stretch with fighter escort, but no fighters were available tonight,' said one of the crew. 'It's all right, though. When we fly so low, it's very difficult for them to spot us in the twilight.' The lights down below suddenly became more numerous, and we flew over a winding canal, running parallel to a coastline. 'Ladoga,' somebody said. Now, above and below, everything merged into one – a dark pearly-grey. We were almost skimming the smooth surface of the water. We could see a faint coastline before us – behind that coastline was Leningrad – and a thin line of fir forests in the south. In the distance, the red beacon of a lighthouse was signalling – was it signalling to us? And down below, in the water, were tiny little islands at regular intervals with anti-aircraft guns pointing upwards. This seemed a whole chain of little artificial islands built in the shallow bottom of the lake. Or were they floats? It was hard to make out; but one realised that here was one of those little things in the organisation of Leningrad's defence which had made the city impregnable.

And then, suddenly, the machine-gunner in the turret became very fidgety. He grabbed the machine-gun and began to twist it about, as though taking aim. There was a moment of suspense. Then he relaxed. What had happened? In the darkness he had spotted a plane flying straight at us. Later he explained what had happened. It had turned out to be another Douglas, coming the opposite way. But for a couple of seconds in the almost complete darkness, he wasn't sure.

And then we reached the opposite coast – the Leningrad coast. For several miles we flew over what looked like more forests; I strained my eyes to see the outline of the city somewhere to the left, but all was dark. Then suddenly several patches of ground were lit up, and a green flare shot up into the air – yes, a flare just like those they fire in Moscow on victory nights. The zoom of the engines began to soften, the propellers turned more slowly, and with a slight bump we landed on the patch of light. Then the lights went out again. '*Priyekhali*,' somebody remarked. 'We've arrived.'

2

First Contact

It was very dark outside, except for several cars and a bus, with their headlights half on. 'How far are we from Leningrad?' I asked. 'Not very far,' one of the crew said evasively. 'Smart work,' somebody said, 'bringing the plane in like this, through the dark. Wonderful fellows, these civilian airmen of ours. They're as nearly infallible as a man can be. Millions of miles some of them have flown, and never a hitch.' We followed a black shadow with a torch, and were taken to one of the cars. An officer with a hard face asked to see our documents. He argued with our colonel, and slowly took down all particulars in the light of his torch. Our colonel showed no impatience, and when at last we were allowed to drive off he said, 'This is Leningrad. This is the Front. They're bound to be sticky.'

At first we drove through the dark along bumpy country roads; then we reached some main road. A good deal of traffic was coming the other way, with dim headlights on. Then we came to the first houses. It was hard to distinguish them, but no sky was showing through the windows – they had not been burned out. And behind some windows there were faint streaks of light. 'It's hard to drive in the dark,' said the driver, an elderly man judging by the sound of his voice. 'It's, my fourth blackout winter.'

'Third,' I thought, and then it occurred to me that Leningrad had been in the war-zone during the Finnish war too – 1939–40 – the winter of 1940–1 alone had been completely peaceful here. The winter of the London blitz.

We drove on in silence, but everybody was straining his eyes to *see* Leningrad. There wasn't much to see. More houses, all seemingly intact, then one or two that were burned out. We were now on the outskirts of the town. Every few minutes an empty or nearly empty tramcar would come in the opposite direction. These places were still unfamiliar to me. 'Okhta,' said the driver, laconically. So that's where we were, on the eastern outskirts of the town, beyond the river. The back of beyond – the subject of an allegedly true funny story I had heard years ago about a drunk who, sticking his head from under the cover of a horse-sledge says in bewildered drunken tones to the driver: 'Driver, where have you brought me?' 'Where you told me to go – to the Vasili Island.' 'You ass,' says the drunk, 'if I had told you to drive me to Okhta, you would have driven me to Okhta, eh? I live in the Nevsky Prospect, near the Admiralty, you ass.' (If it isn't funny, try to imagine the same scene in a London taxi, and replace the place-names by say, Golders Green, Tooting and 'off Trafalgar Square' respectively.) But now Okhta had a modern unfamiliar outline – with blocks of flats and large five- and six-storey buildings. We turned right and crossed the Neva. To the right, against the dark sky, was a cluster of large buildings, with a church dome. 'There's the Smolny,' somebody said. The Young Ladies' Academy, where the Revolution was born; Lenin's headquarters in October. The seat of the first Soviet Government. Then we drove down a long avenue. 'What's this?' 'Soviet Avenue,' said the driver. For the first time I asked my ever-recurring, irritating question: 'What was it called before?' 'Suvorov Avenue,' he said. 'With the Suvorov Museum?' I asked. 'Yes, there it is,' he replied, pointing to a large unmistakably bombed-out house. 'Destroyed in

'41. Pity. I remembered the large mural painting of Russian troops crossing the Devil's Bridge on the Saint Gothard Pass during Suvorov's last Italian campaign. Funny though, to have changed 'Suvorov Avenue' to 'Soviet Avenue' – it was done during the days when Suvorov wasn't a suitable name to give a street. There were few people in the streets, but some traffic, and the trams with the dim little blue lights were still running. It was about ten o'clock. The curfew wasn't till eleven.

Kirochnaya Street, then the Liteiny Avenue – all familiar places. In the Liteiny I distinguished the tall outline of what was once the Army and Navy Club. In 1916, I had come here to hear Skriabin's *Extase* conducted by Kussevitzky. We all went frantic over it then. Tastes change. Recently in Moscow, with the *Poème de l'Extase* in the second part of the programme, I had heard an old lady say in the interval to another old lady, 'My dear, let's get away from the *Extase!*'

We turned into the Nevsky. The dim outline of the Alexandrinka was on the left, and of the Public Library, and the Gostiny Dvor, and then of the Kazan Cathedral, with its colonnade modelled after St. Peter's in Rome. And in front of us was the tall needle spire of the Admiralty.

Just before reaching the Admiralty the car stopped and our colonel stepped out and asked us to wait. He disappeared into a dimly lit doorway, with two soldiers with bayonets outside. Dangulov and I stepped out of the car and walked up and down the smooth clean pavement. We were right in the heart of Leningrad. Before us were trees, and above them, the graceful shape of the Admiralty with its needle spire. All was quiet except for an occasional tramcar that rattled past, usually quite empty, with two dim coloured lights in front, and for the sound of an occasional motor horn. Then, through the stillness of the Leningrad night a loud-speaker began to talk along the Nevsky Prospect: 'This is tonight's communiqué....' More successes in all directions. The houses on either side of the Nevsky looked dark and enormously strange, it felt like being in a great European city.

I still couldn't make out the driver's face, but his voice sounded younger than I had thought at first. 'Bad business, driving at night,' he said. 'I stick strictly to the regulations, but the militia still make a row about the headlights every time they have a chance. Them militia girls are very funny.' 'Have you been in Leningrad these last two years?' I asked. 'Yes,' he said, 'since the start. It's good to be heroes, but we could all do with a spot of ordinary quiet living. Yes, I've been through it all, me and the wife and the kid. Nearly died of hunger myself in '41. It's a lot better now; I get 600 grammes of bread. Not enough, really, considering what we Leningrad people have gone through.' 'Have you had much shelling lately?' 'Yesterday we had twenty minutes of it – the Moscow district got it. Nothing much today, though. But, my God, it used to be bad – especially a few weeks ago. They kept at it for ten days – non-stop; the damn thing went on from dawn till dusk. They're slick sons of bitches – hit the bloody tramcar stop right at the corner of the Nevsky and the Sadovaya – busiest damned street corner in the whole of Leningrad. Everybody was killed or wounded – real nightmare when you see what it looks like. Another day they hit a crowded tramcar. But it's better now than it used to be. They say it's the air force that's keeping them under control. It's easy now, and after what we have stuck, we can manage to stick the rest. It mayn't be long now.' 'Yes,' I said, 'if Smolensk and Vitebsk are taken by the Red Army, they may soon have to pull out.' 'If it happened tomorrow it would suit me all right,' he said. 'From what I've seen of Leningrad – and it isn't much – ' I said, 'there isn't as much damage as I thought. Kharkov certainly looks ten times worse.' 'Oh!' he said, sounding very sceptical, 'you'll see plenty of damage tomorrow.'

At last the dark door between the two sentries opened, letting out a faint ray of light and Colonel Studyonov came out, together with another officer. With a salute, and in very good English, he introduced himself formally, in Red Army style: 'Major Lozak, representative of the Command of the Leningrad Front.' And, turning to the driver, he said: 'To the Astoria.' We drove up the Nevsky and took the first turning to the right. 'Ah,' I said, 'Gogol Street.' 'Quite correct,' said the major. 'Wonderful,' said little Dangulov, with the tone of an impresario showing off an infant prodigy. Of course I remembered Gogol Street; it had a wonderful shop for sweets and chocolates which belonged to a Frenchman or a Swiss called Berrin. The sweets were wrapped in paper with *Berrin, Confiseur, rue Gogol, Saint-Pétersbourg* printed on them. On Christmas Eve or New Year's Eve there used to be crowds of cars and smart horse sleighs outside Berrin's, and luscious displays of sweets and *fruits confits* and chocolates in his brightly lit-up windows. Now Gogol Street was completely dark. Then the car turned a corner and we got out. We were at the Astoria. Turning round, I could see the enormous black outline of the dome of St. Isaac's. The weather had improved; there were a few stars in the sky. Major Lozak said something to a shadowy shape in the doorway and we entered the large marble-lined hall of the hotel. Oh, irony! The first thing I saw was a large notice-board: 'Ausflúge: Leningrad und seine Umgebung,' with a whole long list of excursions to Pushkin, with 'Tsarskoie Selo' added in brackets, Peterhof, Pavlovsk, etc. On the other side of the square marble pillar was a similar notice-board in English: 'Leningrad – this week's entertainments.' But opposite the names of the theatres there were now only blanks. In the far end of the hall, half-lit by green-shaded lamps, came the friendly click of billiard balls. There were some officers there, playing and commenting loudly on the shots. We were escorted by a woman up the stairs to the third floor. 'Sorry,' she said, 'but we haven't got the lift working yet.' The corridors were white and beautifully clean. It was a thoroughly modern hotel, built around 1912 by Lidvall, I think, the most fashionable architect of his day, whom the Petersburg of the 'capitalist' period had to thank for many useful, well-proportioned and never displeasing innovations. To build a modern hotel in one of St. Petersburg's most famous squares, almost beside St. Isaac's Cathedral, required great tact, and Lidvall had it – infinitely more than the Hun who built opposite it the factory-like red sandstone building of the German Embassy – that very German Embassy from whose roof in August 1914 an angry Russian crowd hurled the aggressively virile bronze Teutons and their horses into the street below. Later the crowd dragged the naked Huns across the square to the nearby Moika River, and threw them plunk into the water. At school, we liked to recall that incident in which one or two of us claimed to have taken part. But that is by the way.

It all seemed unreal. We were shown to our rooms. A supper with wine and vodka bottles had been spread out in the sitting-room. In the double bedroom I shared with Dangulov there was very good bedlinen, and a bathroom and lavatory attached, though with cold water only. The colonel took the room next to ours. An amiable old dame, wearing pince-nez and a little purple tartar cap, took charge of us. 'Let's have supper,' said Major Lozak. I could now see him clearly at last. He was young and pale, and very slim, with a regular Roman nose, his fair hair brushed back, and very pale greenish-grey eyes like the Baltic on a rainy day. He had gone right through the Leningrad blockade, and wore on his tunic the order of the Red Star and the Leningrad Defence medal with its pale-green ribbon. Later he told me a lot about himself. We started supper, and were soon joined by a new arrival, Major Likharev, with a pale, rough-hewn face and a heavy jaw. He turned out to be the president of the Leningrad Writers' Union, and had written ten books of verses, most of which, I was ashamed to say, I hadn't read. However, Comrade Likharev said that since the beginning of the war he had been engaged in war work and a large variety of 'organisational' jobs, and that he had in effect abandoned literature for the duration, apart from what he wrote for the soldiers' papers of the Leningrad front.

We had supper and then the officers went off somewhere, to discuss with some military authority the next day's arrangements. I stayed behind with Dangulov and the old dame whose name was Anna Andreievna. It was a pleasant room, with conventional but good-quality hotel furniture, a desk with the inevitable alabaster inkstand and a rack with 'Intourist' notepaper and envelopes, and on the wall a very oily oil painting of a Ukrainian village, with white thatched-roofed cottages and in front of them two girls and a cow with an abnormally large udder – no doubt a symbol of Ukrainian prosperity. Anna Andreievna was an entertaining old dame. She had lived through the whole blockade and seemed none the worse for it. I don't know why, but her conversation was slightly reminiscent of that of *la vieille*, the unforgettable Pope's daughter in *Candide*. 'I am 67 now,' she said, 'but in 1905 I was *camerista* to Prince Muraviav, the Russian Ambassador in Rome. In 1906 he died – very dramatic it was, too. He died of heart failure at the party given – that'll interest you – by the British Chargé d'Affaires. After that I became *camerista* to the Princess Borghese in Rome. Yes, sir, we used to go to Paris every year, to buy linen and lingerie at the Maison de Blanc, and *toilettes* at Worth's and Paquin's. Just the Princess and I. Stayed in the best hotel, of course, the Hotel Vendôme, do you know it? I've been here for four years now. And now that there are no waiters, I do everything.' 'Will you have a little wine, Anna Andreievna?' 'Thanks,' she said. She sipped the Russian madeira. 'It isn't quite what one was used to abroad, when I travelled about with the Princess Borghese,' she said, 'but we can't be too particular these days, can we? 'Why, you're going to make me quite tipsy,' she added with a girlish giggle. 'I'm not used to drink these days, you know.' 'Have a chocolate?' 'Thanks, if you don't mind I'll take it home.' 'Cigarette?' She liked the Lucky Strike. 'Yes,' she said, 'I love foreign cigarettes. When I lived abroad, I used to smoke Egyptian Tanagras.' I couldn't quite figure out what she had done after parting from the Princess Borghese, but for four years now she had worked at the Astoria, and for four years before that at the Hôtel d'Europe. 'I'm an old woman,' she said, 'but I'm as strong as a horse. I carried up all these dishes from the ground floor – all at one go. Didn't turn a hair.' She pointed at the huge waiter's tray on the sidetable. 'I had a son of forty-eight. I was married very young, you see. He was killed in the war – the Finnish war. Yes, sir, forty-eight; great big husky fellow he was, and very fond of his old mamma!' I asked if she'd had a very difficult time during the famine. 'Awful,' she said, 'quite awful. The Astoria looks like a hotel now – but you should have seen it then! It was turned into a hospital. Just hell. They used to bring here all sorts of people, mostly intellectuals, who were dying of hunger. Gave them vitamin tablets, tried to pep them up a bit. However, a lot of them were too far gone, and died almost the moment they got here. I know what it is to be hungry. Just awful. I was so weak I could hardly walk. I had to use a walking-stick to support me. I'd walk down the Vosnesensky to go home. My home is only about a mile away, in the Sadovaya. I'd have to stop to sit down every hundred yards; my legs just wouldn't carry me. Took me sometimes over an hour to get home.'

'It wasn't that I couldn't have lived a lot better than other people if I had wanted to,' she went on, 'but I had six people on my hands. Yes, three old women living in the same house, and a young woman with two children – her husband was at the Front. He has since been killed. And the woman herself died of pneumonia, there was nothing that could save her, because when you're run down, and there's no heating, and you worry a lot, you just die. Now one of the old women, who's her mother, has charge of the children, and the kids are fine, and we all live together.' 'Well,' I said, 'you couldn't have fed them out of your ration, could you? What were you getting during the worst period – 125 grammes of bread?' 'Yes, that's right,' she said, 'and even our Lord Jesus Christ couldn't have fed seven people on that! No,' she said, not without a touch of pride, 'since the Finnish war in which my dear son was killed, I had a feeling that we were in for more trouble before long. Oh, I *knew* it was coming. The fall of Paris, and then all that terrible bombing of London. That winter I bought a few sacks of flour, and a few other odds and ends. And wasn't I glad I had done it! I was so proud every night when I could give a little extra food to the three old women, and the two little children, and their poor dear mother, God bless her soul. You don't know what it was like. You just stepped over corpses in the street, and on stairs! You simply stopped taking any notice. It was no use worrying. Terrible things used to happen. Some people went quite insane with hunger. And the practice of simply hiding the dead somewhere in the house, and using their ration cards was very common indeed. There were so many people dying all over the place, the authorities couldn't keep track of all the deaths. Besides, if a death wasn't declared, how were they to know?' She looked at the packet of Luckys. 'May I have another of your English cigarettes? Just can't resist it! So like the dear old Egyptian Tanagras!' She puffed at it with relish. 'Oh, it's all right now,' she said.

'Now I am as strong as a horse again. Tomorrow there'll be a military banquet for 250 people downstairs; I'll have to be up all night checking the crockery and the tablelinen. I don't need any sleep – couple of hours and I'm as fit as a fiddle. But you should have seen me in February 1942. Oh, Lord, I looked funny! My weight had dropped from seventy kilos to forty-eight.

Dropped thirty kilos, in four months! Now I am back to sixty-two – feel quite plump! Now that the worst is over, I'm sure I'm good for another twenty years. I hope I may go abroad yet. I'd like to see Paris again, and Rome. Walk down that nice street – what was its name again? – yes, the Corso Umberto. Yes, I like Rome, like it better than Leningrad.' She dropped her voice. 'Just getting a little tired of Leningrad, between you and me.' Then, after pressing us to eat more, and offering to make us some hot tea – 'Oh, no trouble at all, or perhaps some nice black coffee' – for all of which we thanked her but said no. She bade us good-night, and departed balancing on one hand over her shoulder the enormous tray with the spoons and forks and bottles and dishes. A remarkable old woman, I thought. So absurdly genteel, and yet with so much character and courage. I could just see her with her pince-nez on her plump little nose, crawling through the snow along the Voznesensky, resting on her little walking-stick, and then finally reaching home, and feeding those children and old women out of her precious hoard of flour. She must have got mighty near the end of her hoard in those four months. She and her dependants were lucky to have had that hoard, luckier than thousands of others. But even *she* had lost four stone in weight. And maybe she *was* getting 'a little tired' of Leningrad now; but she had stayed on during the worst time and ever since. Because of a sense of duty? Or because of those two children and three helpless old women? Or simply because she 'belonged' to the place, as thousands of others had stayed on for precisely the same reason? And at heart she certainly liked the Nevsky far better than the Corso Umberto.

3

St. Petersburg – Leningrad

The next day was that in which I fully realised that the shell was still the same, but that this was a very different city from what I had known it to be. St. Petersburg, Petrograd had gone for ever. This was Leningrad. It had inherited many things from the other two, but it had its own substance, its own personality. Leningrad was not just a new name for St. Petersburg; it was a name that meant a hundred things that the other did not. Similarly, there were hundreds of things that belonged to St. Petersburg which could not be found in Leningrad. Perhaps this distinction was not so sharp three years ago, but today Leningrad had acquired the same distinctive personality as Stalingrad. One no more felt like calling Leningrad 'St. Petersburg' or 'Petrograd' than one felt like calling Stalingrad 'Tsaritsyn.' Perhaps, in the course of years, when thoughts of the siege and the blockade fade in people's memories, they may again colloquially refer to the city by its own name; but it was significant that throughout my stay not one person should have called the city Petrograd or St. Petersburg, though everybody without exception continued to call the principal streets and most of the others by their old names. It was always the Liteiny, and the Nevsky, and the Morskaya – never the Volodarsky Avenue, or the October Twenty-fifth Avenue, or

Herzen Street.[1] People had not accepted these artificial innovations; they had, however, accepted the city's new name – a name full of new associations. St. Petersburg now belonged to literature, and to history, but no longer to real life. And nothing convinced me more of this than the curious personal experience I had that day of revisiting the house where I had spent the first sixteen years of my life, and which I had not seen for more than a quarter of a century.

Dangulov wakened me and pulled aside the blackout curtains. There was a drizzle outside. I could see through the window, on the other side of the street, a beautiful classical baroque building, with long tall windows, rounded on top, and walls of salmon-pink stucco, and flat white semi-pillars. Funny; looking out of a window in Rome one might have seen something very similar. Europe, Europe! it occurred to me. Great French and Italian architects (who were paid fabulous sums by the Tsars and Empresses) and their Russian pupils had really given the city its essential character – this city which had grown and perhaps still remained the western half of Russia's soul.[2] Would I find any traces of 'westernism' in Leningrad today, I wondered. In the days that followed I was to find them, unmistakably.

Anna Andreievna, as bright and chatty as on the previous night, produced a sumptuous breakfast, with a lot of *zakuski,* including pickled *minogi,* a Leningrad speciality, a tough little eel-like fish which you were supposed to eat complete with its spine. The *zakuski* were followed by fried eggs and piping-hot black coffee. At the mention of *minogi* our colonel laughed heartily, and digging Dangulov in the ribs, produced a 'real Caucasian charade' which was even more untranslatable than unrepeatable. 'Didn't they teach you that one at school in Tiflis?' he laughed. Dangulov said he didn't come from Tiflis but from Armavir. To the Russian the Caucasian is what the Scot is to an Englishman, an object for friendly leg-pulling.

Then the two majors arrived, accompanied by a man called Baranov, wearing a semi-military tunic. He was the chief architect of the city of Leningrad, and was going to take us round the city and escort us to some of the places I had asked to be shown. 'It may be a good thing it's raining a bit,' said Baranov. 'They haven't started shelling us yet. They prefer clear days. But it's clearing up, so we may have some yet.' We went downstairs. Already some people, in the far end of the hall, were playing billiards. As we went out into the square in front of the Astoria, here on the right was St. Isaac's Cathedral, with its lofty granite pillars, and its St. Paul-like dome. It was the only thing that looked different – the gilt dome which one could see forty miles away from any height in Finland or from well beyond Oranienbaum, on the southern side of the Gulf, had been dimmed with dark-grey camouflage paint. And in the garden, in front of the cathedral, cabbages were now growing, and among them was an anti-aircraft gun. Opposite us was the absurd former building of the German Embassy, minus the bronze horses and the naked Huns on its roof. To the left was Klodt's equestrian statue of the wicked Tsar, Nicholas the First, he and part of his horse protruding from the tall structure of sandbags and scaffolding. The architect explained that the top part of this scaffolding was just now being renewed. And beyond, at the far end of the square, was the large Mariimsky Palace, where the 'pre-Parliament' used to meet during the last stormy weeks of the Kerensky regime. And to the side of it, straight as an arrow, the narrow Vosnesensky Prospect ran south, a street full of Gogol and Dostoievsky associations. In this street was the barber's shop in which Gogol's Major Kovalev lost his surrealist nose – that nose which he then observed on the following day, driving down the street in a coach and wearing the uniform and the cocked hat of a state councillor. How many other weird visions had risen out of the mist of St. Petersburg, out of the grey cold vapours of the Neva?

We walked round St. Isaac's Cathedral. A few of the granite pillars had been chipped by shell splinters, and the glass was broken in all the windows which were now more or less boarded up. Inside it was no longer a church but a 'museum of religion.' Would it ever be opened as a church again, I wondered, or would the museum – no longer quite conforming with the 'general line' – be put to other uses? St. Isaac's is not 'typically' Leningrad. If anything, it is in contrast with the 'native' architecture, the classical stucco buildings. Here, beyond St. Isaac's, was the real thing: to the left, the magnificent yellow stucco building of the former Imperial Senate, to the right, also in bright-yellow stucco, the massive building of the Admiralty with its wonderful single tower and its needle spire, that tall needle spire which Pushkin watched from his window on those brief summer nights, those 'white' northern nights of St. Petersburg. Even during the brief hour of darkness the point of the spire, still lit up by the last traces of the sunset and the first traces of dawn, continued to shine. In front of us was the wide breezy expanse of the grey Neva, with the Vasili Island opposite, with the University and Academy of Sciences on its Embankment, and the beautiful classical pillared building of the former Bourse, now the naval museum, on its eastern tip. And further to the right rose high into the sky the other needle spire of St. Petersburg, the spire of the Fortress of St. Peter and St. Paul which Peter the Great had built. The spire was no longer glittering, and seemed a little thicker than it should have been, 'There's quite a story attached to that,' said Baranov, the architect. 'We had to camouflage the gilt when the Germans started shelling us in a big way. And it was infernally difficult. We were passing through the worst period of the famine. When a man is hungry he turns giddy much more easily than usual, and to ask anyone to climb up the needle spire of the Fortress was to ask him to take on the giddiest job in the world. To paint the spire would have been too complicated. What we decided to do was to cover it with a long canvas case painted grey. Only who would climb up that spire? We found plenty of volunteers – here in Leningrad you can find a volunteer for anything – but we realised that the fellows were much too weak and would just kill themselves. So we picked on a few who looked less exhausted than the others, and we fed them well for three or four days – and, by heaven, they did the job.'

Somewhere in the distance the shelling had begun. We were standing in the middle of the Senate Square. To the right, where there had once been lawns, more vegetables were growing, and among these cabbage-beds were the elevated openings of dug-outs, and from among them rose a large sandbagged structure. Inside it was the greatest equestrian statue of modern times, Falconet's Peter the Great, the Bronze Horseman. It still stood there, surrounded by sandbags, on its gigantic granite rock which had been hauled with infinite labour from Lakhta, from across the Gulf of Finland, at the behest of Catherine the Great. And when, after nine years of delays, failures and quarrels, the great statue was at last completed, she ordered that the rock be simply inscribed: 'PETRO PRIMO CATHERINA SECUNDA.' Now, around the sandbagged structure, cabbages were untidily growing.

No statue had ever become so much the symbol of a great city as this, or had given men so much food for thought. To Pushkin, Peter was right to have built this strange city, which symbolised, like Peter himself, the new era of Russian history, the 'Window into Europe.' He was right, though it was built on the bones of thousands of serfs who had died in the inhuman effort of turning the swamp into an island of granite. Pushkin knew that Peter's work was ruthless, but he knew that it had to be, and that it was good and right. He loved the city's severe, graceful harmony.

During the nineteenth century the city grew – grew into a city of close on two million people. It was no longer entirely a city of

The Alexandrinka Square.

'severe, graceful harmony,' it had become a centre of trade and industry with hundreds of thousands of newcomers – of traders, and a proletariat, a city of fearful variety, full of human contrast and human conflicts and insoluble contradictions. The white mists of the Neva were blackened by the fog of factory chimneys. Instead of the crisp sunny, winter days of Pushkin came the eerie rainy autumn nights of Dostoievsky and the shadowy unreality of Blok's St. Petersburg poems. And before his death in 1909, Innokenti Annensky wrote his tragic prophecy – his poem 'St. Petersburg' – in which he spoke of Peter's 'cursèd error.' It was no longer the misty lilac St. Petersburg of Blok but a city of cadaverous yellow water, 'yellow' snow. 'And even in May, when the shadows of the white northern night are spread over the waves of the Neva, I feel no more the magic of spring, but only the poison of fruitless desires.' A 'cursèd error!' So the poet felt. Perhaps in terms of geography and economics it was even more so. From 1918 to 1921 Petrograd nearly died of hunger. Thousands died of hunger and two-thirds or more of its population scattered. The first Soviet Government moved 'temporarily' to

Baltic Fleet sentries outside the Admiralty.

Moscow. Petrograd was not only threatened with starvation, but with invasion. It was much more hungry than Moscow. Not until several years later did it become again a great city of three million people. But ten or twelve years passed, and again came invasion, and again came hunger, this time far more terrible than the hunger of the first years of the Revolution. The 'cursèd error' again?

But if so, thousands fought for this error, and died for it. And those who survived meant to persist in it. And yet, will Leningrad, sad and half-deserted and beautiful, be Russia's capital again? I asked many people that question. They all shook their heads, some of them with a faint, slightly defiant smile.

There were ships on the Neva, anchoring in midstream, or moored to the granite side of the quay, opposite the long line of small half-deserted palaces. The ships were painted grey, a few naval craft among them, but mostly former cargo ships. Were they all being used for anti-aircraft batteries? On board, sailors of the Baltic Fleet were busy doing things. Where was the rest of the Baltic Fleet? Kronstadt, perhaps. But I preferred not to ask. And how much of the Fleet was left? Even less did I like to ask that. All I knew was that the Baltic Fleet had done wonders, but that in the early days of the war, in the Gulf of Riga, and at Tallinn, it had suffered many great losses through air bombardment. Today its submarines still continued to be active in the Baltic, and the naval marines, fighting on the Leningrad front, were among the toughest Russian troops. The Germans had an almost superstitious fear of these men who were reputed to be desperate characters, who preferred knifing Germans to any other form of slaughter. In 1917, the bourgeoisie regarded the sailors of the Baltic Fleet as a new variety of *apache.*

And true enough, there were many thugs among them – like the twelve of Blok's poems – apostolic thugs which any Revolution not only produces but needs. They could look ruthless and frightening, and rather romantic. With that long forelock coming from under the sailor's cap, worn at such a rakish angle, with their tattooed chests showing above their striped blue and white jerseys, and that devilish swagger of theirs, they drove all the dishonest women of Petrograd crazy and many an honest one too.

But the Baltic Fleet today was different. Much of the old swaggering tradition was still alive, but they were highly disciplined men now, with infinite devotion and a record of courage and self-sacrifice that matched the record of their southern comrades, the sailors of the Black Sea Fleet and of the marines who fought and died at Sebastopol.

We drove in the car along the quay to the Summer Garden, over the little humped granite bridges across the Venetian-like Winter Canal and the Swan Canal, past the Winter Palace, with its now dirty-grey walls chipped by shell splinters, past the grey Marble Palace overlooking the vast Champ de Mars parade ground, now turned into a huge cabbage field. In the wide space between the Marble Palace and the building formerly the British Embassy, the residence of the last British Ambassador in Petrograd, Sir George Buchanan, stood the statue of Suvorov, clad in Roman armour after the fashion of 1800, and looking as unlike the most popular general of the Russian Army as Nelson would look his own self wearing a bowler hat. Nevertheless, the 'odd' sculptural convention was accepted by the people of Leningrad. Baranov remarked that the authorities were going to sandbag Suvorov, but the soldiers of the Leningrad front asked that this should not be done as they liked to visit the Suvorov statue when on leave.

The famous tall golden railings of the Summer Garden with the shiny granite urns on top were still much the same – those railings which an eccentric English yachtsman had come specially to see. He stepped ashore outside the Summer Garden and, having examined the railings, went aboard his yacht again fully satisfied, and sailed back to England. A favourite, if improbable, St. Petersburg story. So here was the Summer Garden, that piece of primeval forest with lime trees many centuries old, which at Peter the Great's behest a master gardener from Hanover had turned into one of the most famous parks in Europe. In the north-east corner of the garden, beside the little humped granite bridge, Peter had built himself a little house, Dutch in its simplicity. There it still was. During the first half of the eighteenth century the pleasure-loving Empresses had built grottoes and fountains in the park, and they called the little river to the east of it Fontanka, because its waters fed the fountains. Catherine had the fountains and the grottoes scrapped, and the Summer Garden then acquired its definite character – with dark leafy alleys lined by maples and the many centuries-old lime trees. Round it ran a riding path – the Rotten Row of St. Petersburg, and across it, from its pond in the south up to the Neva Embankment ran the famous main alley with its white marble statues of Diana and Apollo and other Greek gods on either side. And near the centre of the garden was the large playground for children, and here in 1855 was erected the large bronze statue of Krylov, the Russian La Fontaine, with bas-reliefs round the pedestal, illustrating his most celebrated fables known by every Russian child. The garden was full of historical and literary memories and was the scene of the first act of Tchaikovsky's *Queen of Spades.*

To me, the Letni Sad, the Summer Garden, was also full of childhood memories – for I was taken there every day for years (at first, no doubt in a pram), in spring, autumn, and even winter, when little wooden houses were put over the Greek gods and goddesses to protect them from ice and snow. But I shall not bore the reader with stories of how I built snowmen or played hide-and-seek among Peter the Great's old lime trees with playmates most of whose names I no longer even remember, and who today may, for all I know, be heroes of the Soviet Union, or white *émigrés,* or nobodies, or merely the flimsy remains of Leningraders who died in the famine.

Through the half-closed main gate on the Neva Embankment, we walked into the garden. It was the same, and yet very different. The alley of Greek gods and goddesses had disappeared. Not only the statues but the alley itself had almost vanished. The statues had been removed to safety, and much of the width of the famous alley was now being used for growing cabbages. There were cabbages everywhere – even in the shaded parts among the old trees, and naturally, over the whole area of 'Rotten Row.' These were plots that had been lent by the Town Council to hundreds of private families. It was hard to find one's bearings. We walked, however, along a narrow path which was the middle of the former main alley, with cabbage beds on both sides, and came to the children's playground around 'Grandpa Krylov.' It was astonishing: all the trees, even the centenarian lime trees, some of them propped up as before with rusty iron supports, were intact except for a few that had been shattered by shells. The truth is – and this ranks as a particularly remarkable fact – that although in the winter of 1941 thousands died of cold, nobody was even tempted to cut a tree in any of Leningrad's historic parks. Krylov still sat on his pedestal, reading his own fables. The statue had been sandbagged only half-way up. 'You see,' said the architect, 'we started on this job during the worst possible time. And people were just too weak and too hungry to finish it. And later there were more important things to do, so the job was never completed.'

The garden was almost deserted. There were few people around and there was a strange stillness everywhere, except for the distant thud of exploding shells. There was scarcely any sound of traffic, and that most familiar sound of the Summer Garden was absent – the harsh cry of the hundreds of crows that used to live on the tops of the old trees. I remembered those crows, fluttering among the bare tree-tops in the early purple twilight of St. Petersburg's winter evenings which came about three in the afternoon. There were no crows in the Summer Garden now, and one could guess their fate. No birds, and few people. Only at the far end, near the pond whose large slopes presented a curious decorative pattern of very regular carrot and cabbage beds, and with the famous granite vase sandbagged in front of it, we came across some people – half a dozen cheerful and healthy-looking little children from a children's home, accompanied by a young woman teacher, and two elderly women digging cabbages. The children joyfully surrounded our majors and insisted on playing with their medals and decorations. The shelling had by now become louder – the shells were exploding in a part of the town much nearer the centre, but nobody seemed to worry. We were now on the Moika River at the south end of the garden. On the other side of the granite-lined river rose from among the autumn trees the majestic red stucco building of the Mikhailovsky or Engineers' Castle – more a castle indeed than a palace – once the residence of Catherine's heir, the 'mad Tsar,' Paul the First. It looked all right from here, except for broken windows, but Comrade Baranov remarked that the building had been very badly damaged by a ton bomb on the other side, and that it had suffered greater damage than any other historic building in Leningrad.

We had told the driver to meet us at this end of the Summer Garden, and we then drove from here to the house where I had once lived. This was a very badly bombed area – no one could quite say why. And it all looked wretchedly shabby and deserted – the narrow Panteleimon Street running east from the Summer Garden, a street – as I knew it before – of elderly and rather nondescript large houses and smallish shops, mostly grocers' shops, bakeries, and small haberdashery and iron-mongers' establishments, and at right angles to it, the sedate and wealthy Mokhovaya. Now it all looked deserted and pitiful. Not only had all the shops disappeared – both streets, formerly so different in character, being united in the same drabness – but this was the nearest I saw in the centre of Leningrad to a blitzed area. Half a dozen houses in the Panteleimonskaya had been wrecked by large bombs and in the Mokhovaya eleven houses – all four- or five-storey buildings – had been destroyed. When we turned into the Mokhovaya, I saw the tall bay-windows of number twenty-nine, a hundred yards down the street, and the top one of these bay-windows had been my own room. It came back very vividly – the nickel bed in the corner nearest the door, and the open fireplace with a framed photogravure of the Bay of Naples above the mantelpiece, and the two large cupboards full of Russian, English, French and German books, and the desk inside the bay-window and on it a large, bronze electric lamp with its large orange shade with silk tassels. The best things in the room were a big Persian rug my father had brought back from the Caucasus, and the all-round view from the three windows round the desk – I watched from here the rioting and shooting going on during the February Revolution with excited crowds running this way and that, and one day smashing up a police station just a little down the street. The worst things in the room were the above-mentioned photogravure of the Bay of Naples, a pair of stuffed squirrels I had shot myself, and two monstrosities somebody had brought from Egypt – a stuffed baby crocodile which stank, and some sort of unusable Oriental smoking contraption made of ivory and an ostrich egg. How different from the charming collection of Japanese ivories and embroideries and Chinese paintings and wood carvings my father had bought during his five years in the Far East many years before, and which were assembled in the little yellow 'boudoir' (as it was called) next to my room. The house opposite, a plain square box of a house with dirty-yellow stucco walls, was now partly smashed by a bomb. It was notable only for the marble memorial plate outside it – Dargomyzhsky, the composer who wrote *Rusalka*, had lived here in the fifties or sixties of last century. From my window I could also see on its second floor the large shop sign, 'Rau Relieur,' French, like so many other shop signs in St. Petersburg. In the next house was another shop with, similarly in French, 'Fleurs de Nice' above it. The mysterious 'Rau Relieur' was actually an old Jew who looked like Socrates; he never managed to fill his orders in time, and, wringing his hands, he always blamed his dark, sulky daughter for what he called the 'chaos' in his bookbindery.

Number twenty-nine was part of what was known as the 'House of Russia,' 'Russia' being the name of the insurance company which owned it, and had built it in 1899. The date was still marked on the little weathercock on the roof. Number twenty-nine was composed of three large flats, each with very high ceilings which accounted for this three-storey house being as high as most other four-storey houses. On the ground floor lived some Baltic baron called Osten Sacken, and on the first floor an extremely senile former Tsarist Minister of Finance, called Timiriazev. He lived there, seemingly in great seclusion, with an old spinster of a daughter to keep him company and to play the piano to him. The top floor had been my home. Number twenty-nine was separated from number twenty-seven – which was also part of the 'House of Russia' – by a large courtyard with a garden and a big clock in the middle and separated from the street by tall iron railings and a gate. In the block at the back of the courtyard there used to live the notoriously reactionary former Minister of the Interior of the name of Durnovo. I remembered the servants referring to this wicked pillar of Tsarism with anger and derision. In number twenty-seven there used to be the Tagentsev Gymnasium, the once well-known girls' high school. My cousin, Olga, used to go to it. After the Revolution she became a doctor and a whole-hearted supporter of the new régime, and the last I heard was that she was working on the Volga during the famine of 1921. I never learned what happened to her afterwards. Rumour had it that she died of tuberculosis a year or two later at the age of twenty-four, but where or in what circumstances I was never able to discover.

It was odd to be here again. When I rationalised it, it was the same place. And yet, apart from the actual walls of the houses – and even they were grubby and shell-marked – everything was completely changed. The front door, with its brightly polished glass panes and brass handles, had gone. Efim, the middle-aged porter – the *schveitzar* – with his little goatee beard, red tubercular cheekbones and kindly smile and his little colloquialisms – he died of tuberculosis early on in the Revolution, leaving behind two small orphan boys – Efim, with his gold-braided cap and blue uniform with brass buttons, was now an infinitely distant memory. The heavy brass handles had disappeared heaven knows when, and the carefully polished little glass panes had been blasted away. The door was covered with plywood and on it a notice said 'A.R.P. Post. No access to the attic from here.'

We knocked on the door and rang probably a dead bell, but nothing happened. An elderly man going past said we should try to get in through number twenty-seven. We went past the yard with the iron railings. These also were closed. The little garden had been turned into a vegetable plot, and although the iron skeleton of the clock was still standing, the clock itself had been blown out by blast. At length we penetrated through a passage in number twenty-seven into this yard, and here a middle-aged woman, looking us up and down with great suspicion, came up. She wore a reddish-brown woollen coat and had a muffler round her head. 'I'm a member of the house committee,' she said, addressing herself to the three officers, 'and I can't allow strangers to walk round like this without asking what they want.'

It was a slightly awkward moment. 'I'm a representative of the Leningrad Command,' said Major Lozak, 'and these people here are with me. You see – ' he seemed slightly embarrassed, 'here is a British correspondent. Used to live here some years ago. He'd like to have a look at the house where he lived.' 'Which flat?' said the house committee woman. 'That one, up there,' I said, pointing at the study and the dining-room windows, 'number twenty-six.' She seemed slightly reassured at my knowledge of the correct number. 'I see,' she said. 'Well, the front door is locked, but you can go up the back stair.' We penetrated into the dark courtyard and the back of number twenty-nine. Everything looked very deserted. There were no people about except for the house-committee woman and she was not very communicative. 'Who's living there now?' I asked, but she ignored my question. I remembered that back stair. At the bottom of it was the dark little lodge where old Efim and his two little boys and the deceased wife's sister, a little monkey of a woman, a terribly humble little thing who always showed infinite gratitude for ten- or twenty-kopek tips, used to live. Efim used to complain of his lodge, and would say it was damp, and was making his tuberculosis worse. He used to feed the little monkey woman and pay her four roubles a month and she looked after the children and the miserable little house on the dark ground floor. I also remembered the back stair because it used to have a pungent smell of cats. I missed this smell of cats now. It merely smelt dead and musty – faintly reminiscent of the graves of Orel.

Taking the porter's route, we emerged from the first floor landing of the back stair into the 'hall' of the front stair, just outside the Baltic baron's door. Then we climbed up two more flights. It was exciting and yet very odd. It was all different. The white imitation marble walls were covered with dark, dirty-brown paint and there was no sign of the well-scrubbed wooden steps with the red carpet and the carefully polished brass carpet rails. And then we reached the top landing. This was 'home.' The oval window above the door was broken. The door was covered with the same dirty-brown paint, but the place where the old brass plate had once been could still be seen with the four screw holes still showing. The door was half open. To the left was the long corridor leading to the kitchen. At right angles on the right was the narrow passage leading to my own room. The hall was dark and empty. No mirror, no coat-hangers – nothing. Strange. I was going to open the door into the dining-room but found it locked. We knocked. There was no response. With five or six people marching up and down the hall and knocking at doors, we must have made quite a lot of noise. But nothing stirred. I went right and knocked on the drawing-room door. Then left and knocked on the door of my father's bedroom. Then further still I knocked on the door of the billiard room. 'Still nothing. Let's try my own room,' I said to the officers. We groped our way along the dark narrow passage. We stumbled over a hole in the floor. 'Be careful,' said the major. Here, in front, used to be the bathroom and next to it a little lavatory, and to the left of it, my own bedroom with the bay-windows. It was very dark, but I found the door and knocked on it. No response. I struck a match. The door was padlocked. Pasted on the door was a piece of paper with 'Ira, I'll be back next week,' and a scrawl at the foot of it, and it seemed as if the paper had been there for a long time. It seemed that I was not destined to enter a single room of my old home. However, the door of the little lavatory was ajar. It also smelt musty and abandoned. I struck another light. Sure enough, there it was: 'The Tornado – Made in England.'

'Well,' I thought to myself, mildly amused, 'at least I can say I've revisited the Family Seat!' Then we walked to the other end of the house and tried the kitchen door but it also was locked. 'Let's go,' I said. As we went down the grubby stairs I had a moment of irrational annoyance. 'Why has my home become such a slum?'

I thought to myself. 'What was wrong with the red carpet on the stairs and the polished carpet rails?' It was really absurd. What claim had I on the house? And then I began to wonder whether anybody was living there. 'Perhaps soldiers' wives who are out at work all day,' one of the officers suggested. Perhaps. But why this deadly stillness, this absence of any signs of life? Why all these padlocked and locked doors? Had all the people who lived there been evacuated? Or had they died of hunger? And I tried to imagine the people living there; Ira, for instance, who was Ira? and who was the man who was to come back 'next week'? and how did all these people live through the famine and through the terrible bombing of this district, when houses were crumbling all down the Mokhovaya, and the blast was shattering my bay-windows as the bomb fell upon the house of Dargomyzhsky and Rau Relieur? How many dark tragedies had occurred here during the blockade? Damn the red carpet on the stair and the polished brass carpet rails! There was a smell of death about the house.

And then we returned to the yard with the cabbage plot and the skeleton of the broken clock; and here was life. Outside the house where Durnovo lived were a large crowd of children, and with them a teacher, a fat little woman with a pugdog face. She talked to us cheerfully and asked if we'd like to come another time and see the children's home in what used to be Durnovo's house. The children were lively and healthy and rosy-cheeked, and the little boys crowded round the officers and insisted that they bend down to let them play with their medals, while the little pugdog woman talked about life being 'quite easy' now compared with what Leningrad had gone through, and said that these children were mostly soldiers' children, while some had no mothers, and others had mothers who were out at work. The children were all from this part of Leningrad. One lively little red-cheeked boy cried, 'My daddy's at the front,' and another little boy cried, 'And so is mine, and he's got the Order of the Red Star.' 'Do the children sing?' one of the officers asked. 'Of course, of course,' said the pugdog. 'Come on, boys, what'll you sing?' In their high shrill voices, joyfully, without a trace of solemnity, they broke into

> *V'boi za ródinu, v'boi za Stálina,*
> *Boyeváya chest nam dorogà …*
> [Into battle for the country, into battle for Stalin,
> Our soldiers' honour is dear to us. …]

It was the song the Russian troops used to sing in the dark days of 1941 as they went to their death in the battle of Moscow. Here was the real thing. It was strangely thrilling to think that some of these children were now perhaps living in the communal 'slum' which had once been my home. This was Leningrad. And it was alive, as alive as the shrill joyful voices of these children. Petrograd was dead and gone – as dead and gone as the red carpet on the stair, as dead as old Efim with the porter's cap and the brass buttons. But his two little boys? Perhaps, for all one knew, they were the fathers of these children who were now singing, '*V'boi za rôdinu, v'boi za Stálina.*' The visit to Mokhovaya number twenty-nine cured me of much of the old nostalgic nonsense. Leningrad had become the only reality. St. Petersburg, Petrograd – that was now history and literature, and not much more.

4

The Observation Tower

Along familiar streets we drove to the Narva suburb, down in the south-west. And here was real Leningrad, Leningrad in its most tangible reality. Leningrad of the front line. If the Mokhovaya was looking grubby and shabby now and had, to all appearances, greatly deteriorated even before the war, the opposite was true of the Narva Suburb, the Narvskaya Zastava, or the Lenin District as it was now called. Here was a new Leningrad I had never yet seen. The old Triumphal Arch with the horses and chariot on top of it, built to commemorate the return of the Russian troops from France in 1815, was still the same, but the whole environment was different. Instead of the wretched wooden hovels and miserable one-storey houses that constituted this working-class suburb around the Putilov works, a new city had sprung up – avenues with enormous blocks of six-, seven-, eight-storey flats, very much better and more harmoniously designed than similar new buildings in Moscow. Nearly all the windows were broken and replaced by plywood; some buildings had been shattered by shells, and all were pockmarked with shell-splinters. But in the main there was less damage here than in the old Mokhovaya. Not far south of the Narva Gate stood the large new steel and concrete building of the Regional Soviet with a well-designed rectangular tower about 250 feet high.

We went up this tower, climbing its long winding stair. Here, on the top platform which was one of the main observation posts of the Leningrad front were rangefinders, telescopes and other optical instruments. Here were a major and several soldiers, and a captain with half his head bandaged and a large black patch over one eye. From the top of this tower one saw a vast panorama of not only Leningrad on one side but also of the front on the other. Almost below us, in the south-west, was the massive black shape of the main building of the Putilov works, around which were large blocks of houses, some still seemingly intact, others badly shattered, which gave this part of Leningrad the appearance of the outskirts of Madrid in December 1937. It was, on the whole, less bad though than the University City of Madrid where the shelling had given the buildings the weird shapes of prehistoric animals. Here the massive blocks of flats had more or less kept their original shape, though much of the ground between them had been ploughed up by shells. Even so, there were fragments of vegetable plots everywhere around the shell-holes. Along the main road, past the Putilov works, there was a constant though not very thick stream of traffic running to and from the front. It was a cool autumn morning with a haze in the air and broken clouds in the sky. Beyond the Putilov works were the pale waters of the Gulf of Finland with the dark outline of the cranes of Leningrad Harbour only about a mile away, and – on the other side of this inlet of the Gulf of Finland, an inlet scarcely more than a mile wide – were the Germans.

'That's Uritsk,' said the captain with the black patch, 'it used to be called Ligovo.' Ligovo – I remembered it very well – was a nondescript little *datcha* place, almost a village then, and was the first stop on the railway to Peterhof and Oranienbaum. The country house where I spent so many summers and so many weekends in winter was on the hill, three miles beyond Oranienbaum and had a superb view of Kronstadt with its forts and its cathedral only a few miles across the water. And now Uritsk – or Ligovo – was in German hands. One could see from here that it was no longer a village but had really become part of industrial Leningrad in the last twenty-five years. A large white building close to the sea stood out very clearly. 'That's the Pishmash (short for *pishuschie mashiny*) over there,' the captain with the patch explained. 'The big Leningrad typewriter factory. It's one of the German strongholds on this front. They hold about twelve miles of coast here; they hold Uritsk, and Strelna, and part of Peterhof – the so-called New Peterhof – and the front runs between New and Old Peterhof.' So there was a Russian 'bridgehead' beyond that – the bridgehead just opposite Kronstadt, and running from Old Peterhof to some point twenty or twenty-five miles west, beyond Krasnaya Gorka. I felt some satisfaction at the thought that the old country house – if still extant – and at any rate its park with the old oak trees, and the forest beyond, where I had learned to love the Russian countryside – had remained in Russian hands.

It was misty and from the watchtower that morning one could see only the faintest outline of Kronstadt, or rather of the dome of Kronstadt Cathedral. I looked at that dark green coastline, stretching to the west. 'What's that?' I asked, pointing to a large dome-like shape rising from the crest of the hill, a long way down the coast. 'That's the church of Peterhof – or rather what's left of it,' the captain said. 'It's about all that's left of Peterhof,' he said bitterly. 'The palace is burned; the park destroyed, the fountains either sent as scrap to Germany, or mixed up with the earth. I was there not long ago. It's a horrible sight. And how our young people liked to go out to Peterhof on holidays, and spend the day in the glorious park among the fountains. Do you remember Samson? These swine sawed Samson in half and sent the bits away as scrap.' Of course I remembered Samson, the greatest of the Peterhof fountains, finer than anything I had seen in Versailles. And I remembered the puddles on the gravel path around Samson, and the strange, intriguing, slightly slimy smell of the Peterhof ponds and its fountains: a damp, fresh, bright-green smell among the dark-green old lime trees of the park; and the beautiful, baroque palace in white and blood-red stucco. 'You cannot imagine with what reverence our young people tip-toed along the parquet floors of the palace,' said the captain. 'There was no reverence for the wicked old Tsars in this tip-toeing. But there was reverence for this great piece of our national heritage. It belonged to us, to our culture, don't you see, and now, now there's nothing but rubble; and it's the same everywhere,' he added angrily, pointing along the horizon to the left. 'There are the heights of Pulkovo right in front of you. We are holding *them!* But there's nothing left of the Observatory, nothing. Smashed to smithereens. And further to the left are the heights of Duderhof; that's where the front goes further inland. But Pushkin (formerly Tsarskoye Selo), with the great Catherine Palace, and beyond it, Pavlovsk, with the most beautiful park in the world, are still on the other side of the front. The Catherine Palace has been more or less destroyed; certainly everything inside the palace, the famous amber room and all – has been carried away, and the beautiful old park at Pavlovsk has simply been cut down by these swine.' It had indeed been an exquisite eighteenth-century park, with lakes, singularly like that of the Bois de Vincennes, with all sorts of little Temples of Love and Grecian pavilions. One could feel how bitterly all these Russian soldiers of Leningrad felt about this destruction. '*Svolochi* – the filthy scum!' the captain concluded.

To the south towards Pushkin and Pavlovsk, the front was six kilometres away. Further west, on the shores of the Uritsk inlet, the front was no more than three kilometres distant. Here they had been stopped literally at the gates of Leningrad, and for two years they had not been able to advance another step.

'He's a good fellow, the captain,' said the sturdy major, in an aside to me. 'One of our best people. Quite recently he knocked out a German observation post just over there, near the Pishmash – one of the hardest places to get. Knocked it out with a direct hit.' 'Haven't they tried,' I asked, 'to knock you out?' The major laughed. 'Sometimes they fire several hundred shells a day at us, but it doesn't do much good. They hit the tower in several places, but have never been able to knock us out. Of course, we've had splinters, right up here, and some dead and wounded – the captain himself got a splinter in his head just the other day – but he's carrying on as you see. Aren't you, Comrade Captain?' The captain with the patch over one eye smiled a little grimly. 'The doctors say they'll save my eye,' he said. As on nearly all Leningrad faces, the captain's had two hard little lines on each side of the mouth.

We looked through the telescope sights and rangefinders at the German positions and were struck by the fact that everything seemed completely deserted: there was no trace of any living being. 'That's because of our snipers,' somebody said. 'They never even put their heads out if they can help it. This has been the greatest front for sniping. But it has become a disappointing trade; they've become so infernally careful now. They've got stuff about 'Scharfschützen' written up all over the place.' 'For the rest, it's not so difficult now,' said the captain. 'We bomb them every day so that keeps them fairly quiet most of the time, and when we answer their shelling, they soon shut up. They stay in their rat-holes now; in the past they would run around quite openly, gathering in hay, Katyusha had a crack at them on one occasion. It made a nice hay-crop of dead fritzes! They use their six-barrel mortars against us – nasty stuff – but nothing like our Katyusha. Oh, Lord, when Katyusha starts her song, it makes us all dance about up here, with concussion and excitement! And Katyusha has a nice long range – get right to Uritsk!' I noticed a large bell – formerly a church bell – on top of the tower stair and marked 'Chemical alarm.' 'You don't think they'll use gas, do you?'

I asked. 'No,' said the captain, 'not now, but there was a time when we couldn't be sure of anything.'

We were about to leave when things began to happen. A white cloud – a smoke screen – suddenly rose around the Pishmash building on the other side of the water. 'Aha,' said the captain, 'I bet you they'll start some nonsense in a minute or two. They want to hide their gun-flashes. I had better get busy.' Then the German guns suddenly went off with one or two gunflashes faintly visible to the side of the smoke-screen. The Russians got ready to answer. Somewhere high up, a German shell whined, harmlessly, like a mosquito. Then, looking back over the panorama of Leningrad, dominated by the large brown dome of St. Isaac's Cathedral, we saw it land about a mile away, right inside the city. A brown cloud of smoke – or was it dust? – rose from among the houses. 'Fontanka way,' somebody remarked. The major, captain and the soldiers were now busy with their optical instruments, and the captain was shouting instructions' into a telephone to the neighbouring batteries. And these batteries – whose whereabouts could just be guessed, so well were they camouflaged – began to fire. It was pleasantly exciting to see the gunflashes, to hear the loud reports of the shells going off towards the German lines, and a second or two later to see little clouds of smoke rise from the other side of the little gulf. A few shells landed in the water, raising fountains of spray. 'Fifty metres out,' the captain with the black patch and the bandaged head cried into the telephone. 'Fifty metres out!' Again the batteries fired, and this time all the shells could clearly be seen landing and exploding on the other shore, inside the German positions. The Germans were firing back, and we saw two shells again land a mile away, inside Leningrad. It was odd to think that this seemingly harmless spectacle – as harmless as a game of tennis – might mean death to ten, twenty, a hundred people, if either side was lucky. Then a moment later we observed how the Germans were extending their smoke-screen further west. Would the firing die down as a result, or grow in intensity? It might be either. Actually, it died down, and soon stopped completely. 'There's no accounting for what they'll do,' said the captain. 'I think this was just a little nuisance shelling, and when they saw we were answering back at once, they soon stopped. They've got no system. The whole thing is pretty pointless. They can't achieve anything, anyway, and they know it. I shouldn't like to be in their place. Must make them mad to have to live in their rat-holes, with no prospect of any kind, except being sooner or later trapped by us, and to feel that *we* are living in a city, with theatres and cinemas and real houses! They're shelling us now simply out of spite. Miserable idiots!'

5

Sightseeing

We took leave of the major and the captain and the men – all of whom had by this time relaxed – and walked down the winding stair into the street, where the driver was reclining in the car. We drove back into town, past the Narva Arch, and along the Obvodny Canal, with its cabbage-tapestried slopes, and past the shattered Baltic and Warsaw stations – it was from the latter that all the express trains went abroad – to Berlin, Vienna, Flushing and Paris. Less than two days to Paris by the Nord express. And then we drove along the wide Ismail Avenue with the large church with the blue dome and golden stars, built, I believe, in memory of the Balkan War of 1877–8.

In front of it used to stand an enormously tall column with an angel of peace standing on one toe on top of it, and the subject of a lewd quatrain wherein the angel of peace figured as the 'cancan-ballerina.' The famous column had disappeared. Tram-cars were running down the Ismail Avenue, and most of them half-empty – how different from Moscow! The trams were driven by women, and at street corners smart young policewomen in white gloves were standing on point-duty. Right at the corner of the Ismail Avenue and the Fontanka stood the wreck of a large six-storey block – it had been destroyed by that direct hit which was one of the most amazing shots in the 'Leningrad Fights' documentary. We then drove down the Voznesensky, with the Admiralty spire at the end of it, and turned into the Sadovaya, that long crescent-like street, running parallel to the two rivers on either side of it, the Fontanka and the Catherine Canal. The Sadovaya had changed almost beyond recognition. The houses were mostly the same, and what gave the Sadovaya its character was not its houses but its traffic, the Eastern-bazaar-like bustle of the great Haymarket through which it runs, and the noisy and vociferous life of the Apraxin Bazaar, with its endless rows of cheap clothes shops and soft goods shops and wholesale fruit and vegetable stores. And then, beyond the Apraxin Market, came two seats of dignity and architectural restraint – the two great stucco buildings of the State Bank on one side and the Corps des Pages – the guards officers' school – on the other. But no sooner had one passed these than one came to the Gostiny Dvor, the middle-class shopping-centre – a vast quadrangle of arcades with its best side facing the Nevsky. The Sadovaya Street meant trade, it was the great trading street of St. Petersburg. The vociferous calico merchant of the Apraxin Market lacked the gentility of the St. Petersburg shop assistant. He was a byword of Moscow-like coarseness.

As for the Haymarket – the Sennaya – it was overflowing with literary associations and old memories. The Sennaya and the streets around it used to be a chaos of clanging tramcars and hundreds of *izvoschiks* and carts or sleighs laden with food of every description – a Covent Garden that was more like an oriental bazaar, with vociferous old women with shawls round their heads, operating on huge sacks of cranberries and barrels of salt herring and mounds of apples piled up on the pavements. Moreover, there were the covered pavilions with their butchers and grocers and fishmongers – pavilions that filled up a good part of the Sennaya. And to either side of the Sennaya, along the noisy Sadovaya, were rows and rows of other shops. I remembered how on the way to the skating pond in the Yusupov Garden further down the Sadovaya – I was only eight or nine then – I would carefully avoid looking out of the tramcar window lest I caught sight of that most terrifying picture in the big ikon shop at the corner of the Sadovaya and the Haymarket, a crazy-eyed head of John the Baptist floating in its bloody gravy. I had once seen it, and was frightened lest I saw it again. I remembered the exact place of the shop but this time, summoning up my courage, I looked, and was not surprised to find that there was no ikon shop left. Indeed the street was empty; there were no shops of any description anywhere, except an occasional bakery or other food-distributing centre.

The whole nature of the Sennaya had changed even before this war had begun. It was now an ordinary, spacious square, with the same church at one end and ordinary dwelling-houses around it. The pavilions had gone; there was hardly a soul around. Haymarket – the centre of the wild, slummy, picturesque St. Petersburg of *Crime and Punishment!* In the old days it still had all the character of Dostoievsky's Sennaya – with its shouting tradesmen, its tangle of droshki and horse-carts, its dark, deep slums all around where old female money-lenders might well be axed to death by starving 'Nietzscheanising' university students, and with those tea-rooms on the first floor where everything seemed chaos, and where between the bellowing of the barrel-organ and the shrieks of drunken prostitutes, profound, night-marish conversations were perhaps still going on at a far-off corner table between Marmeladov, the sententious dipsomaniac *chinovnik*, and Raskolnikov, or between Raskolnikov and the sinister Svidrigailov, that strange bubble of the St. Petersburg earth.

The shelling had started again by the time we arrived in the Morskaya, outside a sumptuous old building, almost a little palace, which was now the architect's house. The shells whined overhead, and blew up somewhere not far away. 'Let's get inside quickly,' said Colonel Studyonov. He looked slightly agitated. I knew exactly how he felt. He did not want any trouble this time, after the tragedy of the Belgorod road earlier in the month. It was he who had to keep a stiff upper lip during that ghastly night as he sorted out the dead and the wounded. In the large spacious rooms of the architect's house, several people were working at desks, drawing plans and working on blueprints. There was a business-like air about the place and nobody seemed to be taking any notice of the shelling or worrying about the uncomfortably large brightly polished plate-glass windows looking on to the sunny Morskaya. The walls were covered with charts and plans, and one of the architects who took me round showed me various plans for new streets which were going to be built immediately after the war on the south side of Leningrad. It was clear that an enormous amount was being done even now in this planning work. The plans for one of the large avenues on the south side were typical of the conflicting tendencies still existing among Soviet architects. The main tendency of modern Leningrad architecture was clearly to keep to austere classical lines; of the three projects two were classical, with one putting strong emphasis on trees and open spaces, while the third was much more 'Soviet,' with the long row of buildings ending up with a giant Paris-1937-like statue of a worker, or *komsomolka*, or something, sticking a mile out. 'How many houses,' I asked the chief architect who had been accompanying us all morning, 'have been destroyed by bombing and shelling?' He said the destruction of actual housing space did not exceed eight per cent, which, incidentally, was considerably less than the destruction in London, and negligible compared with the fearful destruction of Voronezh, Stalingrad, Rostov, Orel or Kharkov. 'There hasn't been so much bombing,' said the other architect, a little man with pince-nez, and hair turning grey.

'Shells damage a house, but unless it's a very small one they don't destroy it.'

At the architects' house they had elaborated plans for 300 large new buildings and 300 of more 'local importance.' They were working out all the restoration plans for important buildings that had been damaged, such as the Engineers' Castle, the former Mikhailovsky Castle that Emperor Paul had built for himself, the Ermitage, the old Catholic Church in the Nevsky, and others. It was interesting to learn that, of some of the most famous buildings that had been more or less completely destroyed, they had already – before the war – drawn up exact blueprints, so that they could be very accurately rebuilt. They had blueprints of the Pavlovsk, Pushkino and Gatchina palaces; unfortunately, they had none of Peterhof, the greatest loss of all.

'The most difficult problem will be to restore the interiors,' said one of the architects. 'We have full inventories of the things destroyed or looted by the Germans, but it may be difficult to recover everything. We shall have, to a large extent, to work on the basis of equivalent value. What they can't give back they'll have to replace out of their own museums and private collections.' 'You see,' said another man, 'we went on with this blueprint work throughout the winter of 1941–2. It was a double blessing. On the one hand the blueprint collection was by no means complete when the war started, and the work had now become really vital. It was also a blessing for us architects. It was the best medicine that could be given us during the famine – gave us work for which we were fitted. The moral effect is great when a hungry man knows he's got a useful job of work to do. The Leningrad Soviet gave us a credit of one million roubles for this work, and we were thankful to get it. There's no doubt about it: a worker stands up better to hardship than an intellectual. A lot of our people stopped shaving – the first sign of a man going to pieces.

'Most of these people pulled themselves together when they were given work. It was a great thing. But on the whole men collapsed more easily than women and at first the death rate was highest among the men. However, those who survived the worst period of the famine finally survived. The women felt the after-effects more seriously than the men. Many died in the spring when already the worst was over. The famine had peculiar physical effects on people. Women were so run down that they stopped menstruating ... so many people died that we had to bury most of them without coffins. People had their feelings blunted, and never seemed to weep at the burials. It was all done in complete silence without any display of emotion. When things began to improve the first signs were when women began to put rouge and lipstick on their pale skinny faces. Yes, we lived through hell right enough; but you should have been here the day the blockade was broken – people in the streets wept for joy and strangers fell round each other's necks. And now, as you see, life is almost normal. There is this shelling, of course, and people get killed, but life has become valuable again. The other day I saw an unpleasant street accident: a man was knocked down by a tramcar and had his leg cut off by the wheels. Why, our Leningrad crowd nearly lynched the driver! It seemed so wrong that anyone who had lived through the Leningrad siege should lose a leg through the fault of another Leningrader; whose fault it was exactly I do not know, but you see the point?'

After seeing many more projects and blueprints our party drove to the Alexander Nevsky Monastery. This was pure sight-seeing. We visited the grave of Alexander Nevsky and the tomb of Suvorov, the latter inside a small chapel, with some other tombs around it. It occurred to me that here, in Leningrad, were buried three of the great national heroes of Russia, whose example had so often been invoked in this war and in whose memory the three most famous Army Orders of this war had been created: Alexander Nevsky, Suvorov and Kutuzov. A dark red velvet flag with tassels was suspended over Suvorov's tomb, a large flat stone forming part of the stone floor of the chapel and bearing the simple words: 'HERE LIES SUVOROV,' and nothing else. Around Suvorov were other tombs. There was one with the following inscribed in beautiful eighteenth-century lettering: 'Spouse of Lieutenant-General Alexander Alexandrovitch Biron, youngest daughter of Prince Alexander Danilovich Menshikov. Born December 17, 1712. Died September 13, 1736.' A young lady of that frivolous age, between Peter and Catherine, when squabbling female royalty and their German favourites nearly undid the work of Peter the Great. On a small table near the entrance was a visitors' book. I looked at one of the latest entries: 'Having visited the grave of the Great General, at a time when the German Nazis are shelling the town and killing innocent people, I fervently hope that his shadow will help us to defeat these barbarians. There can be no question about it. (Signed) Major…' The scrawl was hard to make out. The date was July 7th, 1943.

Outside the chapel, in the large yard of the monastery, now turned into a large vegetable garden, there was an air of country quiet. The doorkeeper was a very doddery old man, probably one of the oldest men of Leningrad. He might well have been a former monk of this very monastery. On our way back we drove past the Smolny, heavily camouflaged with netting, and the beautiful baroque church that Rastrelli had built, camouflaged green and black. 'We have to repaint it white in winter,' said the architect. 'But the camouflage of this place is so thorough that from 13,000 feet they simply cannot identify it.' Then we drove past the beautiful Tauris Palace, which Potemkin had built for himself, and later the seat of the Duma, and scene of so many historic events during the stormy days of 1917. I remembered those exciting days of April 1917 when crowds around the Tauris Palace with many soldiers among them were clamouring for the resignation of the Lvov–Miliukov Government. Improvised orators jumped on to improvised platforms. Some praised Kerensky to the skies. To them the lawyer who looked like Rachmaninoff, and had such a wonderful gift of the gab was the Man of Destiny. Many ladies thought him a *dushka.* Another orator was being howled down for defending Milyukov, an Imperialist – so his opponents said – who wanted to go on indefinitely with the war, because Russia had been promised the Straits. 'To hell with the Straits!' soldiers in the crowd were saying. 'Down with the war!' A Jewish lawyer with pince-nez was saying to the little crowd around him that Kerensky was the true guardian of Russia's democratic liberties, the liberties the Russian people had won with their blood in overthrowing Tsarism. But a Sturdy soldier angrily shouted he had been rotting away in the trenches for three years, all for the benefit of international capitalism, and that the Russian Army had had enough of it, and he shouted that there was only one man whom the Russian people could trust, and that was Lenin. 'German agent!' the little lawyer cried. 'He came here in a sealed wagon from Germany!' There was now angry shouting on both sides. Unrestrained Russian democracy was living its brief hectic life.

The shelling which had stopped for a while now started again and Colonel Studyonov thought we had better go home and cut out the visit to the anti-aircraft battery. The Morskaya had at one point been roped off: a disposal squad was taking away an unexploded shell. We had to drive round the other way, through half-deserted streets, past Velten's beautiful building of the Ermitage and across that superb square outside the Winter Palace now called the Uritsky Square. The giant caryatids of polished black granite outside the Ermitage had been slightly damaged by a shell, but apart from broken windows the general appearance of the wonderful Winter Palace square was unchanged. There was scaffolding round the giant red granite monolith in the centre of the square, with the angel on top. 'This scaffolding,' said the architect, 'was put up some time before the war. We were not sure whether the monolith could stand the traffic so we were going to test it; but shells have been blowing up all around it, and it's none the worse for it. There couldn't have been a better test!' We went back to the Astoria where the old dame had prepared an excellent dinner for us, and after dinner about five o'clock we drove off to the theatre. All the theatre shows in Leningrad began at five-thirty.

We drove to the Dramatic Theatre on the Fontanka to see Gorki's *Petit-Bourgeois.* I had always remembered it as a rather shabby little theatre, compared with the Big Three, and it looked much the same as before. In the past it used to be called the Maly Theatre. I had gone there to a schoolchildren's matinée once to see *Henry of Navarre* – it must have been in 1913 or 1914. Outside the theatre was a small crowd, mostly soldiers, all wearing the Leningrad medal, and some of them had other decorations. There were also some girls, many of them in khaki, and several wearing the Leningrad medal. There was also a sprinkling of Baltic sailors – officers and ratings – the latter with something of the old Baltic swagger, and the forelock sticking from under the sailor's cap. 'It's no good,' somebody remarked. 'The *trevoga* is still on, and until it's over they won't start the show.' Nearby there was a loudspeaker saying every few minutes: 'Citizens, the artillery shelling of the district is continuing; citizens, the artillery shelling of the district is continuing.' This wasn't very evident, though, for what explosions could be heard could be heard only faintly. And the people stood round the theatre doors totally unperturbed. A militiaman was, however, inviting the public to take cover – though without much success, and not very pressingly for that matter. Our colonel, however, thought we had better go in, and we were escorted into a dark little office with a couple of chairs and an old leather sofa; a Lenin portrait and a large pink theatre bill were on the wall. This gave the repertory of the Dramatic Theatre for the week: *Davnim Davno*, the sentimental and rather silly rhymed play, full of *marivaudage*, about the Hussars in 1812 and the young girl dressed up as a Hussar – a play I had seen at the Ermitage in Moscow in the summer of 1942; also that great nineteenth-century comedy, *Krechinsky's Wedding*, and *The Road to New York*, a light American play, and finally, the Petit-Bourgeois we had come to see. Bad luck. This was really the heaviest of all the plays running in Leningrad that week (even if the lightest of Gorki's plays), but that day there was nothing else to see. Actually there were only two theatres open in Leningrad, this and the Alexandrinka, if one did not count a smaller theatre in the Viborg district on the other side of the river. So we sat in the little office for some time, a little aimlessly. Likharev and Major Lozak were recalling various Leningrad experiences; curious how their thoughts always seemed to run back to those famine months. 'They used to play the comic opera *Bayadère* during the famine,' one of them said. 'They played it here and also went out to the front to play it to the troops. It used to be so frightfully cold in the theatre that the actresses had to play with their fur coats on. Yes, even the dancers wore fur coats. Nobody minded, you couldn't expect anything else. It became a little extra theatrical convention – there are plenty of conventions anyway at the theatre – one had to accept these oriental princesses in fur coats!'

'We became pretty desperate at one time,' Likharev said. 'It was no longer safe to take German prisoners down the Nevsky. And then, there was the famous case of the German plane crashing in the Tauris Gardens. The airman had one of those high decorations they call the Ritterkreuz. He was beaten up by the women. He was certainly in a nice mess when they got him to hospital. And the reason why he crashed was that Sevastianov, our great air ace, had rammed his plane. Ramming was a Leningrad invention. We were outnumbered in the air. Out of a kind of despair, rather than see any of these vultures escape, our fellows began to ram them. It put the fear of death into the Germans. They couldn't take it. Sevastianov. . . . Yes, there was he, and there were several others who developed a ramming 'technique' if you please. It takes guts – my God, it does! We no longer need such desperate remedies now. We are more than equal to them now. We can lick them on equal terms.' And it made me wonder whether this quite extraordinary personal bravery and self-sacrifice had not, in 1941, made that tiny difference which in reality made *all* the difference and saved Moscow, and Leningrad, and was ultimately going to win the war for Russia.

'Funny,' said the major, still thinking back to the dark days of 1941, 'how during those days people never talked about food. It was bad style, it was tactless. But how things changed after February! You cannot imagine what it was like when on April 15th, 1942 – yes, I remember the exact date – when the first tramcar ran down the Nevsky. People ran after it and cheered their heads off. It was like their triumphal chariot, that tramcar.'

Every few minutes the loudspeaker in the room had been saying: 'Citizens, the artillery shelling of the district continues,' but suddenly it said: 'Citizens, the artillery shelling of the district has ceased.' Somebody came in to say the show would now start. It was ten to six – the show had been delayed by twenty minutes.

Meschane – the petit-bourgeois – would not have been much of a play really but for the actors. It was typical young-Gorki stuff which, when you come to analyse it, is not very different from old-Ibsen stuff, full of the correct sentiments and sentences, and with its slightly more juvenile Dr. Stockmanns and slightly less stuffy Noras and Hedda Gablers. The petit-bourgeois household is drab and terribly discontented and unhappy, except the lodger, the young railwayman who 'loves life,' and proclaims this love on every occasion: 'I know Life is difficult, full of violence and injustice, but I am a strong and healthy man, and I know we shall win. And I want to throw myself right up to my neck into Life.' With a capital L, of course. To which the boss of the household – miserable old bully he is – replies: 'Life will just show you where you get off. You must be drunk.' But the frivolous young widow agrees with the hero. She does not vamp him; she tries instead to vamp the helpless, futile young son of the boss but he is mentally too impotent, too henpecked by Pa to react. Equally miserable is the daughter of the household, driven to an abortive suicide by her failure to find a husband. The hero finally goes off with the daughter of the saintly old bird-catcher whom the miserable bully had driven out of his house. All a trifle dreary but for the long spells of comic relief provided chiefly by the philosophising drunk, a sort of unsuccessful tragedian, who hangs about the house. But the acting was so good throughout and the bird-catcher's daughter had such a pretty face and alluring figure that one watched the play with considerable interest. The audience, without being over-enthusiastic, seemed to enjoy it – especially the funny passages. There was much laughter, but not loud laughter; cheering, but not frantic cheering, as one gets in Moscow. But perhaps, I thought, Leningrad had become naturally reserved. For, as the curtain was about to rise after the second interval, the manager appeared before the curtain and announced the fall of Smolensk. It was really tremendous news and news which might, sooner or later, have a direct bearing on the whole Leningrad situation. The audience cheered loudly, but without rising to its feet. It was odd to contrast this calm reaction with the frantic enthusiasm in Moscow, for instance, to the news of the capture of Kharkov. Was Leningrad at heart so absorbed in its own problems still that the news from the 'mainland' seemed a little remote?

6

Kamenny Island

The next day was Sunday. We drove in the morning to the Kamenny Island at the end of the long Kamennostrovsky – now the Kirov Avenue. The Kamenny Island on the north side of the Neva delta measures about three-quarters of a mile from west to east and half that length from north to south. It is separated from the much larger island, the so-called 'Petrograd Side,' through which the Kamennostrovsky runs, by a narrow branch of the delta, and, from the mainland in the north by the small Neva, the main branch of the Neva itself. Separated from the Kamenny by other branches of the delta are the famous Elagin Island in the west, famous for its palace now destroyed, and the 'Arrow,' the Strelka, the westernmost point of the island pointing into the Gulf of Finland. The wooded Elagin Island is one of the beauty spots of Leningrad, and to drive in a horse-carriage round it on a 'white' summer night used to be in the old days one of the favourite pleasures of romantic young couples, and of drunks in need of fresh air after a riotous night with the gipsies or at the 'Aquarium,' the famous nightclub somewhere off the Kamennostrovsky. South-west of the Kamenny Island and south of the Elagin is the much larger Krestovsky Island, chiefly noted in the past for its yachting clubs and its tennis courts. It has remained the sports centre of Leningrad, and shortly before the war one of the largest stadiums in the Soviet Union was about to be completed on its western tip, overlooking the Gulf of Finland.

Unlike the Elagin, which was a great public park, the Kamenny was really a suburban area – though those who lived there would have hated to be called suburbanites. It was stylish to have a villa on the Kamenny Island, and to live there all the year round rather than in Petrograd itself; but it was not very good style, really. Like the Kamennostrovsky, the Kamenny Island had something of the hallmark of the *nouveau-riche.* The father of one of my schoolmates had a huge villa on the Kamenny Island, and he used to ask us out there in winter to skate and play hockey and to toboggan down an enormous artificial ice mountain. The boy was a Swiss and his father was one of the two most expensive tailors in Petrograd. Most of the new villas – and they were nearly all new – were owned by very wealthy shopkeepers or business men.

The Kamenny Island looked beautiful on that sunny autumn morning, with the river dark-blue, a few little white clouds high in the clear blue sky, a cool breeze blowing from the nearby sea, and the trees in the island green and brown and golden and yellow. The island had not changed much except that many unnecessary fences had been removed, and many villas had been smashed by shells, and others completely destroyed by bombing, back in 1941. Here and there whole trees had been smashed by a direct hit. The Huns had concentrated on the Kamenny Island perhaps because they knew that at that time several of the Leningrad hospitals had been moved here. But now the island was Children's Island. Or rather it had been until September 1st. Now the chief purpose the island was serving was that of a rest home for adolescent workers. Fifteen villas were now being used as rest homes. In the summer nearly all were being used as children's holiday homes. The Kamenny was, indeed, a good illustration of the work done by the Leningrad authorities to keep the children of the city fit. Many hundred children had lived here for forty-five days in summer, just as many thousands more had been sent for the same period of time to similar if simpler holiday homes in the *datcha* places north of the city – on the way to Finland – to Pargolovo, Levashovo and Ozerki. Moreover, many children whose health was not very strong were now living in the country all the year round – there were now fifteen or twenty thousand of them, and the *datchas* had been adapted to winter conditions.

By the way, the mention of Pargolovo with its enormous cemetery suddenly reminded me of the fact that all my paternal grandparents and great-grandparents, besides a variety of great-aunts and grand-uncles, were buried there.

We drove up to a sumptuous villa near the water edge on the south side of the island and were welcomed here by two young women. One was tall, fair, rosy-cheeked with a well-chiselled little Roman nose, and a coquettish playful expression, a little like a young and rather inexperienced English schoolteacher who wants to be popular with the children. She wore a large black velour hat and a smart tailor-made costume. The other was more Russian, more Leningrad, despite her non-Russian surname. She was only a little older than the other, but far more mature. She had one of those beautiful pale Russian faces, rather round, with large luminous grey eyes, and a full, well-shaped mouth with large white teeth. This girl – she was twenty-four or maybe twenty-five – was the boss of the fifteen rest homes. She also had on a tailor-made suit and a small brown hat which she wore with that natural smartness which the other girl just missed. She took us into a large room, overlooking the river. 'You haven't come on a very good day,' she said. 'This being Sunday, a lot of the children are away. Several have gone to the children's matinée to see *Wedding in Malikovka* and some of the others have gone to the zoo.' 'The zoo!' I said. 'Have you still got a zoo in Leningrad?'

'Yes,' she laughed, 'it isn't really much of a zoo now. The elephant was killed in an air raid – you may have seen it in the Leningrad documentary – and some of the other animals have died, but in spite of everything we have tried to keep the zoo going. The great attraction for the children is the hippopotamus.' We were sitting in the drawing-room or ballroom of what was once the villa of somebody called Neuscheller, who was chairman of the great Treugolnik rubber factory in St. Petersburg. Marble caryatids supported the ceiling and around the walls there were large mirrors and marble statues of Greek gods: there were also bronze candlesticks on top of the huge fireplace and an enormous crystal chandelier was hanging from a ceiling with more paintings of Greek gods. Catherine Evgenievna Borschenko – for that was her name – said she was a 'pædagogue,' that is, simply, a teacher, and she had been sent down here and had worked here now for over a year. She said that the organisation of rest homes for adolescent workers was something to which the Leningrad Soviet attached the greatest importance. There was no doubt about it: the physical and nervous strain of working in Leningrad, for instance in a place like the Putilov works which was almost in the front line, was very considerable, and it was essential to give these young people a break from time to time. They came down here for a fortnight or a month, and the purpose of this rest was to take these boys' and girls' minds off their daily routine – often a pretty grim routine – and to pep them up physically.

'We have fifteen villas here, some for girls, the others for boys of about fourteen to eighteen years of age. We give them plenty of recreation and extra-good food rations. They get up at 8 a.m., then for five minutes they do light physical exercises; then there's breakfast consisting of *kasha* or a hot vegetable dish, or rice milk pudding, and tea with lots of bread and butter. Altogether they get plenty to eat – meat and fish and thirty grammes of butter a day, cheese and jam, a good ration of sugar and a daily bar of chocolate, sometimes English chocolate, you'll be interested to know. They like English chocolate! Then, after breakfast, there is recreation, music and dancing for those who like it; others go on excursions, others still play football or volleyball, or billiards, and there is also a good library. The girls also do sewing and needlework if they wish. This place here used to be before the war the rest home of the Leningrad metal workers. Now we have between eighty and one hundred young girls staying here, and there are about as many girls or boys in each of the other fourteen villas.'

After taking us past a beautiful Sèvres vase in the hall, Comrade Borschenko and the other girl conducted us upstairs where we saw the beautifully tidy dormitories. We then went into a room where about a dozen young girls were drawing or playing a children's card game. They were all neatly dressed except for their shoes which were all on the shabby side. We stayed with them for quite a while. I remember chiefly two of the girls, Tamara Turunova and a girl called Tanya. Tamara was a little girl of fifteen, very pale, thin and delicate, obviously run-down, with dark hair tied in a knot. On her little black frock was pinned the green-ribboned medal of Leningrad. 'Where did you get that?' I asked. A faint smile appeared on her pale little face. 'I don't know what he was called,' she said. 'An uncle with spectacles came to the works one day and gave me this medal.' 'What works?' 'Oh, the Kirov works, of course,' she said. 'Does your father work there too?' 'No,' she said, 'father died in the hungry year, died on the 7th of January. I've worked on the Kirov works since I was fourteen, so I suppose that's why they gave me the medal. We're not far away from the front.' 'Doesn't it frighten you to work there?' She screwed up her little face. 'No, not really. One gets used to it. When a shell whistles, it means it's high up; it's only when it begins to sizzle that you know there's going to be trouble. Accidents do happen, of course, happen very often; sometimes things happen every day. Only last week we had an accident; a shell landed in my workshop and many were wounded, and two Stakhanov girls were burned to death.' She said it with terrible simplicity and almost with the suggestion that it wouldn't have been such a serious matter if two valuable Stakhanovite girls hadn't lost their lives. 'You wouldn't like to change over to another factory?' I asked. 'No,' she said, shaking her head. 'I am a Kirov girl, and my father was a Putilov man, and really the worst is over now, so we may as well stick it to the end.' And one could feel that she meant it, though it was only too clear what terrible nervous strain that frail little body of hers had suffered. 'And your mother?' I asked. 'She died before the war,' said the girl. 'But my big brother is in the army, on the Leningrad front, and he writes to me often, very often, and three months ago I saw him when he and several of his comrades came to visit us at the Kirov works.' Her little pale face brightened at the thought of it, and, looking out of the window at the golden autumn trees, she said, 'You know, it's good to be here for a little while.'

Tanya was different. She had a bright-green jumper and rosy cheeks, and was much less in need of a holiday than the other girl. She was bright and talkative, and said that everybody at her shell factory was sure that the Germans would be chased away from Leningrad before long. 'Have you ever seen any Germans?' I asked. And, chattering away, she told the story of how she had taken part in the capture of German parachutists in the summer of 1941. 'We were staying in the country at Lychkovo, and there were lots of Leningrad kids – forty of us – and we hunted parachutists. We caught three of them. To be truthful, it was the boys who caught them; the girls were very frightened, for all the Germans had tommy-guns. There was one hiding behind a bush and he was firing all the time, no one could get near him. Several of the boys crawled up to him from behind, pounced on him, bit him and took away his tommy-gun. But he had time to kill one of the boys. This one they handed over alive to our troops, the other two they killed. They would have run away – there was nothing else to be done.'

I liked the story. It showed that the Russian children of Leningrad had never been defeatist – not even during those fearful days of the summer of 1941 when the giant Nazi war machine with its vast superiority in tanks and planes was crawling like a steam-roller towards Leningrad, and when helpless terror would have been such a natural reaction among children. For these boys who were hunting and disarming parachutists, and to whom it was a sort of rough sport, were children of ten, eleven and twelve years of age. There was in all this something of the same daredevilry as was shown by the Moscow boys who, during the first raids on Moscow in the summer of 1941, cheerfully used to grab incendiaries with their bare hands until they were taught a safer method. But parachutists were worse than incendiaries, and there was much bewilderment around, even panic, but the boys were not impressed.

We went on to another of the villas; here, in a classical white drawing-room with chandeliers and white marble pillars and eighteenth-century portraits that looked English, some thirty girls were dancing to the tune of an old-fashioned waltz being played on the grand piano by an elderly woman; it was really an old Varlamov song turned into a slow waltz. Comrade Borschenko explained that once a week the girls received a visit from one of the ballet people who taught them old drawing-room dances. The girls were all in their Sunday best – some in embroidered silk dresses. We did not want to disturb them so we went on to another villa. Here we found that all the boys had gone off on an excursion for the day. In all these villas there were primitive brick stoves '1941 model,' but they were there now only for emergencies, as the central heating was going to work in winter. Outside each villa there were large piles of logs.

We then walked round the vegetable plots which had been cultivated by the children. In the distance, between the trees, I caught sight of the pretentious red-tiled tower of the Tailor's Castle where I used to play hockey as a schoolboy, and then walked along the river with its separate 'beaches' for boys and girls. 'Good bathing here in summer,' said Catherine Evgenievna, 'and we seem to have had a much warmer summer here this year than you had in Moscow.' Just as we were about to take leave a beautiful child of six, a little girl, came running up to Comrade Borschenko crying, 'Mamma! Mamma!' and, burying her face in Catherine Evgenievna's skirt, began to sob. 'It's pathetic,' said Catherine Evgenievna in a whisper, stroking the child's hair and taking her up in her arms and giving her a kiss. 'Her mother died in the famine and her father is at the front, so she calls everybody "Mamma" now.' Then, aloud to the child: 'Now don't cry, Galya, let me dry your tears for you, and now say how'd-you-do to these uncles.' Galya, a beautiful child, rosy-cheeked, and with silky fair hair and little dimples, now smiled happily and shook hands with us ceremoniously.

7

Leningrad Airmen

I should have liked to stay longer in the children's colony but Colonel Studyonov said we were already behind schedule, and looking at his watch remarked that we were expected at the fighter airfield in two minutes. So we said goodbye to Galya and the two women and drove north, first through the golden alleys of the Kamenny Island – 'what a really good purpose,' I thought to myself, 'these villas are now serving' – and then through the narrow belt of the northern suburbs of Leningrad into almost open country. I noticed, off the main road, the large building of the covered tennis courts which had been built in recent years. After a while the soil around grew sandy, and the damp vegetation of the Neva delta was replaced by pine trees. It was like a continuation of the sand dunes of Sestroretsk and the Finnish coast. Among the pine trees were numerous little *datchas*. 'Very healthy air here,' said Major Lozak, 'thousands of people used to come and spend the summer round these parts.' The Finns were only some twenty miles away, but since the Russians had recaptured the old frontier station of Beloostrov the front here had become quite stabilised for more than eighteen months. One did not feel the nearness of the front here as one did on the south side of Leningrad. At length we turned off the main road and, after passing several sentries, to whom Major Lozak showed the necessary papers, we stopped outside the airfield. A soldier on duty went to fetch the major, and the major, a gruff, boisterous middle-aged man – or did he only look middle-aged? – then took us to the officers' mess. 'You'll have some roast goose and potatoes,' he said, in a tone that excluded refusal on our part. 'We had breakfast quite recently,' one or two of us ventured to remark. 'Nonsense,' said the major, 'you will have our roast goose and potatoes, and some hot milk with it. It's good for you.' So we all struggled with the enormous hunks of goose and the good parsleyed potatoes and drank the hot milk, while the major talked about things in general pending the arrival of the colonel, the commander of the airfield. 'Why do you think,' I said, 'the Germans are still so determined to hang on to Leningrad?' Sublimely, the major replied: 'They want to hang on to Leningrad BECAUSE THEY WANT TO PERISH.' We laughed.

'Don't laugh,' he said. 'It's a fact. These sons of bitches want to perish, and they WILL perish.' I asked if there was much air activity in the Leningrad area now. 'No,' he said, 'not very much. The Germans have their main fighter airfields at Tosna and Siverskaya and Gatchina to the south of Leningrad. They haven't any big bomber bases close by. We made it too hot for them. So, already long ago, they moved their bomber bases to Pskov and Vitebsk and further still; so there's plenty of time to intercept them if they try to raid Leningrad. They can't do it on an economic basis any more, so they have practically given up altogether. It's fairly quiet now; they have had to shift a lot of their stuff from here to the Ukraine where things were getting much too hot for them. Comparatively speaking, life is simple now. I remember the days when Leningrad had to depend on the transport Douglases for a bare minimum of supplies. It was a job to keep their fighters away from the Douglases. I remember how Pilutov, Hero of the Soviet Union, took on a whole swarm of Messerschmitts and saved the

Douglases. Those were hard days. Ramming had really become a necessity. It was here at the Leningrad front during the blackest days that ramming was invented – Haritonov, and Zhukov, and Zdorovtsev – these were the ramming pioneers. They have all been killed since.' 'Are there any signs of the Germans pulling out of Leningrad?' I asked. 'They won't get a chance,' said the major. 'Some months ago they brought up one of their divisions to the Leningrad front. It was last July, when they thought they could try to storm Leningrad once more. We let our Stormoviks loose; they destroyed sixty per cent of the railway and motor transport that was bringing up their new divisions. We'll destroy sixty per cent or more of them if they try to pull out.'

The colonel, tall and handsome, and looking younger than the major, now joined us, but declined the major's offer of roast goose and potatoes and hot milk. 'Yes,' he said, 'we have some aircraft the Allies sent us. Some Aerocobras and Kittyhawks. The Aerocobras are very good indeed. Also some British planes – Spitfire-3s and Hurricanes; the Spitfires are oldish models, and the Hurricanes are older still; they certainly aren't very hot stuff. There's one we had recently, and there was something written on the fuselage – said it had taken part in the Battle of Britain! Don't know to this day how it got here. For night work we use Boston bombers – and they're not bad.' 'Have you any Lancasters?' 'I'm afraid not,' he said, 'except those we see in the *Britansky Soyuznik!*' He added that he and all the airmen liked to read the *Britansky Soyuznik* – it gave them quite a lot of information about England, and was a very popular paper in Leningrad. You found it in all the soldiers' clubs and reading-rooms.

Least of all did I enjoy the next quarter of an hour. The colonel and a whole crowd of airmen showed me the new Petlyakov divebomber, also widely used for reconnaissance work. It is remarkably well constructed for observation purposes since it gives the pilot an unusually good all-round view. Its speed, I was told, was 540 kilometres per hour. It makes me feel a bit of a fraud when, as a special privilege, I am shown such a thing as a new aeroplane. What made it worse was that the young pilot would rattle off a whole long series of technical details which were just Greek to me, but I kept nodding knowingly, afraid to ask any questions that would give away my abysmal ignorance of mechanics – which would have made, not only me, but much worse, my escorting officers, look a trifle foolish. And I even wrote down some notes, which I could neither decipher nor understand afterwards!

It was a relief when the inspection of the divebomber was over, and some of the pilots came up and talked to us, and at the colonel's suggestion told of their various individual exploits. I can't say that these make good reading, so I shall not record them one by one. But the gist of all the stories was that the Germans were now less strong, less bold and less skilled. In the past they used eight to ten planes for interception, where now they used only two or three. The Russians had definite superiority over the Germans in the Leningrad area now. And even when they didn't have it, it didn't always matter. The stories told by the various pilots were mostly to the effect that the Germans nowadays evaded battle. One to one the Germans hardly ever took on a fight. 'I've known occasions,' one of the pilots said, 'when four Messerschmitts ran away from two Kittyhawks.' And a young lad, with a pockmarked peasant face, said, 'That's just what happened to me one day at Siniavino. But yesterday it was even worse. We went on reconnaissance – two of us. And here were seven Messerschmitt 109-Gs, damn good machines, mind you. But no! They buzzed off. Honestly, made one feel ashamed of them. So we freely wandered around enemy territory as if it were our own.' 'Yes,' said the colonel, 'one may really say that as a rule the Germans take on a fight only if they're in a very favourable position from the start. I don't know what it is, shortage of stuff or lack of guts. Certainly they aren't the same as they were in 1941 or even last year, and that's not simply because we've got more planes. The quality of their men has clearly deteriorated. They've lost all their best men, and we've lost most of ours – there aren't many fighter pilots left who have been at it since the 22nd of June – but we've been building up new cadres all the time.'

The colonel then took us round the officers' quarters – a large well-scrubbed wooden hut. They had a billiard table, and a reading room with large numbers of papers and periodicals from Moscow and Leningrad and, true enough, the *Britansky Soyuznik* – a well-fingered copy too. The curious thing about the place, however, was the slogans on the walls. They were quotations from a text book on officers' etiquette written by a teacher of the name of Kulchitsky of the school for guards' officers, the Corps des Pages. In fact it was the colonel who told me exactly who Kulchitsky was. Here are a few of the slogans:

'AVOID GESTICULATING AND RAISING YOUR VOICE.'

'A SOVIET (the word 'Soviet' must have been substituted for the word 'Russian') OFFICER MUST BE A MODEL OF DISCIPLINE, SMARTNESS AND SELF-POSSESSION.'

'NEVER DISDAIN ANYBODY'S ADVICE. IT IS YOUR RIGHT TO FOLLOW IT OR NOT TO FOLLOW IT.'

'AN OFFICER'S STRENGTH IS NOT IN IMPULSIVE ACTS, BUT IN HIS IMPERTURBABLE CALM.'

'TO AN OFFICER HIS HONOUR IS A SACRED THING.'

'ALWAYS REMEMBER THAT YOU ARE AN OFFICER.'

Back to the Tsarist Army? No. Why should they? But clearly it was realised that the Revolution, like all revolutions, had gone too far in certain directions and had, together with the undesirable things, discarded some desirable things, at least things which in certain conditions created by the war had become desirable again. Not a full swing-back of the pendulum but a slight return of the pendulum.

8

A Factory in the Famine

We drove through the Viborg District, past the Finland Station. Lenin had arrived here in 1917, and to commemorate that far-reaching event a statue of Lenin had been erected in the square outside the station. It was also from this station that so many Russian troops went north to storm the Mannerheim Line. One of my majors said, 'Here in Leningrad the war against Finland is considered more than justified, not least justified by what has happened since. Long before the Finnish war, Mannerheim and his gang had been in closest contact with the German General Staff and an eventual German attack on Russia was clearly going to use Finland as one of its springboards.... And, with Belooströv only twenty-six miles away it would have been suicide for Leningrad to allow the Germans and Finns to go on hatching their plans. We have very little use for the Finns,' he continued, as we drove through the Viborg District – this, like the Narva district, had also been enormously modernised, and most of the wooden houses had been used up last winter for fuel – 'and we find it a bit absurd all this American tender-heartedness for dear little Finland, chiefly because she paid her five dollars a month regularly – or whatever it was. And the sooner the Finns give in, the better will it be for them. The Germans are hanging on to Leningrad because they want to keep the Finns in the war – at least that's one of the reasons – and as long as the Finns are in the war, the Germans will try to hang on.'

'There is a theory among diplomats in Moscow,' I said, 'that the Finns are afraid of throwing in their hand, because while they are in the war they are still getting some food from Germany, and who is to feed them once they give up?' 'Oh,' said the major, 'there'll be plenty of tender-hearted people in America to see to that. And meantime – until the American supplies arrive – well, I don't think it would be unfair if Leningrad were to take charge of Finland's food supplies – what about a couple of months during which they'd get the old Leningrad ration of 125 grammes a day? Didn't their papers gloat in those days about our Leningrad famine when thousands died daily? We don't gloat, but it couldn't be a bad thing to give them a little of their own medicine and make them forget all their insolent rubbish about Greater Finland that they would set up with Hitler's help, and about Leningrad being part of the hereditary Finnish *Lebensraum!* Superior race indeed! Superior to us who built Leningrad, one of the half-dozen greatest cultural centres of the world!'

We were now driving through the Okhta district, beyond the Neva, to the east of Leningrad. Okhta had been little more than a large village of little wooden houses before. Now many large factories and seven- and eight-storey apartment houses had sprung up here, and there seemed to be relatively less damage here than in other parts of Leningrad. As in the Viborg District, so here most of the smaller wooden buildings had been used up for fuel during the previous winter. We pulled up outside a large factory building, the outer brick walls of which were marked with shell-splinters. Comrade Semyonov, the director of the factory, with a strong hard face, and wearing a plain khaki tunic to which were pinned the Leningrad medal and the Order of Lenin, was a typical Soviet executive to look at and to listen to – very precise and to the point. He took us into his office; on the mantelpiece was a collection of various things the factory was now making – bayonets, detonators and large optical lenses, and on the wall were portraits of Stalin and Zhdanov, the picture of the man who conducted the defence of Leningrad being almost as usual here as that of the great chief in Moscow. Altogether, I had noticed in Leningrad a slight aloofness towards Moscow, a feeling that, although this was part of the whole show, it was also in a sense a separate show, one in which Leningrad had largely survived thanks to its own stupendous efforts and those of its local chiefs, Zhdanov and Popkov. In a way, it is part of that Leningrad 'superiority complex' which never died, not even after the capital had been moved to Moscow.

Comrade Semyonov began by giving an account of this factory which in wartime has no name but only a number. It was, he said, the largest factory in the Soviet Union for optical instruments, ranging from the most elaborate optical instruments used in the navy to cinema projectors and cheap cameras. Millions of cheap cameras had been made here before the war, and practically all the cinemas in the Soviet Union had received their projectors from here. 'During the very first days of the war,' said Comrade Semyonov, 'the bulk of our optical equipment was evacuated east, because this was considered one of the key factories for defence. One couldn't afford to take any risks with it. Early in 1942 we had a second evacuation, and those of the skilled optical workers who hadn't gone in the first evacuation were sent away – that is, those who were still alive. Already in the first weeks of the war, when most of our equipment and skilled men had been sent away, we started here on an entirely new basis – we started working exclusively for the Leningrad front and had to make the things for which we had the equipment – and there wasn't much of it. Our people had no experience in this kind of work. Nevertheless we started making the things our Leningrad front needed most – shells and hand grenades and especially detonators for anti-tank mines. We made hundreds of thousands of these. We had never made any of these things before. But Leningrad, as you may know, has a great industrial tradition, a great industrial culture, and our hand-grenades turned out to be the best of any made. Not very long ago we had a visit from a soldier who had formerly been a worker in this place, and he said 'Congratulations! Didn't know you went in for making this stuff. But I've now been using your grenades and they're grand; thanks for keeping up the standard of the old firm!' We also started making bayonets. That was chiefly during the blockade, when it had become terribly difficult to make more elaborate things.' He picked up from the mantelpiece the flat, dagger-shaped bayonet. 'The German hates the Russian bayonet,' he said. 'He's not much good at hand-to-hand fighting. We should have liked to make the four-edged Suvorov bayonet, but we hadn't the stuff. So we started making this thing, which has come to be known as the Leningrad bayonet. For some months now we have actually been exporting some of these bayonets to the mainland, and also very considerable quantities of our detonators. Throughout the blockade and since we have also been repairing the smaller arms, rifles and machine-guns; and in the last few weeks we have started working on optical instruments again, especially on polishing lenses and on repairing range-finders, periscopes – yes, submarine periscopes too, because our Baltic Navy isn't idle you know, least of all under water.'

I asked Semyonov to tell me something about life at the factory during the hunger blockade. He was silent for a few seconds, as if collecting his thoughts. 'Frankly,' he said, 'I don't like to talk about it. It's a very bitter memory. However, I'll tell you a few things. Perhaps your people in England should know what we Leningrad people have gone through. By the time the blockade started half of our workers had been evacuated or had gone into the army, so we were left here with about 5,000. I must say it was difficult at first to get used to the bombing, and if anyone says it doesn't frighten him, don't you believe it! Yet this bombing, though it frightened people, also aroused their frantic anger against the Germans. When they started bombing us in a big way in October 1941, our workers fought for the factory more than they fought for their own houses. There was one night when we had to deal with 300 incendiaries in the factory grounds alone. Our people were putting the fires out with a sort of concentrated rage and fury; like a thousand squirrels they rushed around, putting out the flames. They had realised by then that they were in the front line – and that was all. No more shelters. Only small children were taken to shelters, and old grannies. And then, one day in December, in twenty degrees of frost, we had all our windows blown out by a bomb, and I thought to myself: 'No, we really can't go on. Not till the spring. We can't go on in this temperature, and without light, without water, and almost without food.' And yet, somehow – we didn't stop. A kind of instinct told us that we mustn't – that it would be worse than suicide. That it would be a little like treason. And sure enough, within thirty-six hours we were working again – working in altogether hellish conditions, with eight degrees of frost in the workshops, and fourteen degrees of frost in this office where you are sitting now. Oh, we had stoves of sorts, little iron stoves or little brick stoves that warmed the air a couple of feet round them. The conditions of work were really incredible, but still our people worked, worked with a kind of frantic determination, with furious defiance. And, mind you, they were hungry, terribly hungry.'

Comrade Semyonov paused for a moment and there was a frown on his face. 'Yes,' he said, 'to this day I cannot quite understand it. I don't quite understand yet how it was possible to have that will-power, that strength of mind. Many of them, hardly able to walk with hunger, would drag themselves to the factory every day, eight, ten and even twelve kilometres. For there were no tramcars. We used all sorts of, you would think, childish expedients to keep the work going. When there were no batteries, we used pedals from a bicycle to keep the lathes turning. Somehow, people knew when they were going to die. It was uncanny and hard to understand. People always thought of their families in such cases, and tried to spare them unnecessary worry. I remember one of our older workmen staggering into this office one day and saying to me, 'Comrade Chief, I have a request to make. I am one of your old workers and you have always been a good friend to me, and I know you will not refuse. I am not going to bother you again. I know that today or tomorrow I shall die. My family are in a very poor way – very weak. They won't have the strength to manage the funeral. Will you be a friend and have a coffin made for me, and have it sent to my family, so they don't have the extra worry of trying to get a coffin? You know how difficult it is to get one.' That happened during the blackest days in December or January. And such things happened day after day. How many workers came into this office saying, 'Chief, I shall be dead today or tomorrow!' We would send them to the factory hospital, but they always died. All that was possible and impossible to eat, people ate. They ate cattle-cake, and mineral oils – we used to boil them first – and carpenter's glue. People tried to sustain themselves on hot water and yeast. Out of the 5,000 people we had here, several hundred died. And a very large number of them died right here. The factory was the thing that mattered most to them. It looked as if they wanted to die here rather than at home. Many a man would drag himself to the factory, stagger in and die. It was like a call of duty to come here. Everywhere there were corpses. But some died at home, and died together with the rest of their family, and in the circumstances it was difficult to find out anything definite. The bodies were taken away, and there was really nobody who could report the man's death to us. And since there was no transport, we weren't usually able to send people round to inquire. This went on till about the 15th of February. After that rations were increased, and the death-rate dropped sharply. Today it hurts me to talk about these things.'

Comrade Semyonov sighed, then slapped the table and smiled. 'But now,' he said, 'it's almost like a birthday party. Our only real trouble comes from the shelling. It's a big nuisance. We've had many direct hits, and quite a number of casualties. Six were killed a fortnight ago, it went straight through the roof into one of the workshops. But we don't take shelter until a shell drops within less than 500 metres of the factory. The really big danger comes from the first shell for it comes quite unexpectedly. And the Germans have now also started shelling the town indiscriminately, and no longer by districts as they used to, and that makes it more difficult to follow any precise rules.'

We went through various workshops, all of them dark and dingy because there was no glass in the windows, and some of the premises were lit only by faint electric bulbs. Along long rows of lathes women and girls, some fresh but others with tired faces, were toning out little gadgets which were detonators for anti-tank mines. In another brighter and whiter workshop, together with many other girls, Lucia Kozlova, aged fifteen, young and cocky, rosy-cheeked and fair-haired, wearing a blue overall and talking in a baby voice, was polishing lenses. 'I've worked here for six weeks now,' she said, 'and am already exceeding my norm – did 110 per cent yesterday.' She was pleased with herself. 'Where is your father, Lucia?' 'At the front,' she said. 'He was wounded in May, but now he's back again.' 'And your mother?' 'She works here, in the other building, where they had a shell last month. 'Aren't you frightened of shells?' '*Niet, ne strashno* – no I'm not frightened,' she squeaked in her baby voice, and went back to polishing the lenses. In another large workshop, obviously stripped of its usual machinery, expert male workers were repairing sights and periscopes with large gashes made either in the metal or the glass by shell splinters.

We walked through the factory grounds with their wide-open spaces, partly covered with vegetable plots and partly with heaps of rubble. 'All this is badly smashed up,' said Comrade Semyonov. 'Before the war there was a lawn here with a fountain in the middle, and over there is what's left of the open-air stadium' – and pointing to a badly shattered building – 'and this used to be our concert hall. We used to have real symphony concerts here. Our workers are very keen on music. In 1937, we had the Leningrad Philharmonic playing to us, with Albert Coates conducting. He was in the Soviet Union on a tour then. Very, very good concert. I remember they played Tchaikovsky's Fourth Symphony.'

9

Sunday Evening in Leningrad

We drove back to the Astoria along the Liteiny Prospect and turned into the Nevsky. I noticed that the old eighteenth-century guns – relics of the wars of Peter and Catherine – which lined what I think was the old Liteiny foundry, had disappeared. 'They haven't been used up as scrap, have they?' I asked. 'Good God, no,' said Major Lozak, scandalised at the suggestion. 'They are historically very valuable, those guns. They've been taken away to a safe place.' How typical of Leningrad to have gone to all the trouble of moving those big bronze and iron monsters. They were not outstandingly valuable, except as something to which everybody in Leningrad had become accustomed, still less were they vulnerable; but they were 'part of Leningrad,' one of those things that everybody in Leningrad knew and remembered.

It was Sunday afternoon. The Liteiny, so famous in the past for its numerous secondhand bookshops – there did not seem to be many there now – looked rather deserted except for the regular traffic of half-empty tramcars and occasional army lorries. We drove past a big block of flats where an aunt of mine had once lived, and as we crossed the Basseinaya I looked down that street, and remembered that in number seven, I think, there once lived a girl called Gasya, with whom, at the age of fifteen, I was violently in love – until the day when she discarded my unrealistic calf-love, with its literary talks and its evenings of Chopin, in favour of some elderly bloke's substantial offer of marriage. Of course he was elderly – he was twenty-four and she was sixteen. To add insult to injury I was made to be a *shafer* – one of the best men – at the wedding, and had to take my turn in holding the golden crown over the bride's head while the priest was doing his stuff. Where was Gasya now?

But no sooner had we reached the corner of the Nevsky and the Liteiny than the scene changed. In spite of sporadic shelling, the Nevsky, and especially the famous crossroads, were crowded as they had always been. Thousands of people – workpeople, soldiers and girls – were walking up and down the Nevsky on that Sunday afternoon. What was the eternal attraction of that corner? In the past it used to be one of the main centres of prostitution in Petrograd. There was no suggestion of anything like that now, nor were there any cheap eating places, frequented by students, such as the famous Dominique with its billiard rooms, open in the neighbourhood. But the corner still had a sort of magnetic attraction. At this corner I had for the first time in my life talked to a prostitute. She had accosted me and asked me for a cigarette. I was fourteen, and said I hadn't any, at which point the silly, giggly, clumsy, pale-faced girl said, 'A great big boy like you ought to learn to smoke, and to make love to the girls'; I was seized with panic and saying I was in a great hurry, I ran away.

At the Astoria, 'Mamasha' (as we had all come to call her by now) had prepared the usual dinner, and after that we drove to the Alexandrinka to see *The Princess of the Circus.* Though played inside the august walls of the Alexandrinka – more august than anything outside the Comédie Française – this was the most frivolous show I had seen ever since I arrived in the Soviet Union in July 1941. In this sense it was a typically Leningrad-in-wartime show. Leningrad was obviously needing the lightest and brightest recreation available, and it had been so ever since the beginning of the blockade.

Throughout the blockade the operetta had gone on functioning. According to one story I heard (which I mentioned before) it was so cold in the theatre that the dancers appeared on stage wearing their fur coats; according to another version they appeared in tights in spite of the frost and danced with their faces all blue and their teeth chattering. It seems that both things happened; perhaps the alternative costumes were determined by the mercury being above or below a certain point.

The Princess of the Circus is by the same man as *Sylva* which has been the popular favourite in Moscow for years; Kalmann, I think, is the composer's name; clearly something central-European, probably Viennese, and full of trivial but pleasantly catchy tunes. But, as performed by the Russians, it was extraordinarily like an English musical comedy, with its glamorous and sentimental princess, and fatuously beautiful tenor of a hero, and above all, the whole collection of various 'silly asses' and terrifying old dames and comic slapstick waiters. The main 'silly ass,' played by that admirable comedian, Kedrov, was 'Count Frederix,' the name of the last Grand Chamberlain of Nicholas II. But the Frederix of the Alexandrinka was not as gaga as his namesake; he was, as he himself said, 'the Silenus of the stalls, gallery and other places,' and looked, in his Ruritanian uniform, and with his handlebar moustache, extraordinarily like the late Marshal Pilsudski. The hero with the domino and the top hat was 'Mr. X,' the celebrated acrobat and in reality 'Prince Clery,' but the heroine did not know this, and swooned at the discovery that she was in love with an acrobat. It doesn't matter about the plot – it consisted of the usual musical comedy rubbish and ended as happily as all these things do. Where the action was supposed to take place is equally unimportant – actually it shifted quite irrationally from the entrance to the celebrated Ciniselli Circus in St. Petersburg to Count Frederix's sumptuous mansion on the Neva – with the windows naturally looking on to the fortress – and ended up in the Erzherzog Karl restaurant in Vienna. 'You will be my guest to-night,' said 'Pilsudski.' 'Lend me a hundred roubles.' And at the great fête in the second act there was a dance of vamps with yellow shawls and in golden snakescaled frocks. Frederix incidentally spoke with a comic German accent, no doubt like his namesake, the gaga Grand Chamberlain of the last Tsar. But the really uproarious stuff came in the last act, which was pure slapstick. And the simple, if still very funny jokes – so like English silly-ass jokes – kept the Leningrad audience rocking with laughter. This sort of thing: the terrifying old lady in the Erzherzog Karl restaurant: 'Speaking of rubbish – WHERE is my husband?' And then there was Pelican, the comic senile waiter who kept dropping from the dish a cardboard duck and kicking it around the place. It was curious to think of even a cardboard duck being kicked about the stage during the Leningrad blockade. But now the audience roared with laughter at the cardboard duck till the tears ran down their faces. And Pelican's jokes were on these lines: 'Madam, the lobster is boiling, I just poked it with a fork and it's still hard,' or, 'I had to sack the other waiter because he poured all the sauce down Countess Metternich's bosom,' or, when Herr Schrank, a very nondescript customer, asked Pelican why the latter always addressed him as 'Herr von Schrank,' Pelican replies, 'Because, in our establishment we always call a baron a prince; an ordinary person a baron, and the scum of the earth we call "von."' And then, licking his chops, Pelican said to a new arrival, 'Ah, the pheasant is lovely and tender – but there's none left' (which, I bet, is a Russian addendum). And finally – this was very English-musical-comedy: 'Baron, why is your hair white and your moustache black?' 'It's because my moustache is twenty years younger than my hair.' It was all very unworthy of the stage of the Alexandrinka where Gogol's *Revizor* and so many other famous plays were performed for the first time, and which for nearly a hundred years had been trod by the most famous tragedians and especially comedians of Russia. But there it was – Leningrad was needing complete comic relief, and nothing was as good as this slapstick. In fact, the people were about as much 'front' as Leningrad – with the vast majority of the audience, including the women, in uniform.

In one of the intervals we were invited into a large dressing-room, where we met 'Pilsudski,' and the beautiful hero, and the Princess of the Circus, and Pelican the waiter. The talked about the bad old days of the blockade when they lived on 125 grammes a day. 'God, they were skinny in their tights,' said 'Pilsudski,' pointing at the ladies. 'Regular scarecrows! But now you're quite nice and plump again, girls, aren't you,' he added, pointing at the Princess and the other actresses. 'Oh, we're all right now,' said the Princess; and then they told how they had travelled almost daily to the front during the darkest days, how they had nearly died of exhaustion, but had tried to keep the soldiers in good humour. 'And, except for a very short time, we did get a few little extras to eat – the Leningrad Soviet certainly did their best to keep us alive – and there was nothing to equal the generosity of the soldiers; they would press food on us, though heaven knows they were on iron rations themselves – worse than iron rations. But we certainly cheered them up a lot, at a time when they needed cheering up!'... There were still old photographs on the wall, pictures of Savina and Varlamov and Davidov, and other great Alexandrinka stars of the distant past. Whose dressing-room, I wondered, had 'this been? But what did it matter? For here, today, one had another little glimpse into that immense human drama through which every man, woman and child of Leningrad had lived.... 'God, weren't they skinny in their tights!'

We spent a pleasant evening around the supper table that night. The colonel was again pulling Dangulov's leg with *kishmish* and other standing Caucasian jokes. But in Leningrad, sooner or later, the conversation always seems to get back to the black days, to the winter of 1941. Major Lozak, with his pale face, eyes and hair, and Roman nose, and aristocratic little burr, recalled what Comrade Semyonov had told us at the factory that day. 'It's quite true,' he said, 'in those days there *was* something in a man's face that told you at once he would die within the next twenty-four hours. Life had become terribly cheap.' The major had lived in Leningrad all his life, and he had his parents in Leningrad too. 'They are old people,' he said, 'and I had to give them half my soldier's ration or they would certainly have died. And as a staff officer I was, naturally and quite rightly, getting considerably less than the people at the front – 250 grammes a day instead of 350. I shall always remember how every day I'd walk from my house near the Taurus Gardens to my work in this part of the town, a matter of three or four kilometres. I felt very exhausted. I'd walk for a while, and then sit down for a rest. Many a time I saw a man suddenly collapse on the snow. There was nothing one could do. One just walked on. And I remember how, on the way back, I would see a vague human form covered with snow on the spot where in the morning I had seen the man fall down. One didn't worry – what was the good! People didn't wash for weeks; there were no bath-houses and no fuel. But at least people were urged to shave. And during that winter I don't think I ever saw a person smile. It was frightful. And yet, there was a kind of inner discipline that made most people carry on. A new code of manners was evolved by the hungry people. They carefully avoided talking about food. They tried to talk about all sorts of things. I remember spending a very hungry evening with an old boy from the Radio Committee. He nearly drove me crazy – he *would* talk all evening about Kant and Hegel. Yet we never lost heart. The Battle of Moscow gave us complete confidence that it would be all right in the end. But what a change all the same when February came and the Ice Road was opened! Those tremendous parcels that suddenly started arriving from all over the country – parcels of honey and butter and ham and sausage! Still, our troubles are by no means at an end. This shelling can really be very upsetting. I was in the Nevsky once when a shell landed close by. And ten yards away from me was a man whose head was cut clean off by a shell spinter. It was horrible. I saw him make his last two steps already *with his head off* – and a bloody mess all round before he collapsed. I vomited right there and then, and I was quite ill for the rest of the day – though I had already seen many terrible things before. I shall never forget the night the children's hospital was hit by an oil bomb, many children were killed, and the whole house was blazing, and some perished in the flames. It's bad for one's nerves to see such things happen; our ambulance services have instructions to wash away blood on the pavement as quickly as possible after a shell has landed.'

The major said that he often visited the front lines, and as he also knew German well he saw a lot of German prisoners. 'At first, you know,' he said, 'our people didn't much believe in German atrocities until they saw them with their own eyes. At Tikhvin, where the Germans were for a month, they hanged a lot of people. When I talk to war prisoners now, I am struck by the remarkable change in their attitude to us. In 1941 and even in 1942 they were arrogant, almost without exception. Now they have deteriorated both physically and mentally. They are verminous to the last degree; and an infantry officer whom I questioned the other day, said, '*Wir leben im Dreck. Es ist aussichtslos.*' (The infantry people are terribly jealous of the Luftwaffe who have an easier life, much better food and better quarters.)

'In the past, the most one could ever get out of a German was a recognition of our having guts. But at heart every German remained convinced that, technically, we were vastly inferior to them, and that sooner or later our guts would give way, and then it would be quite easy, and Hitler would win the war. But they've learned a lot of things. They know that it wasn't only tremendous guts but wonderful organisation that enabled us to hold Schlusselburg fortress throughout the blockade. And they've learned a lot of other things at this front – not to mention Stalingrad and all that's been happening since the 5th of July this year. They know that our guns and mortars are better than theirs and our fortifications as good as theirs, and our tanks at least as good, and our infantry about as well armed as their infantry. And now they also know that there's superb confidence in victory on our side and only *Dreck* on their side. They've got very tough troops, though. Their S.S. troops took a big part in the Mga operation this summer, when they made their last desperate bid to break through to Leningrad. But the general level is much lower than it was, and they've been diluting their own troops with a lot of international rabble. There's a lot of rabble at this front. There are, for instance, the Spaniards. The Falangist officers are about as low a bunch as you've ever seen. They spend their days gambling, and take bribes from the soldiers for all sorts of little favours. And the Spanish troops – they are a mixture. About half of them are composed of anarchist rabble from Barcelona while the rest are political prisoners who have been released on the condition they go to Russia to fight. A lot of them try to escape to our lines. But it's difficult, because they are carefully watched, especially by the Germans. Recently a tragic thing happened. Seven of these Spanish Republicans tried to come over to us but just before they had reached our lines they were discovered, and six were killed; only one got across, and wounded at that. Others who often try to surrender and sometimes succeed are the Alsatians. But this is a very static front, and it is much more difficult for them to come over here than it is on the southern front where the war is so much more mobile. But it is comic some of the things that do happen these days. The funniest thing is the latest German leaflets. They must be hard up for new ideas, for do you know what they put in their leaflets now? 'The Duce has been rescued!' They drop these in thousands over our lines. Our soldiers' comment has invariably been, 'So what?''

Major Likharov, our other host, said that in September, when the Germans were approaching Leningrad, his wife got into a slight panic and bought 'just in case' an enormous eight-kilo tin of fresh caviare. 'When I saw it I said to her, 'the stuff will just go bad; I think you had better take it back to the shop,' which she did. Oh, Lord! didn't we regret it afterwards. Throughout the months of the famine we were haunted by the memory of that eight-kilo tin of caviare. It was like Paradise lost!' Likharov, though unpoetic to look at with his rough-hewn face and heavy jaw, was a good poet, but as he said, he was now working almost entirely on propaganda, writing articles and sketches for front newspapers; this meant a lot of travelling about the front and seeing a lot of people, and he was collecting masses of material which he would use after the war. Altogether he thought there would be an enormous crop of literature produced in Leningrad after the war. A lot of people had kept diaries throughout these two years which would make first-class material.

'It was certainly a job travelling about during the worst days of the blockade,' he said. 'I shall always remember my journey to Tikhvin in December 1941. The Germans had just abandoned the town after holding it for a month. They abandoned it on December 12th. It was dreadfully cold, and I travelled there on board a railway engine – had to stand practically all the time. The journey took thirty-six hours – a day and a night and a day. The words 'I'm from Leningrad' were magic words. You can't imagine the way people outside Leningrad reacted to them. They overwhelmed you with kindness. I remember how at night our railway engine arrived at a little station; I was hungry and I hadn't been in bed for weeks; the engine-driver and the stoker were terribly dirty; but when a railwayman heard we were from

Leningrad, he took us to his little house and insisted that I sleep in his clean white bed, with its lace cover and its embroidered pillowslips. He produced the food he had hidden away from the Germans, and gave us a meal the like of which I had not seen for months. I had by that time already lost sixty pounds in weight. He also insisted that my two companions should sleep in his house and have a good rest. All three of us were complete strangers to him – but we were from Leningrad. It was like a passport and a ration book all in one. It warmed my heart to feel how deeply the rest of the country had been worrying about us during those critical weeks of October and November.'

10

Children in the Famine and Now

The south side of the Obvodny Canal to the east of the Warsaw Station used to be one of the worst slum areas of old St. Petersburg. It was here, in one of the streets off the canal, that we visited the next morning a large modern school that had been built in 1936. The rest of the street looked very different from what I had remembered this district to be. Most of the houses were modern brick houses; it was really a brand-new part of Leningrad. It would have looked even better but for the rather extensive damage caused by shelling. For one thing, there was hardly a whole pane of glass anywhere; plywood, which gives houses that dead blind look, was in all the windows. Usually, only one small glass pane per window was put in for giving the room some light. The school in Tambov Street was a large brick building with long white-washed corridors, decorated with portraits of Stalin and Zhdanov and posters. A girl of seventeen or eighteen with dark hair and bright-red cheeks, very lovely and as fresh as a Canadian apple, and wearing a Pioneer uniform with a red neck-tie, very like the uniform of the Girl Guides, took us into Comrade Tikhomirov's office. He was the headmaster and had the very unusual distinction of ranking as a 'Teacher of Merit of the U.S.S.R.' in the Golden Book (or whatever it is called) of the Commissariat of Education.

Tikhomirov was an elderly man with a grey moustache, and a kindly intelligent face. He had started life as an elementary-school teacher under the old régime back in 1907, and had fought in the German war (for that's what 1914–18 is usually called in Russia now) and in the civil war, but had after that returned to the profession he loved most. 'Well,' he said, 'I never thought that when I started teaching I'd ever have to face the problems we have all had to face these last two years! But I'll tell you about that later; there's an arithmetic class on just now, wouldn't you like to go in?' Since the recent abolition of co-education this was now a purely boys' school; the boys now attending were aged eight to thirteen; the older boys wouldn't start coming to school until October 1st. We went into the classroom, there were about forty twelve-year-olds there; they all stood up as soon as they saw the headmaster and the rest of us come in. I did not think an arithmetic class would be very exciting, but even arithmetic, as I soon discovered, was used as war propaganda. The maths teacher, standing on a little platform below the blackboard, was an elderly woman with bobbed grey hair, tired yellow skin and a reddish nose; she obviously felt fatigue and strain, and yet – every word she said was uttered with great animation bordering on exuberance. She wore a smart black skirt and a white blouse and neck-tie, and good-quality black shoes. Her job was to make the lesson sound interesting, and with genuine exuberance she presented the problems to the boys in the following manner: 'Now boys, I want to tell you about a young girl in a factory who decided that she must celebrate somehow the glorious victory of our Red Army at Chernigov. So what do you think she did? No, she didn't go to the pictures. She decided to increase her output. The first day she exceeded her norm by fifteen per cent, the second day by twenty per cent…' I forget all the details of the problem, but soon after the teacher had stated it several boys put up their hands and announced, with obvious approval, that the answer was this: 'In one week the girl exceeded her production norm by 184 per cent.' 'Quite correct!' said the teacher, 'and in doing so, the girl proved that she was a real Stakhanovite, and that she really loved her country.' The rest was much on the same lines. The boys were all in excellent physique, and most of them seemed very bright.

The same was true of another class of thirteen-year-olds, where the headmaster said I could take the teacher's chair and ask them any questions I liked. This was very sudden; I saw the boys surveying me with critical interest as I sat down, and I had an attack of acute stage-fright. However, I pulled myself together and after talking of the fall of Smolensk I asked one of the boys where he thought the Germans would retreat to now. 'They will retreat all the way to hell!' the boy exclaimed. 'And they'll get to hell out of Leningrad, too,' another one spontaneously cried. I didn't think the strategic discussion was getting us very far, and turned to vegetable growing and wood cutting – questions on which the children were great experts. I picked the boys at random and was astonished at the ease and fluency with which each of them gave a detailed account of how he had taken part in planting cabbages and in watering and looking after them. Then I asked some personal questions, but soon had to stop this because the first boy said that his father had died in the famine, and the second one that his had been killed at the front, and the third one that his father has also died in the famine.

Then I asked one of the boys what he knew about England. He said he didn't know much, and then pondering for a moment, he added, 'Oh, no, I do know a few things; one is, that London is the capital of England, and that it was bombed by the Germans,' 'Quite right. Anything else?' He didn't know any more. But another boy raised his hand. 'Yes?' 'I also know,' said the boy, 'that the English haven't opened the Second Front yet.' Several boys laughed. Another hand went up. 'The English have a very good air force, and they bomb the hell out of the Fritzes, and they also have a good navy.' This sounded more encouraging. 'Can anybody tell me anything about America?' Two hands went up. One of the boys said, 'They've got skyscrapers 150 storeys high.' 'They make a lot of trucks for the Red Army.' 'We get American chocolate.' 'The Americans are very rich,' came the replies. 'Have any of you ever seen an American?' Nobody had. 'Had anybody ever seen a German?' A whole forest of hands went up. They had seen German prisoners. 'And what were they like?' 'They looked just like Germans – a lot of *svolochi*,' one of the boys said, and the other boys laughed. I felt that these boys had the minds of boys but the character of grown-up men. They had learned hatred at a very early age. They hadn't been taught it, they had learned it from life itself.

It was one of the points Comrade Tikhomirov made when he took me back to his study and talked to me about the school in general. Before that he took us through the 'military cabinet,' with a large display of brochures on elementary military training, and with an impressive collection of rifles and hand-grenades and even one machine-gun. 'At fourteen they start getting their elementary military training,' he said, 'they learn to use a rifle and to throw grenades; and they also have bayonet practice. Moreover, they receive a rudimentary knowledge of the machine-gun, and also some elementary facts about tanks and artillery. That, by the way, is one of the reasons why our government decided to abandon co-education. The curricula for boys and girls are going to be rather different now, at least they will be from next year.'

Then, taking me into his study, he said that the school had been smashed four times by shelling, but only once very badly – that was in October 1941 – at the worst possible moment. The boys cleared away all the glass, bricked up the walls that had been smashed, put plywood in the windows. 'On the next two occasions the damage was relatively slight, but on May 1st this year a shell landed in the yard, and one of our woman teachers was killed. Eighty-five per cent of the children's fathers are – or were – at the front; I say 'were' because many of them are dead. Nearly all the mothers are working in factories in Leningrad, or on transport, wood cutting, or A.R.P. Nearly all the fathers are actually on the Leningrad front; so there is the closest contact between our school and the front lines. These boys are terribly grown up for their age. We don't have to teach them political consciousness – or hatred. They have learned it all in the hard school of life.'

'Can you tell me something about this school during the famine?' I asked. 'Yes,' he said, 'I can tell you a few things, and then I'll show you something that'll interest you.' Then he said earnestly, 'We stuck it, and stuck it well. We had to be worthy of our city. We had no wood, but the Lensoviet gave us a small wooden house not far away for demolition, so we could use the timber for heating. The bombing and shelling used to be very severe in those days. We had about 120 pupils then – boys and girls – and we had to hold our classes in the shelter. Not for a day did the work stop. It was very cold. The little stoves heated the air properly only a yard around them, and in the rest of the shelter the temperature was below zero. There was no lighting, apart from a kerosene lamp. But we carried on, and the children were so serious and earnest about it all that we actually got better results out of them than in any other year. Surprising, but true. We had meals for them: the army helped us to feed them. Several of the teachers died of undernourishment, but I am proud to say that all the children in our care survived. Only, it was pathetic to watch them during those famine months. Towards the end of the year they hardly looked like children any more. They were strangely silent, with a kind of concentrated look in their eyes.

They would not walk about, still less run about; they would just sit. But none of them died; and only some of those pupils who had stopped coming to school, and stayed at home, died, often together with the rest of the family.'

Comrade Tikhomirov pulled out a drawer of his desk and produced from it a large hand-bound volume. 'This is our Famine Scrapbook,' he said. 'It has copies of a lot of essays written by the children during the famine, and a lot of other material.' I asked – and it was asking a lot – whether I could borrow it till the next morning; and, after receiving every assurance from our majors that it would be safely returned, the headmaster, a little nervously, agreed that I could take it away.

We were seen to the car by the headmaster and by the Pioneers' guide, the lovely child with the dark hair, lively dark eyes and fresh red cheeks. Pointing across the courtyard, she said, 'That's the place where one of our woman teachers was killed by a shell on May 1st.' And as we went out into the street, with its eyeless houses, she said, giving me a friendly feminine smile and a friendly manly handshake, 'You will come to see us again next time you are in Leningrad?' And as we drove down towards the Obvodny Canal with its cabbage-tapestried slopes, I felt that here was one of those Russian girls who in no time can set a man daydreaming, and suddenly make him think of his life in terms of 'ifs' and 'if only's.'

That evening I looked through the large scrapbook bound in purple velvet, and with margins composed of rather conventional children's watercolours depicting soldiers, tanks, aeroplanes and the like. These surrounded little typewritten sheets which had been pasted on to the thin cardboard of the scrapbook. These sheets were copies of typical essays written by pupils – mostly girls – during the famine, and a survey written by the headmaster himself. I wrote a few at random.

One young girl wrote: 'Unlike June 22nd everybody had work and a good life assured to him. That day we went on an excursion to the Kirov Islands. A fresh wind was blowing from the Gulf, bringing with it bits of the song some kids were singing not far away, 'Great and glorious is my native land.' And then the enemy began to come nearer and nearer our city. We went out a dig trenches. It was difficult because a lot of the kids were not used to such hard physical labour. The German General von Leeb was already licking his chops at the throught of the gala dinner he was going to order at the Astoria. Now we are sitting in the shelter, round improvised stoves, with our coats and fur caps and gloves on. We have been sewing and knitting warm things for our soldiers, and been taking round their letters to the friends and relatives. We have also been collecting non-ferrous metal for salvage.'

Valentina Solovyova, an older girl of sixteen, wrote: 'June 22nd! How much that date means of us now! But then it seemed just an ordinary summer day.... Before long the House Committees were swarming with women, girls and children who had come to join the A.R.P. teams, the anti-fire and anti-gas squads.... By the end of September the city was encircled. Food supplies from outside had ceased. The last evacuee trains had departed. The people of Leningrad tightened their belts. The streets began to bristle with barricades and anti-tank 'hedgehogs.' Dug-outs and firing-points – a whole network of them – were springing up around the city. As in 1919, so now, the great question arose: 'Shall Leningrad remain a Soviet city or not?' Leningrad was in danger. But its workers had risen like one man for its defence. Tanks were thundering down the streets. Everywhere men of the civil guard were joining up.... A cold, terrible winter was approaching. Together with their bombs, enemy planes were dropping down leaflets. They said that they would raze Leningrad to the ground. They said we would all die

Young Leningrad girl on an anti-aircraft observation post. In the background is the Admiralty.

of hunger. They thought they would frighten us, but they filled us with renewed strength.... Leningrad did not let the enemy into its gates! The city was starving, but it lived and worked, and kept sending to the front more and more new detachments of its sons and daughters. Though knocking at the knees with hunger, our workers went to work at their factories, with the air raid sirens filling the air with their screams.'

From another essay on how the schoolchildren dug trenches while the Germans were approaching Leningrad: 'In August we worked for twenty-five days digging trenches. We were machine-gunned and some of us were killed, but we carried on, though we weren't used to this work. And the Germans were stopped by the trenches we had dug.'

And here is how, according to the same Valentina Solovyova, work continued at school during the worst time of the blockade: '...It became very difficult to work. The central heating was, of course, out of action. It became terribly cold. One's hands and feet were quite numb, and the ink froze in the ink-pots. We hid

Cabbage plots in the Champ de Mars.

our faces inside our coat collars, and wrapped scarves around our hands, but it was still terribly cold. Antonina Ivanovna, our chemistry teacher, came into the classroom and teased us for sitting there all huddled up. Feeling a little ashamed, we put down our collars and took off our gloves. She was always cheerful, and always managed to cheer us up. She made jokes which made us laugh. . . . Only thanks to this moral support we received from all the teachers and the headmaster did we stick it at all. Otherwise we should have stopped coming to school. . . . But we had to give up using the shelter as a classroom. And the reason for this was quite simple. There was no more light in the shelter; so we had to move back to the classroom. Not that this was very bright either. For there was only one small pane of glass in the window. And so we continued to sit around the little *burzhuika* stove – and so we continued till the spring. Sometimes the stove smoked terribly. And altogether, it was dangerous to sit too close to it. Often there was a smell of burning *valenki* in the class, and gloves went on fire, and even the clothes sometimes began to smoulder.'

Another girl of sixteen, Luba Tereschenkova, described the same strange scene as follows: 'At the end of January and in February, frost also joined the blockade and lent Hitler a hand. It was never less than thirty degrees of frost! Our classes continued on the 'Round the Stove' principle. But there were no reserved seats, and if you wanted a seat near the stove or under the stove pipe, you had to come early. The place facing the stove door was reserved for the teacher. You sat down, and were suddenly seized by a wonderful feeling of well-being; the warmth penetrated through your skin, right into your bones; it made you all weak and languid and paralysed your thoughts; you just wanted to think of nothing, only to slumber and drink in the warmth. It was agony to stand up and go to the blackboard. One wanted to put off the evil moment. It was so cold and dark at the blackboard, and your hand, imprisoned in its heavy glove, goes all numb and rigid, and refuses to obey. The chalk keeps falling out of your hand, and the lines are all crooked and the figures deformed.... By the time we reached the third lesson there was no more fuel left. The stove went cold, and horrid icy draughts started blowing down the pipe. It became terribly cold. It was then that Vasya Pughin, with a puckish look on his face, could be seen slinking out and bringing in a few logs from Anna Ivanovna's emergency reserve; and a few minutes later one could again hear the magic crackling of wood inside the stove.... During the break nobody would jump up because no one had any desire to go into the icy corridors.'

In another essay the same girl wrote: 'One day we were sitting silently round the *burzhuika* warming our numb fingers. The bell had rung several minutes before. We were waiting for our teacher of literature. Instead of him, Yakov Mikhailovich arrived and announced, 'There will be no classes today. We must all go and take to pieces a wooden house because our wood supply is at an end, and we must get more wood in.' Well, it couldn't be helped. It was terribly cold outside. A piercing wind was blowing, freezing our faces and stopping the blood in our veins.'

And here is more, from another essay by the same girl: 'The winter came, fierce and merciless. The water pipes froze, and there was no electric light, and the tramcars stopped running. To get to school in time I had to get up very early every morning, for I live out in the suburbs. It was particularly difficult to get to school after a blizzard when all roads and paths are covered with snowdrifts. But I firmly decided to complete my school year.... One day, after standing in a bread queue for six hours (I had to miss school that day, as I had received no bread for two days), I caught a cold and fell ill. Never had I felt more miserable than during those days. Not for physical reasons, but because I desperately needed the moral support of my schoolmates, their encouraging jokes.'

Not everybody could take it. Leonchukova, one of the teachers, wrote: 'Not everybody could face all the ordeals of the war and the blockade. Some people left the city and departed to more quiet places; others gave up school and went to work in factories; some were defeated in this unequal struggle with calamity, but the strongest held out till the end.'

None of the children who continued to go to school died. But several of the teachers did. The last section of the Famine Scrapbook is introduced by a title page with a decorative funeral urn painted on it in purple watercolour. And the text that follows is by Tikhomirov, the headmaster. It is a series of obituary notes of the teachers of the school who were either killed in the war or who died of hunger. The assistant headmaster was killed in action. Another was 'killed at Kingisepp' – in that terrible battle of Kingisepp where the Germans broke through to Leningrad from Estonia. Another teacher 'died of hunger', so did the teacher of geography. Comrade Nemirov, the teacher of literature, 'he was among the victims of the blockade,' and Akimov, the history teacher, 'died of malnutrition and exhaustion, despite a long rest in a sanatorium to which he was taken in January.' Of the teacher of literature, the headmaster wrote: 'He worked conscientiously until he realised that he could no longer walk. He asked me for a few days' leave in the hope that his strength would come back to him. He stayed at home, preparing his lessons for the second term. He went on reading books. So he spent the day of January 8th. On January 9th he quietly passed away.'

What a human story there is behind these simple words!

11

The Bristles of the Hedgehog

No fortress is impregnable; the only question is what price is one willing and able to pay. People in Leningrad have told me: 'Of course, the Germans can, theoretically, take Leningrad. But it may cost them half a million men to break through our outer defences, and perhaps a million more before they get the whole town. And even then it's not certain. Even if they got as far as the Neva, they'd still have to cross the Neva and get to the Petrograd side and to the islands. Even Hitler would be mad enough to try it, especially as he is bound to know that, sooner or later, he'll have to pull out of here anyway – considering the way things are going further south – in the Smolensk and Nevel areas. He's sufficiently crazy as he is, to tie up all these troops of his between here and Riga, when he is so desperately in need of troops elsewhere. On the other hand, we also could break the German ring round Leningrad – it isn't really a ring any longer, but let's call it that for convenience – if we were prepared to pay a very heavy price. But there are more economical ways of relieving Leningrad. Leningrad will not be relieved by a breakthrough right here, but by a breakthrough on the Volkov, Kalinin or central front, or by a combined breakthrough on all three. We know that, sooner or later, they'll have to pull out, and we are ready to put up with the shelling – this completely senseless shelling – because we know that this shelling kills incomparably fewer people than would an attempt by our Leningrad troops to storm the so-called German 'iron ring.' Besides, there is no longer today the same need for breaking through the blockade as there was before. The blockade is now far from complete; the German 'iron ring' has large gaps in it. First of all, there's Lake Ladoga; and the ice road across it saved us from starvation during the terrible winter of 1941–2; then in the summer of 1942 we transported our supplies across the lake in barges and steamers under fighter cover. The only time when we were really almost completely cut off from the mainland was during those four terrible months – October, November, December, January and the first part of February. Even then, the situation looked slightly more promising after we had recaptured Tikhvin on December 12th. But while Tikhvin was in German hands – it had been in their hands for a month – we were completely cut off except for transport planes. . . . However, Lake Ladoga was not a very satisfactory supply route as you may imagine, especially in summer. Our breakthrough at Schlusselburg last February has made a very big difference. Through that Schlusselburg gap there now runs a railway which links up with the rest of the country. The link of thirty-five kilometres was built in twenty-two days – at Stalin's express orders. We now get everything we really need.'

The tremendous chain of Russian fortifications round Leningrad was something that had been built up in process of time – during the last two years. Even now they were continuing to be perfected. In the past, at the beginning of the siege, the fortifications were much thinner. Now nothing was being left to chance. Even parts of Leningrad that seemed least likely to be attacked had been powerfully fortified now; the Krestovsky Island in the north, the Delta which might conceivably be attacked in winter, across the ice of the Gulf of Finland, had now been turned into a powerful bastion. All the approaches to

Leningrad from land or from the frozen sea had been made as impregnable as was humanly possible. But that wasn't all. The defence of Leningrad had developed in the last two years on the principle that the Germans might well attempt to storm the city, and that, if they were prepared to pay a sufficiently heavy price, they might capture, say, the first line of defence, and perhaps even the second, and might even, if they were determined to progress at any price, break into the city itself. Therefore defence in depth had been organised on a scale probably unequalled anywhere. On the southern part of Leningrad every house had, in effect, been turned into a fortress, with the principal machine-gun nests and anti-tank strongholds set up in the basements and ground floors of large buildings dominating crossroads and main thoroughfares. This network of little fortresses – cemented, sandbagged, and propped up with masses of steel girders and wooden walls nine, ten, twelve logs thick – extended with varying degrees of density across the whole of Leningrad. In the southern part of the city these powerful firing-points were to be found in almost every house, in other parts at every strategically vital street corner. Many of these firing-points in the basements and on the ground floors were so large and 'basic' that they were visible to any passerby.

But I gathered that, in the event of trouble, hundreds of other firing points, invisible to the outsider and concealed at various levels of the houses, would come into action. Besides, in the southern part of the city, there were many barricades still, with anti-tank guns and machine-guns behind them, and several streets were lined with masses of anti-tank hedgehogs which, in case of necessity, could simply be put in a solid mass across the street. This stupendous work was done by the army, and even more by the civilians, and done in incredibly difficult conditions, with a shortage of certain building materials, and with the people not in the best condition for hard physical labour. And outside

Leningrad proper there was the front, with its numerous lines of spaced-out trenches, with minefields and masses of barbed wire in between. This front zone stretched in an irregular crescent from the German Uritsk–Strelna–Peterhof foothold on the Gulf of Finland to a point on the Neva west of Schlusselburg, to that Schlusselburg-Ladoga corridor through which Leningrad's essential overland lifeline now ran. And further west, a similar but shorter Russian crescent of minefields and trenches and barbed wire was defending that Russian bridgehead on the south side of the Gulf of Finland opposite Kronstadt – the Peterhof-Oranienbaum – Krasnaya Oorks bridgehead. That day – it was after the visit to the Tambov Street school – I saw something at first hand of those Leningrad fortifications and of the soldiers manning them. We drove down to the Narva district, past the Narva gate and the damaged houses around it, with the heavily sandbagged firing-points on their ground floors, but instead of driving south-west towards the Putilov works, we took the road going due south towards Pushkin (the former Tsarskoye Selo). Some distance away on the right was the large black shape of the Putilov works. On either side of the road were large new workers' dwellings, many of them badly shattered by shells. All the large spaces between the houses were being used as cabbage plots. We drove up to a large dug-out, scarcely noticeable at more than a few yards away so well was it camouflaged on all sides, except for the entrance at the back. Above the low, wooden door hung a poster of a ragged and distressed-looking child against the background of a burning village: '*Papa, ubei nemtsa* – Daddy, kill a German!' We were met by a sentry who took us into the 'blockhouse.' Inside was a large gun, and the blockhouse, with steel girders and wooden walls twelve logs thick on the side facing the enemy, and almost as thick on its other sides, was a powerful piece of engineering. A lieutenant and two privates showed us the gun, and one of them observed that the blockhouse had actually received a direct hit not long ago, just above the embrasure – but the shell had hit the twelve logs and no harm had been done. Little short of a direct hit into the very muzzle of the gun itself could knock this firing-point out.

We were then taken down some wooden steps into what turned out to be a light and remarkably spacious dug-out, with a little window on the side facing Leningrad. There were bunks on either side of the dug-out, a table with books and magazines, and an emergency foodstore and first-aid outfit. Several other men were in the dug-out – some were lying on their bunks – and they rose to greet us. They were all strong and bright and cheerful-looking lads, but very tough and hardened by the war. 'Nearly all of us,' said the lieutenant, 'have been here since February 1942, the time when this blockhouse was built – largely by ourselves.' All of them had the Leningrad medal, and three or four had other decorations; besides, all wore the guards badge on the left side of their chest – they belonged to a crack artillery regiment. 'Looks pretty cosy down here,' I remarked. 'Yes,' said a bright young fellow, speaking with a strong Ukrainian accent, 'it's become like a second home to us.' He laughed. 'It's grand to feel heroes, but it would be nice to have a quiet life for a change. We've lived here for eighteen months now – more, nearly nineteen months!' There was another soldier there with a long curly moustache and laughing blue eyes, and also speaking with a Ukrainian accent. 'It's all right down here, but we've had our hot moments – plenty of them. When the Germans start shelling Leningrad we come into action at once, and try to shut them up. Of course they do their damnedest to shut us up too. We've probably got a record for accurate firing. Not long ago we were much bothered by a German battery four-and-a-half kilometres away which kept pounding at us all the time. We called it 'target 230.' So we decided to have a real crack at it. And would you believe it – after three shells within sixty-five seconds – we silenced the battery completely. It's never shown any signs of life since! We've sometimes been shelled by eighteen German batteries all at once. You'll have noticed how everything around is pretty well ploughed up.' 'But,' I said, 'you've still got those vegetable plots. Whose are they?' 'Oh,' said one of the soldiers, 'each guncrew has its own vegetable garden. The Germans sometimes make a terrible mess of it, but there's something always left, and we have a lot of our own home-grown vegetables to eat in addition to the usual army rations!' Nearly all the men were Ukrainians, and the remaining two were Siberians. I commented on this. 'We're not from Leningrad,' one of them said, 'and yet we are. Two years here have made this place mean more to us than any other. There's little hope, anyway, of seeing the old folks again. They've been under German occupation for over two years, in a place near Kiev, so what hope is there of ever seeing them again? We can take it out of the damned parasites here. It's all part of the same show anyway.'

'How far away are we here from the front line?' I asked. 'This is really part of the front line,' said the lieutenant. 'You could get a little further along the Puskhin road, but there isn't really much more to see; a lot of trenches and a couple of miles of minefields and barbed-wire entanglements. That is, strictly speaking, the front; here you are on the outer defences of Leningrad. This is one of the bristles of the Leningrad hedgehog,' he said, obviously enjoying the simile. 'And a hedgehog has a lot of bristles, hasn't it?' I said. 'Indeed it has,' he said, and the soldiers nodded approvingly. 'Thick with bristles,' he added. 'Do you always stay here, or do you ever go to Leningrad?' I asked. The fellow with the blond moustache replied: 'We don't go much to Leningrad really. We only go when there's motor transport available, and only a few of us at a time. But it's much too dangerous to go to town in a tramcar,' he added quite seriously. I must have looked a bit startled, for he explained: 'Well, you see, the way we feel is this. Tramcars, as you know, are dangerous. Many have received direct hits and everybody inside was killed. If any of us get killed right here – well, it's normal, it's part of the job. But to be killed while having a joyride in a tramcar – it would be too silly!' 'You may think it funny,' said another soldier, 'but it's quite true. We don't often go to Leningrad for that reason. We, have a very good club right here – in the basement of one of the big blocks of flats. You can see it from this window.' 'Is anybody still living in the house?' I asked. 'Yes, quite a number of people. Not right up on the top floors, they've been badly smashed up and are not – well, not very quiet; but there are people living there, right up to the third floor. There's an old man on the third floor who refuses to leave his bed at night, whatever happens. Only once is he known to have gone downstairs, one night when it was really quite exceptionally bad. He says that he is very hard of hearing, and that the shelling doesn't bother him much.' The soldiers laughed. 'Yes, you'd find some queer characters round here,' one of them said, 'especially among the old Putilov workers.'

'And it's not a healthy spot,' another soldier said, young and fair-haired. 'It's much easier for the parasites over there really. They've got their batteries hidden in forests and we are here right in the open. One day they fired no fewer than 600 shells at us. They landed all round, but not one of us got as much as a scratch. Often we have to fire right in the midst of their shelling us. We've got much better than we were in the winter of 1941. We hadn't much experience then.' 'When were you made into a guards regiment?' I asked. 'In March 1942.' 'And how far are the German guns?' 'They vary a lot,' the lieutenant said. 'Their far-range batteries are as much as thirty or thirty-five kilometres away, and the air force has to take care of them. The 152-mm shells they fire at us from a distance of seventeen kilometres. But they use bigger stuff too – 203 and 210 and even 240-mm shells.'

As always, the conversation sooner or later drifted back to the winter of 1941–2. 'Those were fearful days,' one of the men remarked. 'It was much worse for the workers and the civilians, though, than it was for us. Everything was done to keep the front going; but what it could, the front gave back to the civilians. Only there wasn't much of a margin to spare. We had only 350 grammes a day – and it wasn't even real bread, but a mixture. We got to know many of the railwaymen during those days, and the railwaymen have since put us under their *chefstvo* (patronage), and we take an interest in their doings and they in ours, and we often meet at our club and have discussions with them, and we send one another parcels – there's a real comradeship we've established with the railwaymen.' Another soldier remarked that in winter they would all get a bit of a holiday. Each one would be sent for ten days to a rest-home somewhere outside Leningrad. 'It isn't very easy work really,' he said. 'Nobody ever writes about us in the papers, and we are never mentioned in the communiqués. People know much more about the snipers, for instance, than about us. But I think we are doing a steady, useful job – not very spectacular, but important all the same.' It seemed that these men of Leningrad's defences, of this essentially static front, felt a slight twinge of envy for the airmen and tankmen and gunners of the more mobile fronts, where there was more room for personal enterprise and more opportunities for individual fame. . . . At the same time there was, at least to me, something gratifying in the thought that there were a great many 'dull patches' like this between Murmansk and the Black Sea, or rather along the northern half of the front where it was, relatively speaking, 'all quiet,' and where comparatively few Russians were being killed daily. As for the Germans – well, there were the Russian snipers who were making the Germans' lives miserable even on the 'all-quiet' parts of the front. During the quietest month on the

Leningrad front, snipers, I was told, had managed to kill 6,000 – that is 200 a day.

'We must show you this,' said the lieutenant, as he opened a little storeroom attached to the dug-out. Here were several barrels. 'All homemade. Pickled cabbage from our own vegetable plot around here, and salted cucumbers!' 'It'll come in useful in winter,' one of the men said. 'Very welcome in winter,' he added, 'we'll also start getting again our 100 grammes of vodka per day.' The lieutenant grinned. 'It gives one an appetite,' he said.

We saw that day other bristles of the Leningrad hedgehog; but I remember particularly well that drive to the Krestovsky Island in the afternoon. It was a beautiful sunny autumn day as we drove down the Kamennostrovsky to the 'Islands' on the north side of Leningrad. As usual, the smart, rather *nouveau-riche* Kamennostrovsky (now called the Kirov Avenue) most of whose houses were built in the first fifteen years of this century, had a half-deserted look, and there was little traffic apart from the half-empty tramcars. Yet on this sunny day the great avenue looked cheerful, with the trees of the park round the fortress all golden in the sun, and the bright-blue tiles of the Mosque, half-way up the street, making a dazzling splash of southern colour in this essentially northern city. And it was good to feel that, in spite of everything, Leningrad had not changed so very much outwardly, and one could already visualise very clearly a sunny Sunday morning – a day just like this – not so very long after the war when thousands of young people would again be driving and walking and cycling up to the 'Kirov Islands' for the day. Kirov – many things are 'Kirov' in Leningrad today, the Kamennostrovsky, and the Islands, and the Putilov works. This man who had been killed on December 1st, 1934, was not only

Leningrad's party boss; he was widely considered as the second man of the Soviet Union, Stalin's right-hand man and eventual successor. Few leaders in Russia enjoyed the immense personal popularity that Kirov enjoyed. In many Leningrad homes, for years afterwards, and probably to this day, December 1st was observed as a day of mourning. The energetic, jolly, very human and approachable Kirov who, moreover, represented in the eyes of so many people of Leningrad such a welcome reaction against pompous, vociferous Zinovievs who had irritated the city for so many years by their manners, appearance and ideas – became, after his death, almost a legend – more than a legend, a spirit that continued to dwell in Leningrad. In the dark days of the winter of 1941, Kirov walked through the black starving streets of Leningrad. 'Do not lose heart; Kirov is with us!' Nicolai Tikhonov said so in his poem called 'Kirov is with us' – a poem of faith, faith in miracles, perhaps the most inspired poem Leningrad produced during the blockade – and the most popular.

The Krestovsky Island, which juts further out into the sea than any other of the islands of Leningrad proper, is even now only half inhabited. It had at its eastern end a famous yachting club and tennis courts, but the rest was a marshy waste. Even before the war, apart from a few modern flats built on its eastern end, it was 'waste land' – to be built over in time. It was one of the areas of the new Leningrad – of the Leningrad of the future. Now, only a half-completed road ran through the middle of the island from the east to that wide half-circle of a promontory jutting far into the Gulf of Finland. We drove along this one mile of road, and the waste land on either side had been turned into cabbage and potato fields, intensively cultivated. Right on the promontory was now an enormous circular structure of cement. This was the giant stadium for 200,000 people which had been nearly completed when the war started. The marshy wastes on either side of the now muddy road leading to the stadium were to have become sports grounds, and gardens attached to little villas, in a few years' time, if only there had been no war. The name of the stadium was naturally the Kirov Stadium. Though deprived by the war of its proper function, it was, however, to play a part in the defence of Leningrad. The large concrete slabs with which it was built were used up there and then for fortifications. I cannot describe in detail all that has been built on Krestovsky Island, but I can say that here, with the help of the stadium cement slabs and other building materials which had been accumulated before the stadium was completed, soldiers, assisted by many hundreds of Leningrad women, had built, in the last year, as perfect a network of powerful blockhouses as has yet been seen. The promontory jutting into the Gulf of Finland had become a powerful fortress dominating with its guns every approach to Leningrad from the sea. It is important because in winter the shallow and almost fresh-water sea freezes sometimes several feet thick, and there would be little that could prevent the Germans from attempting to storm Leningrad from the west, across the ice, if these western approaches were not fortified as they now are. Here are powerful anti-tank guns peering out of blockhouses of concrete and timber, here are anti-personnel mortars and machine-guns, and the men inside the blockhouses are protected against gas. The all-round 'circular' defence is complete, closely co-ordinated with all the other defences of Leningrad, and the Krestovsky promontory dominates every possible German approach across the ice – from south, north or west. All the necessary precautions are also taken against the possible danger of enemy landing barges. Colonel Smagly of the engineering service, red-faced, and with his turned-up nose and a black 'Italian tenor' chin, and accompanied by a handsome dashing young officer called Vinogradov, took us round all this high elaborate chain of fortifications, with its gas-proof blockhouses and walls made of enormous slabs of cement from the stadium up above, which looked from here like a half-dismantled Colosseum. 'Made by the hands of our women,' he kept on saying, with a note of affection in his gruff, soldierly voice.

But again, I confess, I was less interested in the technical details of these fortifications than in the actual scene. This was Russia's window into Europe. It was a glorious sunny autumn day. A high mellow wind was blowing from the Baltic bringing in the smell of the sea – a smell I had missed for nearly two years in Moscow. At the back of us, to the left, was Leningrad, with the brown dome of St. Isaac's Cathedral and the two spires – that of the Fortress and the Admiralty – and factory chimneys in the south and east dominating the city's skyline. In the foreground was a branch of the Neva, dark blue under a bright-blue sky, and with little white waves tossing about the small craft moored to the flat banks.

Leningrad has the skyline of a great city, and there are not many cities that have a great skyline. Paris has it, and London, and Rome. But how many more cities in Europe? Moscow – scarcely, in spite of the Kremlin; Berlin ('whose only *raison dêtre* is human slaughter,' Saltykov wrote nearly seventy years ago) not at all.

To the right, a little further inland than the tip of the Krestovsky, was the green and golden park of the Elagin Island, and in the sky above the cluster of trees a rainbow was faintly glittering. A thin line of fir and pine forests, coming right to the edge of the water, stretched to the north-west to the Lisi-Noss – the Fox's Nose – promontory, some ten miles away, and beyond it, some thirty miles away, stretched the slender black line of the wooded Finnish coast. The sea, with little white waves, was a milky blue and the horizon was lost in a mist. But out of the mist rose the tiny lilac shape of another dome which from here looked like a tiny miniature of St. Isaac's. It seemed to rise out of the water – far, far away. It seemed, indeed, slightly submerged. It was the cathedral of Kronstadt, on its narrow strip of an island. And in the south one could see from another angle what we had already seen from the observation post in the Narva district, the large white houses of the typewriter factory at Uritsk, some five miles away from here, and the German coastline running as far as Peterhof, with the ruins of the church high on the hill, and beyond it, the stretch of coast which was part of the Russian 'bridgehead' of Oranienbaum. It was strange, the peace and loveliness of this delicate seascape, so delicate in colouring and so majestic in outline. There was complete silence around, except for the gusts of the west wind coming in from the sea and the chuffing of a little brown tug which was towing a large barge from one island of the delta to another, through waters dangerously exposed to the German guns. This, then, was the window into Europe, and for centuries Russians had fought and died to gain it, and then to preserve it. Again, lines from the *Bronze Horseman* ran through my head:

> On the low banks of these desolate waters,
> He stood, filled with mighty thoughts,
> And looked into the distance....

It was the Peter of Pushkin's vision, planning to build his new capital on the sea.

> From here [he reflected] we shall threaten the Swede;
> Here shall be laid the foundations of a city,
> To foil our arrogant neighbour.
> Nature has chosen this spot for us.
> Here our axe still hacks our window into Europe.

12

Endurance: The Kirov Works

When I look back on those days in Leningrad there is one memory which stands out more clearly than anything else. I mean my afternoon at the Putilov (or Kirov) works. Here, even in September 1943, one had a glimpse of the Leningrad of the darkest and grimmest days. To the Putilov works the dark days were not a memory of the past; in a sense the people were continuing to live here through a peculiar kind of hell, and they continued to live this life voluntarily, feeling that it was their duty to do so. That it was a fearful nervous strain to go on working in these munitions works, almost in the front line and under almost constant shellfire, nobody denied; perhaps at heart some would have liked to be moved to a quieter spot, but no one would admit it. To these people it had become a point of honour to hold on to the end. To be a Putilov worker, a Kirov worker, and to stick it to the end had become to these people like a title of nobility. The workers here were not soldiers. Sixty-nine per cent of the workers were women and girls – mostly young girls. They knew that this was as bad as the front; in a way it was worse, because you did not know the thrill of direct retaliation. To work right through the war on the Kirov works was, these people felt, something of which you would always be proud, whatever the sacrifices, whatever the risks, whatever the possible or probable after-effects on your nerves and health. How many of the Kirov workers of today will live to an old age? Probably very few.

This devotion to the Kirov works had a quality of its own. A quality which was composed, not only of profound patriotism, both local and national, but also of a revolutionary fervour that was essentially working-class, and enthusiasm that was in the revolutionary tradition of the Petrograd of 1917. In many places in Russia today the war is, first and foremost, a national war, a war for national survival and national victory; at the Putilov works one had the feeling that, to the men and women who worked there, this war was also a consciously revolutionary war which was being fought to preserve at any price not only the Russian national heritage, but the heritage of the Revolution and all that Leningrad, 'the City of Lenin,' represented. Nazi Germany to these people was not merely the enemy of the Soviet Union, it was the enemy of the working class, of the Russian working class, which was proud of its revolutionary conquests, and was now fighting to defend them.

The story of the Kirov Division – the division composed of Kirov workers – which fought, together with other Leningrad Workers' Divisions, a grim rearguard action at a time when the enemy was advancing inexorably on Leningrad is essentially a working-class story, reminiscent of the early days of the Revolution and of Yudenich's march on Petrograd in 1919. It is significant that time and again I heard people say in Leningrad: 'Our Opolchenie – our Home Guard – and our Workers' Divisions played an absolutely *decisive* part in saving the city in September 1941.'

There is little doubt that, during the big German advance on Leningrad, after the disastrous battle of Kingisepp near the Estonian border, and the equally dangerous German advance from the south-west on Luga and beyond, the Red Army, shattered, bled white and ill-equipped with tanks and planes compared with what the triumphant Germans had, would not have withstood the final onslaught on Leningrad but for the decisive aid it received from Leningrad itself, from its people and its workers, at the most critical moment of all. And I now understood far better than I did at the time the full significance of the famous Voroshilov–Zhdanov–Popkov appeal of August 21st declaring Leningrad to be in danger. I understood now why there was a greater emphasis on the revolutionary greatness of Leningrad than on its national greatness. It was intended to rouse to a white heat of old revolutionary fervour the workers of the 'City of Lenin'; the appeal to the workers was most important, because they were going to be the shock troops of Leningrad's resistance. The rest of the people would follow – whether driven on primarily by a spirit of revolutionary self-sacrifice or by the spirit of a national *lutte à outrance.*

When we drove up to the enormous black mass of buildings alongside the Peterhof *chaussée* – these large black buildings did not seem to have changed much externally since 1917, and the newer parts of the plant were further off the road – the whole place looked deserted. Nobody was outside except a woman soldier with fixed bayonet, and in the road itself there was no traffic, except one astonishing sight. A dilapidated old droshki was driving two officers – to the front, a couple of miles down the road. ... The two pedestrians I saw were a girl walking arm-in-arm below the factory walls with a Baltic Fleet sailor with a turned-up nose; the sailor was clearly a dashing flirt; he was squeezing the girl's hand and making her giggle all the time. The girl on sentry duty, after scrutinising our papers, let us in, and a handsome young woman secretary emerged from a small building and offered to conduct us to the Director's office. She had well-groomed fair hair and red finger-nails, and wore a smart tailor-made costume with a Persian lamb collar; her pretty face was discreetly rouged and lipsticked, and there were large turquoise earrings in her ears. The gate through which we had passed was badly battered, and there were signs of serious damage all round. However, the director's office was in a relatively safe place, on the north side of a solid brick building. In Leningrad, as in the old days in Madrid, there are differences between safe and unsafe houses; one facing the front is obviously more dangerous than one with its back turned to it. Half a dozen walls and partitions constitute a certain measure of protection against an average shell. We were welcomed by the Director of the Kirov works, a relatively young man with a strong but careworn face. He was tall, wiry, and must have been very handsome a few years before. He wore the usual plain khaki tunic of the factory executive, and spoke rapidly and to the point in a deep bass voice. He was much the same type as Semyonov at the optical instruments factory whom we had seen on the previous day. There were many points in common between the stories the two men told; especially their experiences during the famine were very similar; but the Kirov works held an altogether exceptional place in the history of wartime Leningrad, and what Comrade Puzyrev said to me is, in a way, a historical document, because it was the first detailed interview ever given to any correspondent by the head of the Kirov works. It was not easy to gain access to the Kirov works, and the Leningrad authorities certainly made a very great concession in granting my request to see these works and to meet Mr. Puzyrev.

Puzyrev, like nearly every Russian, had an extremely good narrative gift and sense of human drama, and my condensed account of what he said does not fully render the real qualities of his conversation, which went on for over an hour.

'Well,' he said, 'you are certainly finding us working in unusual conditions. What we have here now isn't really what is normally meant by the Kirov plant. The Putilov works have existed for 150 years, but now the greater part of the plant has been moved to the east. Before the war we had over 30,000 workers; now we have only a fraction of these.' He gave me the exact figure, but I am not at liberty to quote it. 'And sixty-nine per cent of the labour is now female. Hardly any women worked here before the war. Before the war we made turbines, tanks, guns; we made tractors, we supplied the greater part of the equipment for building the Moscow–Volga Canal. We built quantities of machinery for the navy. Already in the last war we made masses of guns and other military equipment. But the plant has since then been at least doubled, and before this war started we began to make tanks in a very big way and diesel engines for both tanks and planes. Practically all this production of equipment proper has been moved to the east. Now we repair diesels and tanks, but our main production is that of munitions, and of some of the smaller arms. As for guns, well, the truth is that the Red Army has so many guns today that it doesn't require any from us now. This, however, was not the case eighteen months ago.

'Those were difficult days,' he continued, 'and things are much easier now. A few times a month we get a pretty stiff dose of shelling, but on the whole it isn't as bad as it's been in the past, and what is much more important, German aircraft do not bother us any longer. In spite of very difficult conditions – and you will see later the conditions we work in – we are managing to increase our production steadily and to supply the Leningrad front with a very large proportion of its shells and mortar mines.' Again he quoted a figure of the output of shells on the Kirov works; without being stupendous, it was impressive, all things considered.

And then Puzyrev spoke of the early days of the war on the Kirov works. It was the story of that *lutte à outrance* of the people and workers of Leningrad. Like one man they reacted to the German invasion, but the highest pitch of self-sacrifice was reached as a result of the 'Leningrad in danger' appeal made by Voroshilov, Zhdanov and Popkov on August 21st. 'The workers of the Kirov plant,' Puzyrev said, 'were in reserved occupations and hardly anybody was subject to mobilisation. Yet no sooner had the Germans invaded us than everybody without exception volunteered for the front. We could have sent 25,000 people if we had wanted to; we let only 9,000 or 10,000 go. Already in June 1941 they formed themselves into what became the famous Kirov Division. They had done some training before the war, but you couldn't consider them fully trained soldiers; but their drive, their guts, were tremendous. They wore the uniform of the Red Army, but actually they were something different – they were part of the Opolchenie, the Leningrad Home Guard, except that they were rather better trained than other Opolchenie units. Several such Workers' Divisions were formed in Leningrad – ours, and those of the Moscow district, and those of the Viborg district, and, in practice, they turned out to be first-class crack divisions. Many tens of thousands of them went out from here to meet the Germans – to stop them at any price. Our Workers' Divisions were fighting at Luga and Novgorod and Pushkino, and finally at Uritsk, where, after one of the grimmest rearguard actions in this war, our men finally managed to stop the Germans – just in the nick of time. And while this was going on, 400,000 women and boys and children went out to dig trenches and build fortifications, all the way from here to Luga, 100 miles away, and in doing so they also helped to delay the German advance on Leningrad. And when the Germans, already wearied by all the unexpected resistance, reached the outskirts of Leningrad, they came up against these trenches and fortifications newly built by the hands of women and children. It was all a horrible business. The Germans had superiority in the air; they butchered our women and children, but in spite of the bombing and machine-gunning our people never gave up. Young girls went on digging with a frenzy you can hardly imagine. They went on digging even when the palms of their hands, unaccustomed to such work, were reduced to a bloody pulp.'

Lutte à outrance – I kept thinking of that phrase, and all that it meant. Here in Russia there was only an 'unreasonable' Paris, an 'unreasonable' Tours (perhaps it was no coincidence that Tours was 'unreasonable' again in 1940, even when everything seemed lost). There was no reasonable Versailles anywhere in Russia, no conflict like the eternal conflict between Paris and Versailles. If in 1792 Paris had not been complete master and Versailles had not been silenced, history might have taken a different turn. The spirit of Leningrad in 1941 was like the spirit of Paris of 1792. It was much the same everywhere in Russia, but in Leningrad this spirit could be observed in its purest and most tangible form. The *sans-culotte* was able to fight his great battle, unhampered and unpoisoned by Versailles or Vichy. *Lutte à outrance* – Leningrad did what, after the fall of France, Churchill said England would do if she were invaded.

'The fight put up by our Workers' Divisions,' Puzyrev went on, 'and by the people of Leningrad who went out to stop the Germans was absolutely decisive in the battle of Leningrad. It is no secret – a large proportion of the Workers' Divisions never came back. Their losses were very heavy. Many of the men are now in the regular army, while some we have managed to bring back, especially skilled workers who are invaluable in industry.' When Puzyrev spoke of industry, one felt how deeply conscious he was of the great tradition of craftsmanship which had been built up in Leningrad for over a century. Leningrad had, indeed, the most highly skilled workers in the whole Soviet Union, and one felt that Puzyrev regretted at heart that such fine industrial material should have had to be sacrificed on the battlefield. But clearly in 1941, when it was touch-and-go – touch-and-go both outside Leningrad and outside Moscow – such fine points as the most rational and productive use of a Russian man had to be put aside, at least for a short time. Yet the fact that some of the Putilov workers had been taken out of the army when the worst of the crisis was over was typical of wartime Russia.

'The formation of the Kirov Division wasn't everything, though,' Puzyrev continued. 'It was essential to defend the plant itself – defend it against the possible breakthrough by German tanks (and heaven knows they were not far away, and in those days there weren't all those miles of minefields and barbed wire that separate us from the Germans now), and against paratroops. The Germans were using paratroops in a very big way on this front in 1941, and often with serious results for us. So we had a large artillery unit composed of our own men, permanently stationed on the Kirov works, and also a tank brigade, and a complete anti-paratroop organisation. All three were on duty night and day.'

Puzyrev then spoke of the autumn and winter of 1941. 'We were shelled for the first time on September 8th and on September 15th they started against the Kirov works a terrible, merciless artillery bombardment. For days and weeks we were shelled almost ceaselessly. Yes,' said Puzyrev, 'that 15th of September was one of our blackest days. The greater part of our second shift were living at Strelna, eight or nine miles down the Gulf. And that day the Germans broke through to Strelna and Uritsk, and a large number of our people were cut off.' 'What happened to them?' 'Quite a number of them got away to Peterhof where they joined our troops, as for the rest – ' he shrugged his shoulders. 'I hate to think what happened to them.

'The shelling was so heavy during that month of September, and the Germans were so near,' he continued, 'that we decided to evacuate part of the plant to less threatened places in Leningrad – on the other side of the Neva – to the Petrograd District, somewhere off the Kamennostrovsky, and to the Vasili Island. For, mind you, in those days we had to be prepared for the worst. The loss of the southern half of Leningrad was not entirely out of the question. It is horrible to think of it, but at that time one had to consider the possibility of seeing the Germans in the Winter Palace, and of shelling them from the Fortress on the other side of the Neva. Nobody really believed that it would come to that. But people like us, in charge of munitions, had to prepare for any eventuality. We also sent part of the equipment to the Viborg district. If the Germans had broken in, Leningrad would have been defended, house by house, and reduced to a shambles, as Stalingrad was.'

And I remembered what somebody had told me on the previous day: when the Germans were approaching Leningrad, they dropped leaflets on the city saying Leningrad must follow the example of Paris and proclaim itself an open city. To the people of Leningrad the whole idea was entirely incongruous.

'In view of the very grave situation,' said Puzyrev, 'it was decided in virtue of a government order of the middle of October to evacuate a large part of our equipment to the east. I was then the foreman of the tank department. At that time, however, it was found possible to evacuate only one complete workshop – 2,200 people and 525 machine tools and other production units. For by that time the black days had begun. In November and December we were busy packing the equipment which was going to be sent east. But actually nothing could be sent away till the spring. However, our most highly skilled workers, who were badly needed in Siberia and the Urals, were evacuated by air, together with their families. They were flown to Tikhvin, but after the Germans had taken Tikhvin we had to fly them to other airfields, and from there the people had to walk to the nearest railway station, walk through the snow, in the middle of a bitter winter, and often they had to walk dozens and dozens of kilometres.

'The bulk of our equipment did not leave till the spring, or rather till the summer, by way of Lake Ladoga. But already in the early winter of 1941 a lot of equipment from Kharkov, Kiev, and other places in the Ukraine, and also some from Moscow, had reached the Urals, and our skilled workers were badly needed to handle the stuff and to organise production. Cheliabinsk, for instance, had never made tanks. It was essential to start this tank production going in the shortest possible time.

'We were then in the middle of that critical transition period when industry in the west had ceased to function, and had not yet started up in the east. What was so remarkable, when you look back on it, was the tempo, the speed with which Cheliabinsk, which had never done anything on these lines before, proceeded to turn out tanks, diesel engines and high-precision instruments which only highly skilled workers could make. The people who left here in October were already working at full speed in their new place, 2,000 kilometres away, by December!

'It was one of the greatest organisational achievements of our Soviet Government,' Puzyrev said, 'to have managed to carry all the necessary equipment and men to those invulnerable places. And in what conditions it was done! Trains carrying the equipment were attacked from the air, and so were the transport planes which were taking the skilled Kirov and other workers and their families from Leningrad. Fortunately the percentage of transport planes shot down was not high. The flying had to be done mostly at night, in very difficult conditions. The whole thing was tremendous really – I call it a technical super-victory, our greatest organisational victory which was to pave the way for military victory. If it had not been achieved, Allied supplies could not have made much difference. We should have been pretty well sunk.'

During the black days of the famine the Kirov works lived through much the same sombre experiences as the rest of

Leningrad. 'Those were terrible days,' said Puzyrev. 'On December 15th everything came to a standstill. There was no fuel, no electric current, no food, no tramcars, no water – nothing. Production in Leningrad practically ceased. We were to remain in this terrible condition until the 1st of April. It is true that food began to come in in February across the Ladoga ice road. But we needed another month before we could start any regular kind of output at the Kirov works. But even during the worst hungry period we did what we could. With small cadres we managed to do odd jobs. We repaired guns, and our foundry was kept going, though only in a small way. It felt as if the mighty Putilov works had been turned into a village smithy. People were terribly cold and terribly hungry. It is no secret that a large number of our people died during those days. And it was chiefly our best people who died – highly skilled workers who had reached a certain age when the body can no longer resist such hardships.

'It was at that time that I was made chief engineer of the Kirov works. Now, when I look back on it, I already find it hard to imagine or describe how people lived during those days. As I said before, there was no water and no electric current. All we had here was a small pump which was connected with the sea down there; that was all the water supply we had. Throughout that winter – from December to March – the whole of Leningrad used snow for putting out incendiaries. There were very few big fires in Leningrad, the largest was that of the Gostiny Dvor. Here, on the Kirov works, not a single workshop was destroyed by fire.

'People were faint with hunger, and it was necessary to preserve their strength as much as possible. So we organised hostels so that they could live right here. We authorised others who lived at home to come only twice a week. The anti-paratroop and fire-fighting squads were on duty day and night. In December we had to call a meeting and announce that a reduction of the bread ration from 400 grammes to 250 for workers, and to 125 for employees and dependants – and very little else besides – had become necessary. They took it calmly, though to many it was like a death sentence. Nobody raised objections. The motion approving the reduction was voted unanimously. If only as a protest they could have voted against. But nobody protested. They knew there was no other way.

'You know, the army on the Leningrad front asked the High Command to reduce its rations so that so drastic a reduction should be avoided in the rations of Leningrad's civilians. But the High Command decided that the soldiers were receiving just a bare minimum for carrying on, and would not agree. The soldiers' rations then were 350 grammes a day.

'We tried to keep people going by making a sort of yeast soup. It cost only four kopeks, with a little soya added. It wasn't much better, really, than simply drinking hot water, but it gave people the illusion of having 'eaten' something. In that 250 or 125 grammes of bread, forty or fifty per cent was substitute stuff anyway. I don't want to exaggerate. I am an engineer, not a politician, but the courage, the guts our people showed in those fearful days was truly amazing. A very large number of our people died. So many died, and transport was so difficult, that we decided to have our own graveyard right here. We registered the deaths and buried the corpses. People were hungry. But there was not a single serious incident. When the bread vans arrived, there was not a single case of looting. Now and then there were some rows, but never anything serious. Frankly, I find it hard to this day to understand how people resisted the temptation of attacking bread vans or looting bakeries. But they didn't. Never, not once. Sometimes people came to me to say goodbye. They wanted to come to say goodbye because they knew they were going to die almost at once. Later, already in the summer of 1942, a lot of the people who had stayed on through the winter were sent east where they supplemented their comrades from Kiev, Kharkov and other places.'

'And now?' I said.

'Now,' said Puzyrev, 'we've got problems of a different order. Difficult, but not as desperately difficult as those of the winter of 1941.

'Many of our workshops have been badly damaged. No wonder! They've been plastering us for over two years. And yet we are carrying on, and as I've already told you, we are steadily increasing our output of munitions. But it's a big problem all the same, this shelling of the Kirov works. Here, in this small room, facing north, and with thick walls and other buildings on all sides, one is relatively safe, but you just can't choose relatively safe places for everybody on an enormous plant like this, working, as it does, right under the Germans' noses. A few times a month now we get a real plastering. And then there are also the occasional stray shells which come without warning. We have, however, greatly reduced the danger of fire – for the Germans also use a lot of incendiary shells. We had all the wooden buildings on the Kirov works pulled down. They came in very useful as fuel last year.'

'But how,' I asked, 'can you carry on at all when shellfire is heavy? Have you heavy casualties? And how do your people stand up to it?'

'Well,' he said, 'I suppose there is a sort of Kirov works patriotism. Except for one or two very sick people, I have never yet come across anyone here who wanted to quit, and get a quieter job elsewhere. What is also very characteristic is this.' He pulled out a drawer of his desk and brought out a pile of forty or fifty envelopes with postmarks. 'These have come in the last two days only. They are all requests from our workers, now in the east, to be allowed to come back to Leningrad. They know how difficult conditions of work are, but at the same time they know that the transport problem of Leningrad has been settled, and that they wouldn't present a food problem. So they are begging us to let them return, alone, or with their families. But we can't agree to it. These skilled Kirov workers are doing highly valuable work out there; here we haven't much equipment, and the place is run as a sort of emergency war factory. Not unlike Kolpino, some ten miles away from here, in the south-east, where munitions are turned out in underground foundries – right in the front line.

'The way we keep the place going is by having decentralised it. The important thing is not to hold up production, not to lose too many machine tools and too many people if and when there is a direct hit. That's the principle on which we work. We have divided up the work into small units, with only a corner of each workshop, or quarter of a workshop taken up with people and machinery; and this section, as far as possible, protected against blast and splinters. But misfortunes – or rather a certain normal rate of casualties – will occur. In September to date, for instance – this is the 28th – we have had forty-three casualties (it's been a fairly good month, I must say) – of these, thirteen were killed, twenty-three wounded, and seven cases of shell shock.

'You also ask how they take it? Well, I don't know whether you've ever been for any length of time under shell fire. But if anybody tells you it isn't frightening, don't you believe it. He's a liar. There is no soldier and no civilian who is not frightened. I am the director here, and I am frightened. But the real thing is not to show it. And I don't. And everybody else here knows how to act and how to behave in a bombardment. But this frequent shelling nevertheless has an effect on people's psychology. In our experience a direct hit has a very bad effect for twenty-four or forty-eight hours. In a workshop that's had a direct hit, production slumps heavily for twenty-four or forty-eight hours, or stops almost completely, especially if many people have been killed or injured. It's a horrible sight, all the blood, and makes even some of our hardened workers quite ill for a day or two. But, in the long run, it doesn't matter. Two days later, they are fully back at work again, and do their best to make up for the time lost by what's called 'the accident.' But we realise all the same that working here is a perpetual strain, and when we see that a man or a girl is going to pieces, we send him or her to a rest-home for a fortnight or a month.' I said I had seen the Kamenny Island rest-homes.

'Besides, when a shell lands close by everybody immediately takes shelter; it's a rule. And it has saved a lot of lives. So it is only the first shell that's really very dangerous – the shell that comes without any warning. But more often than not the first shell hits nothing in particular, so one's chances of surviving till the end are still fairly good! Yes,' he said, giving the pile of envelopes before him a friendly pat, 'all our old workers, and the families of those who are here, would give anything to be able to come right back now; they'll come back in time. Meantime we are carrying on. The people here are the nucleus who are going to prepare the Kirov works for its complete restoration after the war.'

He ended with this optimistic flourish, and then offered to take us round some of the workshops. 'The Germans have been unusually quiet today,' he said, 'you are very lucky.' Just then a single gun fired one round somewhere in the distance, and a shell whined faintly overhead. 'I spoke too soon,' said Puzyrev, and our colonel looked a little agitated. However, nothing more happened, and we were able to spend another hour or so on the Kirov works, almost undisturbed.

We went out. The enormous plant was, I could now see, much more badly smashed up than its outside view from the street suggested. In a large open space, with badly shattered buildings around, stood an enormous blockhouse. In it were a number of machine-guns, and the roof was made of powerful steel girders, and the cemented walls were twelve bricks thick. 'Nothing but a direct hit from a large gun at close range can do anything to this,' said Puzyrev. 'It was built during the worst days when we thought the Germans might break through to Leningrad. They would have found the Kirov works a tough proposition. The whole place is dotted with firing-points like this one.' A number of guns were fired, quite close to us. 'That's all right – those are ours,' said Puzyrev.

I cannot describe in detail all that we saw that day at the Kirov works, with the Russian and German guns close by, fighting their sporadic duel, and the German lines, down there by the Uritsk Inlet, scarcely two miles away. The factory buildings, spreading over a wide area, were battered; some were almost completely destroyed; but many of the workshops carried on behind their chipped and pockmarked brick walls and heavily sandbagged windows. 'This is the workshop,' said Comrade Puzyrev, pointing to a half-dilapidated building, 'where President Kalinin used to work in his youth. He came here several times before the war, and our fellows would tell him: "Don't worry, Mikhail Ivanovich, your lathe is still in good order"'. As we passed another large workshop, Puzyrev said: 'This is the place where the K.V. tank was born in 1939. It was first used in the Finnish war. Oh, it's all a terrible pity,' he said, as we walked across a wide open space among several of the factory buildings. 'There were lawns here, and flower-beds, and a fountain, and it was such a joy to watch the great new K.V. tanks roll out of there.' In place of the flower-beds there was now a wide expanse of rubble and large shell-holes, many of which, judging from the fresh cement, had been filled up only quite recently.

We went into several of the workshops. They were organised just as Puzyrev had described them. Production was split up into small units everywhere. Lathes which were turning out the same kinds of shells could be found in different parts of the plant. It was, as Puzyrev had said, no use having too many machines and too many people knocked out all at once. Nearly everywhere, in these dark noisy workshops smelling of machine oil, were the shells being turned out by girls, some in overalls, some in ordinary clothes; and nearly all wearing cloth slippers; mostly young girls with tired faces and a hard concentrated look in their eyes. I remembered Tamara, the little girl in the island rest-home, and what she had told me. These young girls also had seen accidents and were working under great strain. Perhaps they were not always conscious of it, but it was there. It was dark and terribly noisy in those vast, half-empty workshops of the Putilov plant where these girls and a few men, split up into small groups, each with its own set of lathes, were turning out the shells – it was dark because of the sandbagged windows and because electric current was being economised. In a passage just outside one of the workshops a middle-aged worker with a grey moustache was busy demonstrating a machine to two girls; these were newcomers. Out of the workshops all the time fresh shells were being wheeled away in noisy little wagons.

Then we went into one of the foundries. One end of this large foundry was quite dark, but behind a strong brick partition the other half was lit up by the flames inside the open furnaces, with their red-hot walls. Dark, eerie shadows of men, but again mostly of young girls were moving about in the red glow. The girls, with patched cotton stockings over their thin legs, were stooping under the weight of enormous clusters of red-hot steel they were clutching between a pair of tongs, and then you would see them – and as you saw it, you felt the desperate muscular concentration and the will-power it involved – you would see them raise their slender, almost child-like arms and hurl these red-hot clusters under a giant steam hammer. Large red sparks of metal were flying and whizzing through the red semi-darkness, and the whole foundry shook with the deafening din and roar of machinery. We watched this scene for a while in silence, then Puzyrev said, almost apologetically, through the din: 'This place isn't working quite right yet. I had a few shells in here the other day,' and pointing at a large hole in the floor now filled with sand and cement, 'That's where one of them landed.' 'Any casualties?' 'Yes, a few.' We walked through the foundry and watched more closely all that the girls were doing. As we were going out, I caught the glimpse of a woman's face in the red glow of the flames. She had a long black scarf over her head and her shoulders, though she could not have been cold there. Her face was grimy. She looked an elderly woman – almost like an old gipsy hag. And from that grimy face shone two dark eyes. There was something tragic in those eyes – there was a great weariness in them, and a touch of almost animal terror. How old was she? Fifty, forty, or maybe only twenty-five. Had I just imagined that look of terror in her eyes? Was it that grimy face of hers and the eerie shadows around leaping up and down in the glow of those red fires that had given me that idea? I had seen some of the other girls' faces. They were normal enough. One, a young thing, even smiled. Normal – yes, except for a kind of inner intensity and concentration – as if they all had some bad memories they could not quite shake off.

Curious, all the same, how in a corridor, outside this inferno, we saw a wall newspaper displayed on a noticeboard. It made one realise how all this human drama was really only part of the life of these people. It was not all heroics, this life of theirs. Much of it was plain, straightforward work, regulated by much the same rules as anywhere else in the Soviet Union. The wall newspaper contained funny drawings, and announcements of club meetings and political lectures, and praise for the Stakhanovites and others who had exceeded their norm, while one worker received a severe telling-off in these terms: 'Shame! Shame that a highly skilled riveter like Comrade Gusev should have failed so miserably in the task which our comrades at the front were expecting him to fulfil without fail. We expect him to pull himself together in future. – The Editorial Board.'

How lovely the blue sky seemed, and the golden autumn leaves as we came out of the dark foundry! But suddenly a strange thing happened. Unmistakably there was a bomber overhead, which in a flash brought back to my mind old memories of the London blitz. It was the same zooming sound of the dentist's drill. I looked up, but the blue sky was all clear, and then glanced inquiringly at Puzyrev. He smiled – perhaps for the first time in two hours. 'We've rung the bell – didn't you hear it a few minutes ago? It's a signal telling our people not to worry. There is no plane. But just beyond that building over there we are testing the diesel engines.'

We now came to the main building of the Kirov works, a large brick structure heavily battered by shells and with large pieces of its broad façade chipped off, and all its windows sandbagged. 'But don't you think this is symbolic, all the same,' said Puzyrev, pointing to the top of the façade decorated with greatly enlarged reproductions, in coloured tiles, of the three great Orders of Merit the Kirov works had received from the government – the Order of the Red Banner and the two Lenin Orders. The Kirov works was *trizhdy ordenonosny* (thrice decorated). And here were the three enormous decorations on top of the battered building. And they were unscathed, though the whole wall around was badly chipped and blasted. As we went back to our car, we noticed, hidden in a safe place between two large buildings, a couple of ambulances. 'We have them on duty day and night. One never knows. You've been very lucky. Actually, anything might have happened at any moment.' Before saying goodbye Puzyrev said: 'Now there are a few things concerning the exact sort of things we make here, and some other details, which I don't want you to write about. It's no good telling the b——s over there too much; for they're sure to see your papers sooner or later, or listen to your radio talks.' He enumerated a few points. 'Is that understood?' he said. 'Yes,' I said, 'it's understood. And good luck.' These people needed good luck.

13

At the Writers' Union

Leningrad has its own literature, its own writers, and is a trifle snobbish about it. It is inclined to look down on Moscow, though heaven knows, some of the most famous Soviet writers of today, such as Sholokhov, Alexei Tolstoy and many others either haven't lived in Leningrad for years, or never had anything to do with Leningrad. I am on dangerous ground here, and that is for a number of reasons. I am far from convinced that in the last ten years Leningrad has produced anything very superior to what Moscow or the rest of the country has produced, and I am not sure that Leningrad has remained anything like Russia's literary capital which it certainly was throughout the eighteenth and nineteenth centuries, and indeed, right up to the Revolution. I am not, however, sufficiently acquainted with Leningrad's literature, least of all of the last two years, to express any considered opinion. This is not entirely my fault, because in the last two years it has been practically impossible to buy or otherwise obtain in Moscow the works of the Leningrad writers, with the exception of what is published in the national press and, occasionally, in the magazines and in small pamphlets.

Naturally, everybody knows the articles of Nikolai Tikhonov in which, month after month, he has reported to the national press the daily life of Leningrad since the war; everybody knows his little books of verse, ranging from what might be called patriotic poster work to a deeply inspired poem like 'Kirov is with us.' Vera Inber has more recently acquired nation-wide popularity with her truly remarkable poem *The Pulkovo Meridian*, that grim, tragic poem of the blockade, written in perfectly chiselled lines and a metre as light as the Byronic octave. The outer lightness of this tragic poem, with such lighthearted similes as that of 'a little coffin like a violin case' in which a Leningrad father takes his dead baby to the cemetery during the famine, not only places this poem in the Pushkin tradition, but reflects, probably more accurately than any louder poem, the ironic resignation with which so many men and women of Leningrad accepted the simple fact of death through hunger.

But it was really only through the fortunate accident of personally knowing Vera Inber, that little grey-haired woman with her fine and sensitive character, that I had a chance of reading the *Pulkovo Meridian* in a daintily published little volume, printed in Leningrad. Otherwise I should probably have read only a few extracts of the poem published in Moscow magazines. Ten thousand copies of the little book were printed in Leningrad and were sold out in two days, after which the 'black market' price of Inber's poem ranged between 400 and 500 grammes of bread – or nearly a whole day's ration. Yet thousands of copies changed hands that way. What poem anywhere outside Russia in recent years has sold 10,000 copies in two days? There are many other Leningrad writers and poets who are widely known throughout the Soviet Union – but more from their articles than from their books, or from occasional poems published in the national press – Alexander Prokofiev, and Sayanov, and Likharev, and Vychnevsky, and that very fine poetess, Olga Bergholz, and Golubeva who wrote *The Boy from Urzhum* (the story of Kirov), and Ketlinskaya who is today writing what promises to be one of the most important Leningrad novels. Of the older men,

Lavrenev and Zoschenko, though no longer living in Leningrad, still consider themselves essentially Leningrad writers. And there are many others, for instance, Sergei Spassky, of whose existence I became aware only after hearing Yakhontov, I think, recite three of four of his poignant little Leningrad poems at a concert in Moscow, and which, hard as I tried, I could never find anywhere in printed form.

The truth is that Leningrad, which remained after the Revolution probably still the largest (at least purely literary) publishing centre in Russia, went on publishing quite a number of books even during the blockade. But paper and labour were limited, and what was printed was rapidly absorbed by Leningrad itself, and few of Leningrad's wartime books reached the 'mainland,' except in driblets. But one still has the impression – and that appears to be the feeling among all the Leningrad writers of today – that the really big literature of Leningrad and about Leningrad is still in the future and that, except for a few small books, like the Inber and Tikhonov poems, and a few others, little of permanent importance has yet been written, and that the great books based on the experience of wartime Leningrad will be written later, with a full sense of perspective, without wartime inhibitions, without material and psychological handicaps. For one thing, a very large part of the Leningrad writers' energies today is devoted not to writing literature, in the full sense of the word, but to lecturing in the army and in factories, and to writing day-today matter for local and army newspapers, etc.

The Leningrad Writers' Union organised a reception one evening at which I was the guest of honour. It was a great event for me, and I was assured that it was also a great event for them. I believe it. Not because they considered me a famous journalist or eminent author – I don't think any of them had ever heard of me before – but because I was the first British correspondent, in fact the very first person from England since the war, to have turned up in Leningrad. The fact that I was also originally a 'native' of Leningrad seemed to make me doubly welcome.

From numerous remarks that were made during the evening I felt how deeply Leningrad still felt its closeness to Europe, how very much alive the 'Western' traditions of the city still were – the traditions of Peter the Great and Pushkin – and what a large place was held in these people's outlook by the sea. More even than in Moscow, perhaps much more than in Moscow, one was conscious, in talking to these Leningrad writers, of a real thirst for close future contacts with the West; they thought in terms of harbours and ships – ships that were carrying passengers to and fro, and goods, and books and music, and paintings and gramophone records. Perhaps I am imagining it, but I had a feeling that these Leningrad writers regarded the semi-isolation in which Leningrad had lived not only during the war, but also before the war, as a deep cause of a certain creative weakness from which the writers, and also the painters, were the first to suffer.

Like most Russians today, many of them felt that a constant flow of ideas between Russia and the West, a continuous contact with other countries, was important, both for the world and for Russia herself, and that, as history in the past had shown, Russia, with her genius for absorbing and transfiguring foreign cultural influences and ideas had flourished most and had herself contributed most to the general heritage of European civilisation when contacts were closest with the outer world. And Leningrad, which symbolised so well the transformation into something purely Russian of so much of European civilisation – Pushkin, for instance, was a typically Russian product of the French eighteenth century and, to a lesser extent, of the English Romantic Revival – felt perhaps more deeply than any other town in Russia its debt to Europe. Russia, though in the seventeenth century as barbarous in its own way as, say, Turkey, Persia or Afghanistan, showed in much less than a century that its soil was essentially *European,* and that European civilisation could flourish on it more luxuriantly than even in most European countries. If at first, therefore, there was above all a desire to learn from Europe, there followed a desire to exchange with Europe. The stage after that would be to want to teach Europe. That by the way is where the Comintern went wrong, because it turned out to be an artificial product, with no deep roots in Russia itself and no suitable soil outside Russia. That, after this war, Russia will have much to teach the world cannot be doubted; the very fact that Russia, despite terrible handicaps, is now winning the war, is enough to make the socially and politically curious ask: How did she do it? And many lessons will be contained in the answer to that question. But in the cultural field in Russia today there is no 'superiority complex' of any kind (except possibly in music), but there is a profound desire among many writers not only to 'exchange' ideas with Europe, but also to learn. When I say Europe, I naturally also mean America; nowhere among writers has Hemingway, for instance, aroused such interest as an artist and as a craftsman as among writers in the Soviet Union.

And all these people today regret the relative cultural isolation in which Russia lived in recent years.

I am not building up here a purely personal theory. During that evening at the Writers' Union in Leningrad much was said precisely on these lines. What I say is also based on what I have been hearing for the last two years from people in Moscow. I think I am right in saying that Alexei Tolstoy's ideas on the subject run on much these lines. And Alexei Tolstoy is, among other things, a political force.

Much was said during that evening at the Leningrad Writers' Union, in their beautiful marble-pillared and marble-staired eighteenth-century mansion off the Liteiny Prospect – unfortunately I did not see the outside owing to the absolute blackout – but naturally, the main subject of conversation was still Leningrad and all its past and present experiences. I find it hard to record fully what was said, or to say exactly who said what. There were many people there; first we sat round a sort of conference table for about an hour, and then round a grand supper table – for a great deal more than an hour. A very large proportion of the talking was done by that tremendous figure, Captain Vishnevsky, in naval uniform and with a dazzling display of decorations. For irrepressible exuberance there was, I am sure, nobody like him for miles around. He had gone through thick and thin, lecturing to the troops, and fighting in the navy and on land, and writing pamphlets and booklets for the Russians and propaganda leaflets for the Germans, and also writing plays and a story or novel (as yet unpublished) about the Baltic Fleet in wartime. Almost equally exuberant was Sayanov, the poet and front reporter for the Leningrad and army press, young and jovial and with a superb blond moustache *à la Budienny.* His main subject was the Russian air force since its pioneer days. These did most of the talking about Leningrad, with a few additions from Alexander Prokofiev, Ketlinskaya and others. Tikhonov and Inber were, unfortunately, not in Leningrad at the time; I had seen Inber in Moscow just a day or two before I left. Heaven only knows what they did not talk about; much of what they said covered fairly familiar ground, but Vishnevsky, in particular, produced much human detail and some new angles. I shall try to restore a few notes I took down during the first part of the evening.

There was a lot of talk about the *levée en masse* and the *lutte à outrance* that had saved Leningrad.

'It's all very well,' Vishnevsky exclaimed, 'for the Germans now to say that the Leningrad line is much stronger than the Maginot line. At the beginning, when they were only approaching Leningrad, there was nothing, not a damned thing. What made

Leningrad impregnable was that a million people went on working day and night on trenches and fortifications. Our youth went into the army like one man. Our Workers' Divisions – and there were several of those – played quite a decisive part during those first stages of the battle for Leningrad. Bessonov, an old Obukhov worker of 67, and all his six sons went off to the front. The old man refused to be left behind. There was a tremendous exaltation among these people. Old veterans of the Putilov and Obukhov works went out to die.... I remember those days in August and September 1941, after the famous Voroshilov–Zhdanov–Popkov appeal. Last spring you could see some of those posters, gone grey with time, on some of the Leningrad houses. The Germans had thrown forty-five divisions against Leningrad. As they were approaching the city, they were setting fire to everything. There was a ring of fires round Leningrad – you could see them at night – it was the villages burning. But people here said, 'We're not going to budge.' Nasty things happened. There were Fifth Columnists in Leningrad; they would fire rockets at night to give guidance to the German guns and planes. Many Fifth Columnists had come in together with the refugees; some conscious, other unconscious – that is, stupid old peasants who were filling everybody up with enemy rumours and enemy propaganda. In my street it was observed how somebody was firing rockets. Inquiries were made, and a bunch of enemy agents were caught.'

'Yes,' said Ketlinskaya, 'an old aunt of mine had some neighbours, and it was noticed how they kept their light on at night, despite the strictest blackout rules. It was found that there was a man there, of German origin, who was signalling to his pals.'

Somebody else said that the most critical day of all was the 14th of September. 'That day our various high school students held together with the Komsomol an enormous meeting, as a result of which every single young man still in town volunteered for immediate service. Hundreds of thousands of young people volunteered that day and in the next day or two.

'Only one thousand did not volunteer. We said, 'We want no cowards here.' And we said goodbye to them.'

That was Vishnevsky speaking, and he said the last phrase in a very ominous tone. The dazzling captain now held the floor again.

'The people of Leningrad knew among other things,' he said, 'that they were fighting for their own skins. General Malwerstedt of the S.S. Polizei Division made it perfectly plain that the S.S. were going to undertake a gigantic purge of the city, that 400,000 people at least would be bumped off or tortured to death right away. He said that the Revolution was a 'concrete thing' and that unless you killed all the people in any way typical of the Revolution, you did not stamp it out at all. It is a principle which, I sometimes wonder, shouldn't we be well advised to apply to Germany in stamping out Hitlerism.... I am glad to say that Malwerstedt was subsequently bumped off by the partisans.

'We weren't going to be taken in by any nonsense. They started by dropping leaflets calling upon us to declare Leningrad an open city. Our people laughed at the idea. It wasn't cheerful laughter, I can tell you, but they laughed. They said, 'Nothing doing.' All the time the Germans tried to frighten us out of our wits. They announced that Field-Marshal von Kuechler, who had smashed Warsaw to smithereens, would do the same to Leningrad. Hitler had already announced on July 16th: 'Ich habe alle Móglichkeiten kalkuliert,' and had announced the imminent fall of Leningrad. Then on November 5th, when the town was already cut off, they dropped leaflets, saying, 'We shall do the bombing on the 6th, and *you* will do the burying on the 7th."

'How the Germans love sadistic jokes!' I remarked, 'especially against people who are down or who they think are down.'

'Yes,' said Vishnevsky, 'they were going to make it hot for us on the twenty-fourth anniversary of the Revolution. On the night of the 6th they dropped 65,000 bombs on Leningrad – mostly incendiaries, but very few started any fires. Our fire-fighting had already been perfectly organised. Then on the 8th Hitler announced that he would starve us into surrender: 'That town will raise its arms of its own accord.' The divine Führer really didn't understand the first thing about our people. He is really a lout like the rest of his lousy soldiery. The German prisoners we get here – they don't understand anything either.

'Those were the days when our soldiers had entrenched themselves and a German breakthrough already seemed improbable. They fought like devils. So did the Naval Infantry. What superb fellows they were! Everybody in the Navy fought who could carry a rifle – the bakers fought and the cooks fought. The Baltic Fleet played its great part, tens of thousands went into the naval infantry, and the Fleet Air Arm was in charge – that was a little later – of protecting the Ladoga ice road. These sailors fought like devils. In one very hot engagement, south of Lake Ladoga, one of our sailors had his foot blown off by a German shell; he stuck the bleeding stump into a large shell-case and carried on till he lost consciousness through loss of blood – which was pouring over the sides of the shell case. There was a sacred frenzy in these men which frightened and bewildered the Germans. . . . Then, at one of the blackest moments, we learned that the Finns had broken into Beloostrov. We had hardly any men to spare. There were no rifles except training rifles. But I shall always remember that grey winter dawn at the Finnish station when 700 men, poorly armed but determined to get Beloostrov back, went north. They got it back, and the Finns have never tried to shoot their necks out again.'

Vishnevsky and others then talked about the famine. Much of what was said I had already heard, but there were a few fresh points.

'The Leningrad Public Library was of great help to us in the blockade. People went there at first – actually before the blockade began – and studied every conceivable book on the sieges of towns. Then during the blockade there were no matches in Leningrad; scientists and others went to the Public Library and looked up books, 100 and 150 years old, books in French and English and German – on all the primitive methods of making matches. There is an old man there, Bychkov by name, one of the curators of the library. He recently celebrated his eighty-fifth birthday. He refused to be evacuated. He said, 'Leningrad won't be taken – to hell with you!' And he refused to go. He was so weak, though, for a while he couldn't walk at all.

'At that time we didn't know yet about the Ladoga ice road and the prospect really was very grim. But we cheered up enormously after the Battle of Moscow. We were all very hungry. To walk up to the third floor was agony. You'd stop a dozen times before getting there. But people didn't complain. They never looted bakeries. Many thousands died quietly every week. The Komsomol did all it could to keep people's morale up. They would drop in on people who were obviously going to pieces and say, 'Look here, old man, it wouldn't be a bad thing if you had a wash and a shave.'

'I myself said at a meeting,' said Vishnevsky, 'that women should use rouge and lipstick, it would make them feel better.'

'The Komsomol and the Pioneers,' somebody said, 'did a lot to help the civilian population to pull through. They'd go to the houses of older people and would help them to change their ration cards which were about to expire. An enormous number of letters kept coming to Leningrad, especially from our own Leningrad front. The children did the work of postmen. They whistled outside houses till the people came down to fetch the letters addressed to them. With food rations what they were, you naturally couldn't expect the children to run up and down hundreds of stairs.

'There was a terrible fuel shortage, of course. One of the most extraordinary stunts of the blockade days was this one. There is a place in the Port of Leningrad where for half a century or more the coal ships from Cardiff used to be unloaded. As you know, when coal is unloaded there is always a certain amount of waste – the stuff drops into the water. Well, large holes were cut in the ice, and divers went down and worked for many days in the icy waters; and they brought to the surface 4,000 or 5,000 tons of coal! Those were the sort of expedients to which we were reduced.

'There continued to exist the closest contact between Leningrad and the front – that front which was so near and whose guns could be heard throughout the dark, hungry winter nights. Women in Leningrad continued to knit comforts for the troops, and people kept sending them all sorts of little presents.

'There was a soldier, a Sergeant Chistov, who wrote a letter to one of the Leningrad papers, saying that he never received any letters from anyone; and he added, 'I am lonely; my heart isn't armoured.' Within a week he received 692 letters from people in Leningrad.

'An enormous interest was shown here in the sniper movement. It was really here on the Leningrad front that it started. The real pioneer of the sniper movement was a Komsomol lad from the Viborg district, now Hero of the Soviet Union Smolyachkov. There's another one, Semenchuk, aged nineteen. He has a sniper's rifle personally inscribed by Zhdanov. He has killed 209 Germans.... And it was also here, on the Leningrad front, that the technique of ramming enemy planes was developed.

'Fearful things were happening all the time. There were dead bodies all over the place. Cats and dogs had disappeared completely. I knew an elderly artist who strangled his cat and ate it. Even last summer I remember taking some small children out to the country, and a little girl began to scream in terror:

'There's a German. There's a German!' What she saw was a pig. She had never seen a pig before, except on war posters. A lot of our children have never seen even a cat or a dog.

'One of the greatest examples of how Leningrad fought for its life was when in the spring 300,000 or 400,000 people came out into the street with shovels – people who were scarcely standing on their feet, so weak and hungry were they – and proceeded to clean up the town. All winter the drains and sewers had been out of action; there was a great danger of epidemics spreading with the coming of the warm weather. And in a few days these 300,000 or 400,000 weak, hungry people – many of them were very old people who had never handled a shovel in their lives – had shovelled away and dumped into the river and the canals all those mountains of snow and filth which, had they remained there, would have poisoned Leningrad. And it was a joy to see the city streets a few days later all clean and tidy. It had a great moral effect.'

Mr. Eliasberg, the conductor of the Leningrad Radio Orchestra, was also there, a middle-aged man with a long thin Jewish face, who talked about the various experiences of his orchestra. This orchestra was the only one left behind in Leningrad during the blockade; it was split into first-aid, A.R.P. and air raid shelter 'groups.' 'I've got a great viola player, Yesenyavsky; I always remember the wonderful way he plays the viola solo in Berlioz's *Childe Harold in Italy.* That man – I have never seen him happier than on the 13th of September; that was the day we had eleven air raid warnings, it was really one continuous raid. But Yesenyavsky was a happy man that day. He had put out his first incendiary bomb.... I also remember another memorable day – the 28th of October, when things were looking very black indeed. We had seven air raids that day. In the morning we had a rehearsal of Tchaikovsky's Fifth which we were going to play that night; it was going to be relayed to London. During that rehearsal four bombs dropped right outside the Radio Headquarters. Several people were wounded, among them two of my musicians. One was wounded in the head, the other in the leg. But they both arrived at the rehearsal, and later at the concert, bandaged up, and they played. I remember how another warning went just as we had started on the third movement, the Waltz; and then, when we were in the middle of the Finale, the whole building shook with a bomb that had landed just outside.'

I remarked that Broadcasting House had had very similar experiences in London during the blitz, and worse.

'Well, yes,' said Eliasberg, 'that side of it must have been much the same; but what happened to us later can't have had any parallel in London. For in November things became more and more difficult. We were constantly going to the front under shellfire, to do what we could for the troops. Many of our people were becoming very weak. In December and January many of them died from exhaustion and undernourishment. For seven long weeks the Orchestra was out of action. Then the party and the Leningrad front came to our rescue. The front gave us eighteen people for our Orchestra – eighteen people whom it was essential for us to have. Thanks to this we were able, on May 7th, to play for the first time in Leningrad Shostakovich's Seventh Symphony. It had been performed only in Kyubyshev before then. Now we have seventy-five people in the Orchestra, and we play twenty-two or twenty-three times a month. Life has almost returned to normal for us, after the great ordeal we have lived through. But there is one thing I shall always remember. During those black days our musicians developed a new quality in their playing; they felt it more deeply, they gave more thought to it. Altogether, people in Leningrad are thinking a lot these days, and reading a lot, most of all our classics – Tolstoy and Dostoievsky, not least his *Writer's*

Diary, in which so much thought is given – whether he is right or wrong is another matter – to Russia's destiny and her place in the world.'

'And people themselves keep diaries,' somebody else said, 'a lot of diaries, with many astonishing details; a lot of this will be the basis for the literature Leningrad will produce after the war.'

Serov, the painter, much of whose work I had seen at the Leningrad art exhibition in Moscow, was also there. The impression I had formed of that exhibition was that, on the whole, Leningrad had maintained a rather higher standard of craftsmanship than most of the Russian painting produced today. The Leningrad artists had, during the blockade – and one realises in what fearful conditions they were working – concentrated on small canvases, on small charcoal drawings and etchings. Much of the work was little more than of documentary interest; but there were many poignant little paintings of the desolate Leningrad streets buried under the snowdrifts, and drawings, notably by Dormidontov, of a bread queue during the worst days of the blockade; some of these drawings, apart from their documentary value, had also a deep emotional content, and unquestionable qualities of composition. But actually, I think, the greatest value of the exhibition was to be found in the portraits, not least in Serov's own portraits. These were the faces of Russian soldiers of the Leningrad front, of partisans, of airmen – faces of men, famous or nameless, all of whom were profoundly typical of the great and terrible years of 1941 and 1942.

It occurred to me then that there was a curious parallel between the art of this Russian war and French art during the Revolution and the Napoleonic wars. The vast canvases of David and the rest were no doubt of greater artistic merit than some of the giant monstrosities one had seen at exhibitions in the Tretyakov Gallery in Moscow: 'The Rout of the Germans outside Moscow,' 'Sebastopol,' and the rest of all those monumental battle scenes, those glorified *images d'Épinal*, with their static tanks spitting tassels of fire – but they were not half as typical of the Revolution or Napoleonic period as the portraits by the same David, Gerard, Gros, Gericault and so many others. In the same way, the *epoch* of this war in Russia – and what an epoch it is – is best of all reflected in the portraits painted by the Russian artists of today. The human material at the artist's disposal is so supremely good that, even with the ordinary academic canons to which Russian artists generally adhere today (for lack of encouragement to follow less academic and more experimental or even plainly modern lines) the result is bound to be good. But Serov was not inclined to discuss painting in theoretical terms; somehow the 'artistic' side of art was something for which he had little interest in the present circumstances; he agreed with me, though, about the historic importance of the portraits painted in Russia today, and said that Leningrad would probably have its portrait gallery of the men who had taken part in the great battle and the blockade. He preferred instead to dwell on the active role played by the artists of Leningrad in this war. Many artists died of hunger, many others were killed in the bombings and bombardments; all, except the old men, had volunteered for the army, and the authorities had to make an effort to keep some of them back. Many of those who had gone into the army were dead now. 'We Leningrad artists,' said Serov, 'were busy preparing a large exhibition for the twenty-fifth anniversary of the October Revolution when the war came and upset all our plans. Those of us who did not go to the front devoted ourselves almost entirely to poster and propaganda work. Like the Moscow artists, many of us joined the Tass poster organisation – the Leningrad 'Tass Windows' are altogether distinct from the Moscow 'Tass windows' – and to nearly all of us ordinary painting really became very much a sideline. But whether we do poster work or simply paint, we painters have come much closer to the ordinary masses of the people. We continuously go to the front, we even live among the partisans, in the enemy rear. Like cinema operators, some of us have been killed. We have much interesting correspondence with soldiers and partisans. There is one young sniper who recently distinguished himself. One of our people painted a very good portrait of him. Having seen the picture, the sniper wrote a few days later: 'You've made my picture. I killed today a German *for you.*' Another soldier who had his portrait painted said to the artist: 'You mustn't show my picture to anybody just now, because I am going into the enemy rear.' Then a few weeks later he wrote: 'I've come from the enemy rear; I've done this and that. You can show my picture now.'

'Yes,' said Serov, 'their portraits are certainly worth doing. Take almost any of our Leningrad soldiers. Usually quite an ordinary face, and nothing in the least heroic about the shape of his nose – but – have a look at him, and he's a lion!'

There was much other talk, but I forget all the details. Somebody again mentioned the German leaflets that were now being dropped over the Russian lines. 'They must certainly be hard up for cheerful thoughts.... The other day our soldiers laughed when the Germans thought they would overwhelm them with the terrific news that Mussolini had been captured by the S.S. 'Serves him bloody well right,' they said. Better still, the Germans have now been frightening our soldiers with, if you please, the counter-revolutionary activities of the Soviet Government. In connection with the election of the Patriarch in Moscow they announced in their leaflets to our soldiers: 'After the war you will again be ruled by the priests!'

We adjourned to the beautiful dining-room with its white-and-golden upholstery – only the paintings had been removed to safety from the otherwise exquisitely furnished building (I didn't ask whose mansion it was before the Revolution) – and here we had a typically Russian party, with lots of food, and vodka and wine. There were first the usual toasts to Anglo-Russian friendship, to speedy victory, to Stalin, to Churchill, to Leningrad, to the Red Army, then, half-way through the supper, Mr. Eliasberg drank a heartfelt toast to Sir Henry Wood; somebody else to a highly elaborate death of Hitler! Then I stood up and quoted words of wisdom from Mr. Eden's latest speech on Anglo-Soviet relations, and everybody drank to Mr. Eden; somebody then said that the Finns had such cold feet that for two months now they had stopped their Russian broadcasts; so we drank to the perdition of the Finns! From across the table Sayanov, with the blond Budienny moustache, proceeded to prove that Keats was a much greater poet than Byron, and it was unfortunate that most people in Russia were unaware of it; so we drank to the memory of Keats. It was altogether a very jolly party.

Then somebody – it must have been Vishnevsky – told funny stories; for instance, one about a soldier who boasted about all the things he would do to the German women when he got to Berlin; he was charged with the use of obscene language, but the colonel intervened and said the soldier had proved himself a true patriot, and one with a solid faith in victory and in the stupendous might of the Red Army. The two or three ladies at the table pretended not to listen. Altogether, I noticed that they drank very little and looked on tolerantly at the rest of the company, though perhaps with a slight touch of disapproval. Heaven knows what else we talked about – Priestley and Hemingway, I think, and Kipling, who for nearly three generations now has been a Leningrad favourite, and the Second Front, and the German working-class's share of responsibility for what had happened, and the London blitz, and the British Navy, and how nice it would be after the war to sail from Leningrad straight to London, and about *Mr. Bunting*, the one English wartime novel everybody had read. The whole party was, to everybody, a deliberate escape, and they were glad to have a complete change for a few hours.

The party broke up a good couple of hours after curfew. I was in the hands of the military, and our car drove us to the Astoria through the blackout without incident. How the civilians at the party got to their respective homes I don't know.

14

All-Day Shelling

I woke up the next morning with a doubly unpleasant sensation. I had a hangover, and Leningrad was being heavily shelled. I had been wakened by this loud thumping noise of shells exploding some distance away. And all that day the thumping went on, non-stop, with often as many as three or four thumps to a minute. The area most heavily shelled was about two miles away, somewhere round the Narva district and the Obvodny Canal. I kept thinking of the Putilov workers and of the children and staff of the Tambov Street school. When I suggested we go down to the shelled areas, Colonel Studyonov merely said: 'Why look for trouble, when for all you know, the trouble may come to you anyway?' Which, I suppose, was reasonable enough.

Altogether it was a disappointing day – I mean the first half of it. Our programme was the sort of programme that would have been dished out in the normal course to the visiting ambassador of a friendly power, or to a delegation of the T.U.C. We spent a couple of hours in a military hospital on the other side of the river, and another hour in a large air raid shelter in the basement of a seven-storey block of flats in the centre of the town (there wasn't a soul there, except the woman in charge of it – even though the shelling outside was pretty heavy) and another half-hour in a training centre for civil defence instructors and instructors in elementary military training. In all three everything was thoroughly organised and the people in charge were thoroughly competent, and that's about all there is to say about it.

The chief surgeon of the military hospital took us round the delousing rooms, and the operating rooms, and the X-ray rooms, and the blood-transfusion place – in fact all the things one was quite prepared to take for granted; they were, to the layman, exactly the same as in any good military hospital in Moscow. He said the hospital had been getting a certain amount of British and American equipment and other supplies and that there was no shortage of anything, except X-ray plates. There was also a physiotherapy department and a mud-bath installation. The hospital had had eight direct hits from shells, but the building was solid and the damage slight and nobody had been killed. There were strong air raid shelters and all the wounded could be taken down there in a very short time. Only a few things in the hospital were peculiar to Leningrad. With the front so close it was adapted to receiving far more wounded in case of emergency than it normally held – three or four times as many. Further, it had its emergency power station, and its emergency water supply, straight from the nearby Neva. The hospital also had its own vegetable gardens – twelve hectares of them, and in a pinewood outside Leningrad a convalescent home. It seems that during the blockade this hospital carried on almost normally; it had enough coal for its central heating, and received absolute priority in everything. Now everything, to use the old cliché, was spotlessly clean – the long white-washed corridors, and the wards overlooking the Neva – most of the windows were intact – and the white overalls of the doctors and surgeons.

Most of the wounded here were officers with arm and leg wounds requiring lengthy surgical treatment, and the hospital specialised in the 'restoration' of hands. Nearly all the wounded with whom I talked had been wounded in the big Mga battle in the early summer; nearly all of these had had their legs damaged or blown off by anti-personnel mines. The proportion of Russian casualties resulting from mines during offensive operations was clearly very considerable and probably even greater in the large sweeping offensives in the south than in the more restricted and more concentrated operations around Leningrad. One or two of the men I saw had been in hospital for a long time, since the famous Schlusselburg rupture of the Leningrad blockade in February 1943. The losses were very heavy then, but the result had more than justified the losses suffered in that bold storming of the German positions across the ice of the Neva.

One of the casualties in that operation was a young officer from Odessa, with a dark, sad face; he said he had always disliked unlucky thirteen; he had never had a scratch; but in the thirteenth attack in which he had taken part he had lost his right leg. He said he had come to love Leningrad more than any other place in the world; he had fought here for two years, and he hoped to stay here after the war; he had only an old mother in Odessa, and he had little hope of her having survived the German occupation. But there was another Odessa lad, a fair and blue-eyed Ukrainian, and as typically Odessa as you make them, in the same ward, speaking that superbly picturesque Odessa jargon which is not only a linguistic but even more so a psychological blend of Russian, Ukrainian, Yiddish, Armenian and possibly Greek. Odessa is Russia's Marseilles, and for the picturesque exuberance with which he told it, no *histoire de Marius* ever surpassed this lad's story of how he and his pals made a surprise attack on the headquarters of an S.S. brigade: 'We came out of the high cornfield – yes, the corn was one and a half metres high – just as the S.S. men were sitting down to supper, see? They just hadn't an idea we were coming. They were sitting around in the garden lolling about in armchairs, waiting for their supper, see? and talking and behaving as though they weren't giving a damn about anything. And just as the soup was being brought in, see? we turned our machine-gun on them. We killed nearly the whole damn lot of them, among them the chap with the soup tureen. And only two ran away, and lord, didn't they run; and suddenly there was one more whom we saw running away. We hadn't seen him before, a great big brute of an S.S. man he was! You see, he had been sitting inside the privy, see? and had realised that something was going on, so he thought he'd better run too, but he hadn't fastened his pants properly, so as he ran they came down, and while he was trying to pull them up again a bullet got him, see? right in his bare behind! Damn fool; if he'd stayed inside the privy, we mightn't have noticed him. Of course, they were going to counter-attack, but by that time we had beat it; it was no use waiting; we had done the job we had come for.

'Our chaps are doing well in the south,' the Odessa lad continued. 'I soon hope to be back home in Odessa-Mamma. Great place, Odessa; the sea is so blue, and the sun warms your bones, and there are all those nice streets in Odessa, the Pushkinskaya and the Deribasovskaya. Nothing like it in Leningrad.' 'Come, come,' I said. 'I know, I know,' he said, 'it's a better-looking city, more cultured, and all that, it's got historic monuments – Peter the Great and Catherine, and Lenin – a more cultured city, one might say, a more historic city. But I don't like it. The climate is all wrong. There's no warmth here as there is in the south, it's kind of damp here all the time. But I'll grant you – Leningrad would be a very nice city – if you put it on the spot where Odessa stands.'

Never mind about the air raid shelter and the civil defence instructors' training centre. But what was interesting that day was our visit to the great Leningrad Public Library. This great library, at the corner of the Nevsky and the Sadovaya – one of the 'danger corners' during the shelling – claims to be, with its nine million volumes, the largest library in the world, or at any rate in Europe, with the exception of the British Museum. In recent years, it is true, the Lenin Library in Moscow is believed by some to have surpassed the Leningrad Library, but nowhere in Leningrad did I find any support for that view. At any rate, for its immense collection of incunabula and first editions, Leningrad is certainly still miles ahead of Moscow. Even Moscow admits that.

It was a beautiful sunny day when we drove up to the public library, but as the Sadovaya street corner is a dangerous one, and shelling had been going on since morning, it was decided that we park the car in the Alexandrinka Square on the other side of the library. Here we were, standing outside the car, and looking at the beautiful building of the Alexandrinka, with its freshly repainted yellow stucco, and with the whole exquisite ensemble of Rossi's stucco buildings beyond, and to the left of us the little square in front of the Alexandrinka Theatre, with the bottle-shaped monument of Catherine, with Rumiantsev and Potemkin and other great men nestling below the sovereign's equally bottle-shaped skirt. It seemed almost miraculous how this beautiful corner of old St. Petersburg had escaped without a scratch. Although the streets were now very deserted – for the shelling was becoming heavier and heavier – this Alexandrinka Square looked more beautiful than it had ever looked. And just then one shell, and then another, crashed into something quite near, perhaps 500 yards away, on the other side of the Nevsky, somewhere behind the enormous granite pavilion with its plate-glass windows, which was once the most Gargantuan delicatessen shop in Europe – Eliseyev. Two clouds of what looked like brick dust shot up into the air. The tramcars in the Nevsky stopped and the few passengers came running out and dived into houses. A few other people could also be seen running for cover. We waited beside the car for a few minutes, not feeling too comfortable, but perhaps reassured by the extraordinary 'luckiness' of the

Alexandrinka Square. An ambulance dashed past, turning into the Nevsky. I uncomfortably recalled Major Lozak's experience of the man who had staggered two steps down the Nevsky already without his head. The firing continued, but the shells were no longer exploding in this part, so we walked into the Nevsky – I had the feeling of slinking rather than walking – and round to the other 'unlucky' side of the State Library at the corner of the Sadovaya where, according to Leningrad hearsay, the Germans had a special knack of landing their shells in the middle of the crowd at the tramstop. Actually it did happen once or twice – hence the legend.

But now there was no crowd at any tramstop, the Nevsky was still deserted except for an occasional army car, half a dozen people on the allegedly more sheltered side of the street, and a policewoman who continued to stand on point duty. Then one of the tramcars with two passengers inside began to move. Clearly Leningrad had learned not to be too lighthearted about shelling.

We were taken up a narrow staircase into the office of the chief librarian, a pedantic-looking young woman with masculine manners, and wearing the Leningrad medal. Her name was Egorenkova. A sort of hard defiance was written on her face, as on so many other Leningrad faces. She showed neither pleasure nor displeasure at seeing us, and simply treated our visit as a small job that had come into her day's programme. Like every other job, she would do it competently. Personally, I had the impression that she was a woman with whom personal reactions no longer mattered; her whole existence had become public service and nothing else. Her one aim in life was to save the Leningrad State Library, and it was a sufficiently large task for any ordinary human being. She was defending 9,000,000 books against 80,000,000 Germans – against those creatures who, for the first time in many centuries in Europe, had made bonfires of books. Leningrad is, in many ways, a fanatical city – only a city with a touch of divine fanaticism could have done what Leningrad did – but in this rather frail, overworked young woman who was the chief librarian of the Leningrad State Library was this inner fanatical fire, a fire of devotion and a fire of hatred particularly noticeable. She said nothing to indicate it; her remark about a shell that had killed a lot of people in the Sadovaya, just outside the library, was made almost casually, with a complete air of 'objectivity,' but I felt she would gladly make any German suffer all the torments of hell for what Germany had done to Leningrad and had tried to do to the State Library.

Perhaps I was just imagining it. For actually Egorenkova was completely businesslike from beginning to end; and yet, I am still sure of it.

'The outstanding fact about the library is,' she began, 'that it never closed down. Not even in December 1941 or January and February 1942. By the time the blockade started, we had managed to evacuate only a very small part of our most valuable things. We had evacuated the most important incunabula and manuscripts, some unique Russian and foreign eighteenth and nineteenth-century books, and our unique collection of newspapers published during the Civil War – 360,000 items in all, out of a total of over 9,000,000. Our staff put in an enormous amount of work for the protection of this library. Our staff filled the attics of the building with sand – carrying there 2,200 cubic metres. To some extent we had to decentralise the library, and also to store away in our basements some of the most valuable items. Windows had to be bricked up and sandbagged; we secured water-tanks, pumps, fire-extinguishers, and large quantities of sand, and organised the whole fire-fighting system with the maximum thoroughness – allowing for the difficulties arising, for instance, from the absence of a normal water supply. Our A.R.P. staff consisted of 102 people. We were lucky though. The only trouble we had from air raids was a few incendiaries in the autumn of 1941. Since then we have had three direct hits from shells; they damaged our roof, but no books suffered, and there were no casualties. A more serious problem was the lack of fuel and the effect of the cold and damp on our books. I shall come to this later.

'Before the war there were seven reading rooms in our main building; we had as many as 3,000 readers a day and as many as 9,000 books were issued in one day; moreover, we had to deal with some 400 written queries a day.

'On June 22nd there was a sudden sharp drop in the library attendance. In August we closed down the main reading-room and opened a safer reading-room on the ground floor, with 150 seats. People who were very nervous could do their reading in the air raid shelter. Not all people react the same way to bombing.

'Our real problems started with the coming of winter. We closed all the reading-rooms but opened two small ones – one used to be the newspaper room, the other was the staff dining-room. Both of these had little brick stoves. But in January 1941 we had to close down the first of these two rooms, and the former dining-room remained the only reading-room in this whole great library. There were days in January 1942 when only five readers came. But we continued to receive queries from soldiers and from various organisations, a lot of them on problems of nutrition, on the manufacturing of matches, and the like.

'In March we managed to open another reading-room – a larger one, and the Lensoviet helped us to fit it with a more satisfactory stove, and we were also given some fuel.

'Today we have about sixty readers a day; the number of readers is growing. We have ten or twelve new entries a day on the average. Now that the various technical and other colleges such as the Polytechnic, the Pædagogic Institute, part of the University are about to open again, the number of our readers is sure to grow in the coming months. But for the present, our principal readers now are engineers, army doctors, scientific workers – in short, specialists dealing with practical present-day problems. We have no young students among our readers just now.'

She was factual throughout, without any expression of approval, disapproval, hope or regret. What she said during our inspection of the library was also confined to statements of fact – without comment.

With its miles of bookshelves, the famous library looked almost normal. Here and there there were large gaps of empty bookcases – for instance a large set of bookcases labelled 'Bibliothèque de Voltaire.' The magazine room was open, with a somewhat scrappy collection of the latest numbers displayed on a large table – the Ministry of Information's *Britansky Soyuznik*, and copies of the *Lancet*, the *British Medical Journal* (about six months old) and (significantly) the American *Journal of Nutrition*, and other scientific magazines.

'These things come very irregularly,' said Egorenkova. 'Our great problem now will be to keep the books in good condition for another winter with little or no heating.' And, pointing at the windows in one of the rooms, with no glass panes in them, she said: 'We have had most of our windows blown out four times, but we are not putting in new glass or plywood just yet; the fresh air coming in is good for drying the books. We shall close the windows when the rainy weather starts.'

On the main staircase was a display of various charts and diagrams, including several depicting the Allies' war effort. On another wall was a display of photographs and various documents on the occasion of the eighty-fifth birthday of Bychkov, the director of the manuscripts department of the library. 'He isn't feeling very well, so he is not here today,' said Egorenkova. 'From the start he has refused to leave Leningrad.' Again no comment.

We then went through the immense main reading-room almost as large as that of the British Museum. Everything seemed in order, but there were no readers. There were ten or fifteen readers in a smaller reading-room nearby.

Then we went down a long corridor which seemed almost interminable; it was lined with card indexes. 'This catalogue was down in the basement at first, and there it got damp,' said Egorenkova. 'We brought it upstairs and dried it; no serious damage was done, all the cards are legible and in good condition now. It was important to save the card index, which is our only absolutely complete catalogue. There's a handful that aren't quite dry yet,' she added, pointing to a number of index cards spread out on a window sill. 'They are the last ones.'

On the second floor were still 3,500,000 foreign books – mostly French, German and English. 'The most important incunabula, both Russian and foreign, we have evacuated,' Egorenkova said. 'We still have here, among other things, the archives of the Bastille – they were bought up for this library by a Tsarist diplomat in Paris.'

Up till now there had been few signs of human life in the enormous building. But now we came into a large room which was buzzing with activity. Fifteen elderly women were here, filling in index cards, writing notes, sorting out piles of material – posters, manuscripts, newspaper cuttings, cartoons, ration cards and what not. 'This is quite a new and special department,' said Egorenkova, 'here we are building up a complete record of the life of Leningrad and the Leningrad front in wartime. Meet Vera Alexandrovna Karatygina, a specialist in the history of Leningrad, Petrograd and St. Petersburg.' No one could be more different than these two women. Karatygina was a handsome elderly woman with white hair, rouge and lipstick, a loud exuberant voice, and the shrill delivery of an enthusiastic school teacher.

'We disdain nothing,' she said. 'Everything that seems of the slightest historical value for the full reconstruction of the history of our defence of Leningrad, we keep and catalogue, and classify. Brochures, and invitation tickets of every kind, pamphlets, leaflets, membership cards – everything is important. Theatre tickets, concert tickets, programmes, concert bills – for instance the bills announcing the first performance in Leningrad of Shostakovich's Seventh – documents relating to our industrial, scientific and literary life; ration cards of the different periods of the blockade and after, a list of all the houses of Leningrad with, as far as possible, details of the number of people living there, damage through shelling, etc., A.R.P. instructions – some printed, other simply manuscripts, photographs, copies of front newspapers and other publications, however ephemeral – all these we are collecting and classifying. We are also compiling large files of newspaper cuttings on every conceivable subject concerning the defence of Leningrad. And just now,' she said, 'several of us are here compiling an album of the rupture of the Leningrad blockade – with letters from soldiers who actually took part in it, and masses of other printed, written and photographic material.'

The old ladies – most of whom looked like rather decrepit old gentlewomen who had seen better times – were up to their ears in cuttings and posters and bills and were so absorbed in their work that they scarcely seemed aware of our existence – any more than of the shelling that was continuing outside. As we went out I remarked to Egorenkova, 'It must give these old ladies great satisfaction to take part in such a highly valuable enterprise.' 'Why do you call, them old ladies?' she said, a little acidly. 'They are not "old ladies," they are fully qualified librarians who have been for years on the staff of the library.'

The Anichkov Bridge across the Fontanka, halfway down the Nevsky Prospect, and the Anichkov Palace, built by Rastrelli and Rossi, on one side of the river, and a beautiful baroque palace in red and white stucco – the name of which I forget – on the other, constitute another of the architectural beauties of Leningrad. The main feature of the bridge itself was now, however, missing – I mean its four famous bronze horses which Klodt made about 1850 and which are as much a part of Leningrad as the Chevaux de Marly – which they vaguely resemble – are part of Paris. There are many stories about the removal to safety of the Klodt horses in the dark days of October or November. It was an arduous job, but it was completed in one night except that one of the horses was left standing in the middle of the Nevsky, waiting for its turn to be removed. People further down the Nevsky rubbed their eyes in the morning when they saw one of the Klodt horses apparently galloping down the street. To the literary-minded, the horse had clearly borrowed the idea of leaping off its pedestal from the *Bronze Horseman*. It is said that an old woman made the sign of the cross at so supernatural a phenomenon, and that another one burst into tears. She was convinced that this was an evil omen – that the horses had leapt from their pedestals so as not to be captured by the Germans who were now going to enter Leningrad.

Long before, in Moscow, I had heard that the Anichkov Palace – now the Pioneers' Palace – had been severely damaged in the bombing. But, whatever the damage, it had now been fully repaired. The old palace of the Empress Maria Feodorovna (sister of Queen Alexandra) was now in perfect condition, except that the more valuable paintings and furniture had been removed to safety. It had become the Children's Palace, and had been that since 1935. Before the war, as many as 13,000 children and 600 teachers could be received at the palace and in the palace grounds simultaneously. Its function then was the same as that of any Pioneers' Palace in any other large town of the Soviet Union. The children came here to listen to lectures, to play games, to read, to listen to concerts and to work in 'circles' – literary 'circles,' dancing 'circles,' musical and dramatic 'circles,' or chemical and other scientific 'circles' – which the children joined in accordance with their individual tastes. There were physics and chemistry laboratories in the palace. Children were encouraged to go in for this 'individual activity' which helped them, outside their school work proper, to develop their own particular talents. For example, a child who in the Pioneers' Palace displayed great musical or dancing gifts had every chance of being passed on, if he or she wished it, to the Conservatoire or the Ballet School. At the same time, the Palace of Pioneers was not only a place of study and entertainment but also one where, in one way or another, the 'solidarity' and' civil consciousness' of the children were being developed.

In Leningrad during the war the Pioneers' Palace had to adapt itself to entirely different conditions; it acquired a different purpose. Its purpose now was to provide the greatest possible moral and physical help to the children. There were many war orphans and hunger orphans in Leningrad, and the Pioneers' Palace was something like a new home for them. Actually they did not live there, but in a large hostel close by, and were always welcome at the Anichkov Palace. Further, the Pioneers' Palace was really the centre from which care and supervision were extended to practically all the children of Leningrad between, roughly, the ages of seven and fourteen. As before the war, so now, there was a close link between the schools and the Pioneers' Palace, both of which belong to the education department of the Leningrad Town Council.

One of the main tasks of the Pioneers' Palace was now to keep watch over the largest possible number of schoolchildren, to organise their time outside school hours, and keep them in good physical and moral condition – both of which were essential in view of the frequent or total absence of both parents, and also in view of the psychological effect of living in a town under almost constant bombardment.

In a large room overlooking the garden, and with Empire decoration and Empire furniture, we were received by the head of the palace, a bright and lively little man called Natan Mikhailovitch Steinwarg; 'Natan,' as everybody called him, was, it appeared, a famous Leningrad character, popular with children and teachers alike. He was certainly a live wire and seemed none the worse for the extremely arduous job he had been doing in Leningrad since the beginning of the war, and right through the blockade.

'There were 500 schools in Leningrad before the war,' he said. 'Now there are 105. Before the war Leningrad was, in fact, the largest educational centre in the whole Soviet Union. We had half a million schoolchildren and 400,000 students – which means that nearly one-third of the population were pupils of one kind or another. It was a city of young people. It is not so now; though even now there is a surprisingly large number of children still in Leningrad – and we are letting them stay on. There is no longer any need to evacuate them.

'What we at the Pioneers' Palace have been doing since the war, in co-operation with the schools, can be stated briefly. For example, we have had to organise holiday camps for 50,000 schoolchildren last summer – that is, nearly all the children of Leningrad, except the very young ones who have their own crêches and kindergartens to look after them. Each lot of children spent at least one and a half months in the country, and we made all the arrangements for their extra food rations. The younger children simply rested and had a good time; the children over ten also worked a lot on the vegetable gardens throughout the summer. During the blockade we had much more difficult jobs to do; together with the schools we had to organise the evacuation of hundreds of thousands of children, and I needn't tell you in what difficult conditions that had to be done.

'The Palace is more than ever the Children's Club – or whatever you like to call it. Here are some of the things the children do when they come here. They have been doing a lot of amateur theatrical work, and they have done their rehearsing here, under the supervision of expert teachers. As a result, in the last eighteen months, they have given as many as 200 theatrical shows to soldiers in the hospitals and to army units not immediately in the front line.

'Most of the children have a father, sometimes a brother, at the front, and there is the closest personal bond, anyway, between the children of Leningrad and the Leningrad front. The children worship the soldiers. Our teachers have been helping them here a great deal in one of their main occupations – the making of presents for the soldiers. They knit and sew, and chisel cigarette holders, and make cigarette cases out of wood, with often quite elaborate designs. They also make and collect all sorts of gifts which they send to the children of the liberated areas. They, and especially the boys, also do bigger jobs; they were, for instance, of enormous help in repairing the serious damage caused to the Anichkov Palace by a bomb.

'They love their palace, and all the children would like to be here every day. But we have to space out their visits, because it is not safe to have too many children all in one building. What we are doing now is to set up a large number of branches of the Pioneers' Palace in the various districts of Leningrad. Now take today, for instance. For seven hours they have been shelling the city – chiefly the Lenin district along the Obvodny Canal. We had to telephone urgently to all the schools in the southern part of the town not to allow any of their pupils to come here today, because the children love coming here; and you know what Russian boys, and especially Leningrad boys, are like; no shelling will stop them if they really want to get to a place. So we have decided, as a precaution, and also as a means of providing practically all the children of Leningrad with the necessary comfort, to open branches of the Palace of Pioneers, and we hope to open most of them by October 15th.

'Comrade Zhdanov and Comrade Popkov are keenly interested in our work, and we are certainly getting every help from the Lensoviet.

'One of our most painful tasks is looking after those little war cripples who have been injured in the bombings and shellings – there are children in Leningrad without arms and legs; though fortunately not very many. From the start our teaching staffs have taken every precaution to save the children from injury. But misfortunes will happen nevertheless. Our shelter rules are strictly observed in the schools.

'But it isn't all so easy for the children. Well, take today, for instance. There are many hundreds, perhaps thousands, of children in this city who have spent the last seven hours in a shelter, with explosions going on around all the time. It does fray their nerves – it is no use pretending that because a child is tough, it can stand anything. And it is therefore terribly important that the Pioneers' Palace and its branches should do everything to take the children's minds off the grimmer side of things. So many of them have seen people lying dead in the street, and other terrible things. So we arrange concerts for them and theatrical shows, and we make them give concerts and theatrical shows themselves, and they come here and play games. But come and look for yourself,' said Natan.

We walked over the parquet floors of several rooms of the Anichkov Palace. Outside, the shells were still thumping. 'That's more than seven hours now,' Natan remarked. In one room a dozen boys were absorbed in games of chess. But several of the other rooms were empty, till we came to what must have been the sumptuous music room or ballroom of Maria Feodorovna's palace. This room was packed. A variety show by the boys and girls themselves was in progress. All the boys, with closely cropped hair, were wearing little blue or grey blouses and red pioneer ties, and most of the girls, many of them with large silk ribbons in their hair, were remarkably tidily and neatly dressed – as though they had dressed up for a birthday party. Altogether, it was a much better-groomed children's audience than you would find anywhere in Moscow, where clothes tend to be – even with children – on the untidy and sloppy side.

The late Maria Feodorovna, who was a kindly woman, would – I am sure – had she suddenly returned from the next world, been pleased to see such a charming children's party in her palace, and also to see in what nice condition her palace was being kept, and to what good use it was being put.

What was going on was *samodeyatelnost*, or 'self-activity.' The children were doing things themselves. As we entered the ballroom, a fair-haired little boy in a blue blouse and a red pioneer's tie was playing on a concertina, with great gusto, Tchaikovsky's familiar little waltz from the *Children's Album*. Then another little boy with a squeaky little voice sang, first a Russian soldiers' song, and then an English romance called 'Annie Laurie.' 'His father,' Natan whispered, 'was killed at the front last summer. A very fine man, a captain. He had the Order of Lenin.'

Then there was a comic, patriotic recitation from a bigger boy, with a lot of jokes about the Nazis. Outside the guns were going hard, but the children all laughed and clapped.

The rest of the programme was more ambitious. Four or five of the children played an amusing little sketch, with a 'winter fritz' as the funny man, and then an exquisite little girl of twelve or so gave a 'rainbow dance,' juggling deftly with streams of multicoloured ribbons and ending up with wonderful vitality in a graceful whirlwind of colour. The child's dance was clearly the product of professional ballet training. 'Yes,' said Natan, 'one of our best Leningrad ballet people comes here regularly and gives lessons to the most promising children.'

The rainbow dance brought the house down. The children clapped and screamed for more, and the dance was repeated, with a middle-aged woman with a red face and a mop of peroxided hair playing on one of Maria Feodorovna's cream-coloured Bechstein grands. Then a tall handsome boy of eleven or twelve played the violin very nimbly – a Weniawski mazurka, and one of Dvorak's Slavonic Dances. 'He's studied the violin for three years now in the musical studio of the Pioneers' Palace,' Natan explained.

It was good to see how happy and cheerful these children were, and how fit they all looked. But one could not help thinking with a pang of the other children who were now spending their eighth hour since morning in an air raid shelter, while shells were smashing houses and killing people around them. Nor could I help thinking of that infernal foundry in the Putilov works. What was happening there? The answer really was that one took things as they came to one. Today it was they; tomorrow it might be these. And, after all, there was no guarantee whatsoever that a shell would not come through the window at any moment and spoil the variety show at the palace completely. One just took chances – within reason – and did not worry.

When we got back to the Astoria about six o'clock there was a message for Major Likharev. His wife had phoned. Had anything happened? He rang up. Five shells had landed all round the house, and had smashed all the windows in his flat. Fortunately nobody had been either killed or even injured. He drove home as his wife, he said, had sounded 'a little upset.' However, he returned in a couple of hours, as we were getting ready to go off to the Smolny.

15

The Mayor of Leningrad Speaks

Two men are largely responsible for the survival of Leningrad – Zhdanov, Leningrad's party chief who also, as a member of the Politburo and as a member of the Praesidium of the Supreme Soviet, could act with all the authority of the highest party and governmental organs behind him; and Popkov, president of the Leningrad Soviet (the Lensoviet) or mayor of Leningrad as he liked to describe himself the night he received me at the Smolny. Actually his opposite number in London (if one can speak of 'opposite numbers' at all) would be the chairman of the L.C.C. rather than say the predominantly decorative Lord Mayor. These were the two men who, together with Marshal Voroshilov, at that time commander of the northern front, signed the famous 'Leningrad in Danger' appeal of August 21st, 1941.

I had seen Zhdanov only once in the distance, at the meeting of the Supreme Council when it was called in June 1942 to ratify the Anglo-Soviet Alliance. I did not see him during my visit to Leningrad, and Zhdanov has thus remained in my mind something of a legend: the man who conceived the Ladoga lifeline, and the man who, in the defence of Leningrad, had shown, in his more limited field, the same qualities of energy, self-possession, and organisational genius that Stalin had shown in the conduct of this war and the leadership of the country generally. To save

Leningrad militarily was Zhdanov's primary concern; I have heard it said that if he had been prepared to take a risk in December 1942, he could have permitted the civilian population slightly larger rations than he actually did permit; but the future of the ice road was still uncertain, and as long as that was so, Zhdanov decided to save up every possible ounce of food for the army, rather than save a few thousand civilian lives. For if these lives had been saved, and at the end of a few weeks the efficiency of the Leningrad front had been impaired through the necessity of applying starvation rations to the front itself, the damage to the country as a whole – and to Leningrad itself – would have been infinitely larger. It was just possible that a German breakthrough at that time, at this or that point of the front, would have rendered the Ladoga ice road impracticable or delayed it, and Leningrad would have had to continue without outside supplies. In other words, more generous rations for civilians in those weeks of uncertainty might have meant the end of everything, and Zhdanov was going to take no such chances. But it takes a man of iron will to take the hardest, most 'civic' and, on the face of it, least 'humane' line when in a grim dilemma of this kind.

So I did not see Zhdanov, the man whom many, thinking in terms of fifteen or twenty years hence, already regard as one of the two most likely successors, or even as the most likely successor. But I was invited to spend an evening at the Smolny as the guest of Popkov, who is, in effect, Zhdanov's second-in-command.

The Smolny is the young gentlewomen's high school, which became, in October 1917, the headquarters of the Bolsheviks. From here they directed the Revolution, and on the 25th the Smolny became the seat of the first Soviet Government. The famous building was wrapped in complete darkness as we drove up to it that night – the night after the eight hours' shelling. A sentry with a flashlight took us across the yard into the main building and there, along those long vaulted corridors through which triumphant Lenin had briskly walked to his office in those historic autumn days of 1917, we were conducted to Popkov's study.

Then, in October 1917, the whole neighbourhood of the Smolny and the long vaulted corridors were swarming with armed Red Guards and sailors of the Baltic Fleet. Now the corridors were empty except for a sentry here and there.

Popkov was a little different from so many of the other Leningrad bosses I had met. He also had a strong, fine face, but it was softer, and brightened by a friendly smile. Often his eyes twinkled, and he smiled almost boyishly, displaying two rows of perfect white teeth. He had one of those good Russian faces that make one feel at ease at once. His whole bearing had a natural simplicity, without any sophistication or the slightest trace of a pose. He was, no doubt, a 'tough baby,' as everybody in Leningrad has to be, especially in a job like this, but he did nothing to emphasise it. And what startled me, this great Leningrad leader did not speak with the usual, rather cold Leningrad precision but in a softer and more flowing Russian, of a kind spoken on the Volga. Actually, as he later told me, he was born in 1903 in the province of Vladimir, between Moscow and Nizhni-Novgorod. 'I come from the family of a very poor carpenter,' he said, 'for two years I worked as a farm labourer, and then for two more years as a baker. Then in 1926 I came to Leningrad to study.' Here he completed his course at the Workers' Faculty, and then at one of the technical institutes. And then – 'Then I just stayed on here, and became a member and then the chairman of one of the District Soviets; then I became first deputy to the chairman of the Lensoviet, and, for six years now I have been mayor of Leningrad! I was thirty-four when they made me mayor.' He liked calling himself the mayor.

The day before my visit, Popkov had asked me to send him a list of questions. Now, as we sat down, he laid the list before him and proceeded to talk. There were several other people in the room to whom I had been presented, several military men, and an elderly man, Professor Moshansky, the head of Leningrad's health department, and Comrade Bubnov, Popkov's secretary, an enormous lanky young fellow with a large turned-up nose and with something of the same *bonhomie* as his chief.

What I had really asked Popkov to give me was a general view of Leningrad both as a city and as one of the key-points of the Soviet–German front. There were also a number of specific questions, answers to which would fill in a few gaps in my reading of the situation. To the question: 'How many people actually died in Leningrad during the winter of 1941–2?' I received no answer, except that 'a few hundred thousand' was as much as could be said for the present. Also, when I asked: 'What is the present population of Leningrad?' Popkov smiled and said, 'Is it really necessary for you to know?'

My own guess was between 600,000 and 800,000, but I did not press the point. 'I'll give you an indication, though,' said Popkov. 'It has a population only a little less than Hamburg.' 'What,' I said, 'before the recent R.A.F. raids or since?' – at which everybody laughed gleefully and Popkov replied, 'No, I wouldn't have compared Leningrad with a rubbish heap.'

For the rest, he talked very freely; though there are one or two points I am omitting at his request.

As regards the military situation of Leningrad, Popkov said: 'The military situation of Leningrad today is more solid and stable than it has ever been since the beginning of the war. This can be proved by a whole series of facts. For months the Germans prophesied the imminent fall of Leningrad, and were planning their great victory banquet at the Astoria. All these plans have fallen through. First, our soldiers and workers smashed the German attempts to take Leningrad by storm. Then the Germans tried the blockade. The blockade also failed, though we lived through some very difficult hours, as you know, especially during the month when Tikhvin was in German hands and we were literally isolated, except for some transport planes. In making the Ladoga ice road we established a narrow link, but still a vital link with the outer world. In this way the German attempt to starve us out, to deprive us of communications, food and fuel, fell through, just as the attempt to take us by storm had failed.

'Today, since the railway link has been restored, through the Schlusselburg gap, we have no food problem at all. This has been solved completely. The civilian rations for sugar and fats are substantially higher in Leningrad today than in Moscow. We are trying to make up for the weight everybody lost during the months of undernourishment.

'The question: Can we or can't we hold Leningrad? no longer arises. The question is: How soon will the Germans abandon their Leningrad positions? The Germans have built very powerful fortifications here, and they would be more than reluctant to abandon them. They will not abandon them voluntarily. But there is one question which here, in Leningrad, is in everybody's mind; and that is the Second Front. Because we are convinced that if only the Germans were compelled to withdraw ten divisions from this front, they would have to withdraw altogether, because we'd push them out then. And the bombardments of Leningrad would automatically cease.

'There are thirty German divisions on the Leningrad front, though looking at the map you see that it isn't a large front. This summer, when the Germans feared we would widen still further the gap in the blockade, they brought reinforcements from the Kalinin front. Among them were troops which had taken part in the storming of Sebastopol. They had another crack at Leningrad in July but with no effect.

'But they will hang on as long as they can. It's a matter of prestige. Leningrad is the second capital of the Soviet Union;

they've also got to consider Finland. If they abandon Leningrad, Finland automatically drops out of the war. But it's all quite pointless, and they can't do anything, except vent their rage and fury and disappointment on our civilian population. They claim to be shelling railway stations and factories. But except the Kirov works, which they can't help hitting, they have never shelled any factory, except by chance. Actually they are trying to spread panic. But it all has little effect, and it's really a waste of shells. We have lived through much worse times than this, and we are determined to stick it to the end. All the shelling does is to deepen the fearful hatred every man, woman and child in this town feels for the Germans. The shelling increases our hardships and sufferings and our death roll, but it does not diminish our powers of resistance – far from it.'

'Today,' I remarked, 'the city was shelled for eight hours. How many casualties were there today?'

'I can tell you exactly,' said Popkov, 'for I have here the latest report, received half an hour ago. The shelling went on from 8.45 a.m. to 6 p.m., with the heaviest shelling in the morning when people go to work, and towards the end of the day. Altogether 1,564 shells were fired. Many houses were put out of action today, some water-mains were smashed, and in twenty-eight places the tramlines were damaged. By eight o'clock tonight the tramlines were already restored to the extent of seventy per cent. By the morning all the damage to the tram lines will have been repaired. And the number of casualties for the day,' said Popkov, 'is sixteen killed and seventy-two wounded.… That's nearly one hundred casualties. It may not seem much, compared with all the ammunition the Germans spent. But these figures mount up, and sometimes terrible things happen, when a first shell lands without warning in a crowd. For instance, one day last May, thirty-two people were killed outright and many others injured when a shell landed among a crowd of people at a tram-stop. But, once the first shell has been fired, people have learned how to take care of themselves.'[1]

Popkov looked at my questionnaire. 'You asked for some details about the present railway link between Leningrad and the rest of the country. The Ladoga road – over the ice in winter and over water in summer – was chiefly used for bringing food into Leningrad. Now, with the railway working, we can bring in anything, no matter how bulky. In addition to food, we can bring in almost unlimited quantities of coal, munitions, cattle, metal, and other raw materials. The Germans claim they are constantly shelling this railway. All I can say is that the railway functions like clockwork. It has fully solved our supply problem. Without it, life would be much more difficult. The Ladoga road was, after all, only an expedient. What's more, we not only import, but we also export – for instance, masses of scrap iron, machinery which can be more profitably used elsewhere, and all sorts of raw materials which we don't need. And also manufactured goods. Militarily, it is extremely important, too; by creating a direct and rapid link with the whole Volkhov front, it has greatly increased the manœuvrability in the whole Leningrad–Volkhov area.' Popkov pointed at the map. 'That's where it runs, linking up Schlusselburg with the main line south of Lake Ladoga. As soon as the blockade was broken last February, we started building the railway. We built the essential forty-five kilometres in twenty-two days, and we doubled this stretch here between Ladoga and Borisova Griva. Forty-five kilometres in twenty-two days – it took some doing!' he added.

'But although Leningrad is now normally supplied – and we shall not need the ice road next winter, we are not keen to let people come back. It remains a military zone. Of course, thousands and thousands of Leningraders are clamouring to come back. But the enemy is still at the gates. The town is being shelled.

If we had more people here, we should also have more casualties. Honestly, if I were in the position of the Germans, I'd pull out. What's the point of hanging on like this? Yet, there is no sign of their preparing to quit. They've got some of their most hardened troops here. There is one Spanish division here – not the Blue Division – that one was wiped out long ago, but some new, rather rubbishy division – but the overwhelming majority of the troops here are German.

'Today,' Popkov continued, 'the food situation is not worrying us any more. We have larger food reserves in Leningrad today than we had at the beginning of the war; and one of the reasons why we were so short of food in the winter of 1941 was that some of our most important food stores were destroyed in an air raid. Thanks to the railway, we have now substantial coal reserves, and the work we have done on the peat bogs round Leningrad has already exceeded our production programme. Although we have the railway we still try, as far as possible, to be self-sufficient. It has not been easy, though. The workers of Lenin's city have made many great sacrifices to supply it with timber. We have only a small territory from which to draw our timber supplies, and, for military reasons, certain woods must not be touched. The problem of timber, the most difficult of our problems, has been solved by the women of our town. We have sent 10,000 women beyond Lake Ladoga to cut wood. It is very hard work, and they work in all kinds of weather. But, thanks to them, we have enough wood to see us through the winter.[2]

'The bulk of Leningrad's industry has been evacuated, also the greater part of the population. We evacuated 500,000 people across the ice road alone. Certain categories of citizens we continued to evacuate even during this last summer. We want to keep in Leningrad only people who are useful. We are, however, keeping all the children here who have remained. There is no longer any necessity to evacuate them. They are quite cheerful here and their cheerfulness is good for the people's general morale. In the summer they all had a spell in the country, an average of forty days. The Komsomol of Leningrad have played an immense part in all the welfare work we are doing.

'We don't want more people to come into Leningrad now. As I said before, the more people we have, the greater will be the number of casualties. We have enough people to keep the life of the town going. Until September 15th, many houses still lacked electric light; now there is electric light everywhere, and it can be used without limit. Our power stations are now burning peat instead of coal, we changed them over for the purpose. Twenty per cent of the water is now wasted and runs into the sewers, because of the water-mains that are still damaged and continue to be damaged; but on the whole, the water supply is satisfactory too, and tap water can be safely drunk. Except for A.A. shells, practically all the shells made by the Leningrad front are made in this city; it means a very large production – well, you saw some of it on the Kirov works the other day – because there is not a front anywhere with the same concentration of equipment on both sides as on this front of ours.'

I asked what the health of the people of Leningrad was like. Professor Moshansky, the head of the Leningrad Health Department, said that 'apart from war casualties, the death rate among children was no greater than before the war. In hospitals, the death rate among adults was high throughout the summer of 1942, because of the after-effects of the famine, but now this death rate had been brought down to its prewar level. One of the most remarkable things about Leningrad,' he said, 'was that there were no cases of insanity or other nervous diseases due to bombing and shelling.' Professor Moshansky then gave a detailed account of the anti-typhus, anti-typhoid and other inoculations which had become the general practice in Leningrad, of the prophylactic measures taken against scarlet fever, and the various prophylactic tablets that were being regularly given to schoolchildren. There were, as a result, very few cases of infectious diseases – very few cases of scarlet fever and even measles; diphtheria had almost disappeared; there was much less dysentery than before the war, very little tuberculosis, and scurvy had now disappeared completely.

All this sounded almost too good, but at the same time it was obvious that with the physically weaker part of the population having either died or having been evacuated, the Leningrad medical authorities were now really dealing with, in the main, a naturally healthy population.

Regarding the elimination of scurvy, Professor Moshansky referred to the important part played in the spring and summer of 1942 by that vitamin drink, so peculiar to Leningrad, and of which I had already heard so often – the drink made of fresh pine and fir needles. 'Thousands of our children and youngsters went out to collect these fresh twigs, and there wasn't a factory canteen, a school, a government office – in fact there was hardly a place in Leningrad – where there weren't buckets of this liquid, and everybody was urged to drink as much as he could of it. It didn't taste particularly good, but people drank gallons and gallons of it, as a sort of duty to themselves and to the common cause! And it certainly made a very big difference to their devitaminised systems.'

'How much of Leningrad has been destroyed?' I asked Popkov.

'Some parts of the town have suffered greatly; but, in the main, the stone and brick buildings have been preserved. What is going on is a race between the German gunners and our repair squads. Up till now we have repaired 860,000 square metres of roofs, and put in three million square metres of windows.'

'What, not glass, surely?'

'Of course not! Glass adds immensely to the dangers of artillery bombardment. Wherever windows are broken we replace the panes entirely by plywood, with the exception of one small pane per room, to let in the light. Seven thousand rooms have been completely restored in 1943 alone, or 103,000 square metres of floor space. What is more, we have carried out a tremendous plumbing job throughout the town, restoring as many as 49,000 main taps, and twenty-five kilometres of water mains. Practically the whole water system had to be restored or repaired after the winter of 1941–2. In 1943 alone we have carried out the equivalent of two years' peacetime work. The Germans destroy, and we restore – that's part of Leningrad's life. We can't quite catch up with the destruction. The living-space 'fund' is satisfactory today, except that there are still 800,000 square metres of living space to be restored. Everywhere the water supply has been restored in houses – the water going up nearly everywhere as high as the sixth floor, and we are also busy repairing the central heating for the coming winter. The tramlines are rapidly repaired whenever hit. We are increasing the length of the tramlines.

'The vegetable plots have been a great help in solving our food problem. We have 12,500 hectares of vegetable plots in Leningrad and the immediate neighbourhood. Moreover, we have some very prosperous state farms outside the city. The only vegetables we import from the 'mainland' are potatoes, but we have enough cabbages, carrots, etc. to feed not only ourselves, but to supply the entire Leningrad front. The vegetable plots are lent by the town council both to organisations and to individual families. For instance, those vegetable plots you saw in the Summer Garden belong to individual families; they take turns in guarding them.'

'In Moscow,' I said, 'a lot of pinching of vegetables goes on.'

'Not here,' said Popkov. 'Ours are very disciplined people, with a great sense of solidarity. Sometimes young children will pinch a handful of somebody else's carrots, but it's unusual. The interesting thing is that in Leningrad in the past people only knew how to eat vegetables; now everybody has become an expert gardener. A lot of lectures are given on gardening, and they are extraordinarily well attended. People have been told: "You'll eat as much as you've planted, so don't expect anything from outside." And the results have been excellent.

'Let me, however, draw a few conclusions about our general situation. I'm afraid that if, from what I said, you got the impression that everything was fine in Leningrad, this impression would be quite wrong. Remember that no town has to work as Leningrad has been, and is, working. Everybody feels that he is part of the show, and that every hour of work he puts in is part of the defence of Leningrad. The impulse to work is, therefore, very great. Only this public spirit of our people has made Leningrad what it is today – a place where life is fairly close to normal. Yet the fact remains that we are still half-blockaded, and that we have some dead and wounded every day. No one in Leningrad will deny that life is very hard. But at the same time you will hardly find anyone wishing to go away. The people of Leningrad have become like a large family, united by common hardships and their common effort. It is this solidarity which has made it possible for Leningrad to look fairly decent again. You should have seen it at the end of the terrible winter of 1941–2. But it has not been achieved at a low cost.

'Think how much labour it has cost, for instance, to repair nearly all the roofs of Leningrad. If, two months ago, you had gone to the top of St. Isaac's, you would have seen many houses with their roofs torn off. You won't see many now. Throughout 1941 and 1942 we usually had 200 or 300 shells every day or every other day. We had about 40,000 shells fired into Leningrad during 1941 and 1942. The shelling now is less frequent, but when it comes, it comes usually in big doses, as it did today.

'One cannot speak without emotion and admiration of our people. They put their heart into everything they do. In the past a man who cut five cubic metres of timber a day was considered a Stakhanovite. Now women, and not very strong women, cut seven or even ten cubic metres.

'It was our people and not the soldiers who built the fortifications of Leningrad. If you added up all the anti-tank trenches outside Leningrad, made by the hands of our civilians, they would add up to as much as the entire Moscow–Volga Canal. During the three black months of 1941, 400,000 people were working in three shifts, morning, noon and night, digging and digging. I remember going down to Luga during the worst days, when the Germans were rapidly advancing on Luga. I remember there a young girl who was carrying away earth inside her apron. It made no sense. I asked her what she was doing that for. She burst into tears, and said she was trying to do at least that – it wasn't much, but her hands simply couldn't hold a shovel any longer. And, as I looked at her hands, I saw that they were a mass of black and bloody bruises. Somebody else had shovelled the earth on to her apron while she knelt down, holding the corners of the apron with the fingers of her bruised, bloodstained hands. For three months our civilians worked on these fortifications. They were allowed one day off in six weeks. They never took their days off. There was an eight-hour working day, but nobody took any notice of it. They were determined to stop the Germans. And they went on working under shellfire, under machine-gun fire and the bombs of the Stukas.'

'The tradition of 1917!' I remarked.

'Not only that,' said Popkov. 'It's much more general. Everybody took part in these tremendous efforts – not only the workers. Really *everybody*. And there was no panic at any time; no hysterics. A great love went into all that work – a great love, and a great spirit of self-sacrifice. We lost many, many valuable people during those months – and since. Yes, the Leningrad medal – which even many of our children have received – means a great deal.

'Well, what more can I say?' said Popkov. 'Perhaps just this relatively small point. Perhaps you don't know that Leningrad is quite an important manufacturing centre for consumers' goods. We supply the army, not only on our own front, but on the other Soviet fronts with a lot of things. We make buttons in Leningrad, and combs, and hosiery, shaving brushes, and shaving powder, and razor blades, and eau-de-cologne for the troops, and even perfumery for the army girls – and for our soldiers' wives and girlfriends! And,' here Popkov grinned boyishly, 'Leningrad has also started producing babies – hasn't it, Professor?' 'Yes,' said the Professor, 'and strong and healthy babies too. Very good quality babies.'

I asked Popkov how he viewed the future of Leningrad after the war. 'Isn't it, industrially, something of an anomaly, with the iron ore and the coal so far away?'

'No,' said Popkov, 'it's like this. Leningrad after the war will be, first, the greatest educational centre in the Soviet Union; already before the war we had 400,000 students here, and we may have more after the war. Secondly, it is going to be a great centre of light industry, because Leningrad is famous for the skill of its workers (most of whom will come back), and for the quality of its goods. After the war we shall at last be able to concentrate on the production of consumers' goods. They were pretty good even before the war. One of our comrades came back from a trip to Paris, and brought his wife some 'wonderful French stockings.' She had one look at them and found that they were our own Leningrad make! Thirdly – regarding heavy industry, you may know that northern Russia will no longer have to depend on the Donbais for coal, or on Krivoi Rog for iron ore. We are developing an important new iron ore area round Vologda just now, and it promises to cover all Leningrad's needs. More important still, you will have heard of the Pechova coal basin in the north-east. A railway has been built right up to the Pechova area; it will supply Leningrad with coal. Although it is a very long railway, it will have little competing traffic – its main purpose will be to bring coal to Leningrad and central Russia. So the industrial future of Leningrad looks more promising perhaps than it has ever been.'

After this long talk we had supper. It was a much quieter affair, though, than the uproariously jolly supper at the Writers' Union. The usual toasts were proposed to Churchill and Stalin, and also to Zhdanov and the other leaders of Leningrad, and Popkov, recalling a message he had received some months before from the Lord Mayor of London, proposed a toast to the Lord Mayor and the people of London. (Which, incidentally, shows that such messages which seem unimportant when read about in the press, do count with the people to whom they are addressed, and create genuine friendliness and mutual interest.) Altogether, one clearly felt at this gathering, as at so many others, the genuine desire of Leningrad to establish close contacts with Britain after the war, and how much the symbol of the window into Europe was still alive.

And I had that curious impression again that Leningrad was a little different from the rest of the Soviet Union; that it considered itself as being just so much better than the average. It was also keenly conscious of having, to a large extent, worked out its own salvation at the most critical moment, when the army was shattered and bled white, and when the nine Workers' Divisions, dressed in army uniform, did so much to save the city. And of these nine divisions, four were practically wiped out in that grim rearguard action they fought in the late summer and the autumn of 1941. These Workers' Divisions and the Baltic Fleet, who held Kronstadt and Oranienbaum, largely saved the situation during the most critical days at the beginning of September. The Army meantime had been retreating. Disguised as refugees, hundreds of enemy agents had penetrated into Leningrad, spreading wild rumours and firing signal rockets to German aircraft. Defeatist leaflets were showered on Leningrad by the thousand. The bulk of the population remained firm. Then sent by Stalin, General Zhukov arrived, instilled new spirit into the troops and re-organised them from top to bottom, thus giving birth to what was to become the 'Leningrad Front.' Leningrad was now fit to withstand new onslaughts.

And yet – what was Leningrad without the rest of Russia? If its spirit never broke, it was ultimately still due to the Russian victory at the gates of Moscow. It put new life and hope into the faint bodies of the people of Leningrad. If Moscow had not been saved, Leningrad would, sooner or later, have died of hunger.

After supper we went to see a film privately shown at the Smolny. It was a new film called *Two Soldiers*. One of the heroes was a delightfully amusing character, and not only looked the very image of the Odessa lad we had seen at the hospital that morning, but he talked in exactly the same Odessa jargon and sang an Odessa ditty which was to become one of the most popular tunes in Russia for months afterwards:

I can't speak to you for all Odessa,
For Odessa – it is very, very large. . . .

At the beginning of supper, Colonel Studyonov had received a phone call with the welcome news that flying conditions were bad, and that we could not fly back to Moscow at 5 a.m. as was originally planned. It meant at least another day in Leningrad.

Men of one of the Workers' Divisions who played so great a part in the battle for Leningrad in 1941.

German prisoners being taken along the Nevsky Prospect. The building on the right is the State Library.

16

The Last Day

That last day – for it was the last, because the weather improved, and we did fly back to Moscow early the next morning – was a day without a programme. I simply wanted to walk about Leningrad, and breathe the air of Leningrad. I had tentatively asked to be taken to Kronstadt, but Major Lozak said it was impossible, because it was an exceptionally dangerous trip, while Colonel Studyonov laughed and said 'Look at the rate his appetite is growing!' Clearly, it was asking far too much, and, as it was, my hosts had gone to infinite trouble, and had let me see more in four days than a journalist normally sees in a few months. So in a way I was glad to spend the last day simply strolling about Leningrad.

It was a cold sunny morning as we walked out of the Astoria and turned right, towards the river, as on the first day. This time we walked; the overworked driver had been given the morning off. (Later he told me that we had driven nearly 600 kilometres since we arrived.) Old memories had become much fainter than they were on my first day in Leningrad. I could see the whole thing in different perspective now. I kept thinking of the Putilov works, and the children we had seen in the yard of the old house in the Mokhovaya, and so many other things and people who were part of Leningrad of its last two years. Yet old memories kept cropping up nevertheless. As we crossed the Horse Guards

Boulevard, running east of St. Isaac's Cathedral, I remembered two things – my Uncle Peter's office in the building of the Olonetz Railway somewhere down this boulevard, and how I made a habit of dropping in to see him after school, and how he always gave me a glass of lemon tea and a biscuit, and, neglecting his work for half an hour, would talk about the new Meyerhold production at the Alexandrinka, or show me the latest copy of the art magazine *Apollo,* for which he wrote book reviews, and of which he kept a file in his otherwise prosaic-looking office. Or, at other times, he would explain to me Dostoievsky or recite bits of Baudelaire. In half an hour with Uncle Peter – that best type of old Russian intellectual – I learned more about books and art and other things that mattered than I learned at school in a month.

I had another pleasant memory of the Horse Guards Boulevard. Here, during Palm Week the Verba or Palm Week Fair was held. It was one of the gayest things I know. They sold there large bunches of *verba* or catkins – these were really the Russian version of palm branches – and all along the boulevard there was a superb display of gingerbread of a hundred varieties, the peppermint gingerbread and the white Viazma gingerbread being the most celebrated. And they sold large coloured balloons on strings – thousands of them – and other balloons which you blew up. The most famous of these was the long red balloon which made loud squeaky noises and was sold under the name of 'Mother-in-law's Tongue.' Another great favourite with the children, and with the boys who sold them, were 'American Inhabitants' – little glass devils inside a narrow glass tube filled with water and with one end sealed up with a thin sheet of rubber; when you pressed the rubber, the 'American Inhabitant' would pirouette joyfully up the tube and blow tiny bubbles. And then there were the furry little monkeys on a pin. They were made of wire with green or red fluff and with two little beady eyes, and these monkeys carried umbrellas and feather dusters and wore the strangest assortment of hats. Verba meant noise and fun, and with its puddles of melting snow it meant the end of winter – and Easter in a few days.

For a long time shall I remember that last morning in Leningrad. We walked across the Senate Square, and then along the Embankment towards the Winter Palace. It was a sunny autumn day, with a strong wind from the Baltic whipping up the dark-blue surface of the Neva, and the waves beating impatiently against the high granite banks, with their long line of deserted palaces, as though trying to wake the great city out of its trance. The grey ships on the Neva were stationary and silent, there was hardly a soul anywhere, and only high in the blue sky were four fighter planes speeding northward across the Trinity Bridge and over the needle spire of the Fortress.

How sad it all was, and yet how beautiful. There are only two other great masterpieces of urban scenery I know which, like this Embankment of the Neva near the Winter Palace, are equally impressive and moving, equally harmonious, and make you feel that you are in the presence of a great work which was somehow built by 'accident,' but at the same time seems to crystallise the genius of the nation that made it. I mean the view of Paris from the Pont des Arts, and the view of London from Westminster Bridge. Just as, during the blitz winter, the sight of London from Westminster Bridge made me clench my fists with rage and fury at the thought of what *they* were doing to London, and made me feel thankful that they had not yet succeeded in destroying St. Paul's; so in Leningrad that morning I was filled with the same feelings of rage and gratitude. What did all this mean to them, to these people who had made Berlin their capital, the most soulless and most meaningless capital in the world – 'with human slaughter as its only *raison d'être*?'

'A bit skinny,' said Major Lozak as we walked past the Winter Palace, with its blind, plywood-covered windows and its chipped grey stucco walls. 'Leningrad is like a person who is run down and has lost a lot of weight. It needs fattening up, with a lot of paint and glass and plaster. But the body is sound. Shells are not like bombs. They are much smaller, and whereas a bomb hits a building when coming down with its maximum speed, a shell usually lands with most of its impetus already exhausted.'

Then we came to the Winter Canal, with its little humped granite bridge on the Neva Embankment, and its Venice-like bridge, like the Bridge of Sighs, a little lower down, joining the Ermitage with the building opposite. Call it imitative, which it originally was; and yet this canal with its bridge like the original Bridge of Sighs, built in this northern setting, had in the course of time acquired a character entirely its own, and had become part of Russia. Pushkin – or was it only Tchaikovsky's librettist? – had made this canal the nocturnal scene of Herman's last tragic meeting with Liza; here Liza threw herself into the canal while Herman in his frenzy was flying to the gambling den to use the secret he had wrenched from the old Countess. In any case the Winter Canal has, in people's minds, become associated with Pushkin; and with Herman, that strange hero to whom a dreamlike St. Petersburg alone could have given birth – a St. Petersburg different from the completely real and harmonious city of the prologue to the *Bronze Horseman.* It is associated with the old Countess, that *Vénus Moscovite* who had known Cagliostro in the Versailles of Louis XV, and who died, her senile mind still filled with nostalgic dreams of the splendour and *volupté* of that eighteenth-century France she had known in her radiant, adventurous youth. And it was also associated with Tchaikovsky who, in the *Queen of Spades,* based on the same Pushkin story, wrote one of his greatest and most inexorably tragic pages, with the Winter Canal in moonlight as its setting.

Russia's most national poet and most national composer – for he is accepted as such whatever the Mussorgsky worshippers may say – had combined to make the Winter Canal, with its Venice-like bridge, a deeply Russian reality.

We walked down the narrow granite embankment of the Winter Canal, to the point where it runs into the winding Moika River; we crossed the bridge, and stopped before number twelve, that beautiful little late-eighteenth-century house, where Pushkin had lived, and where he died in terrible pain, three days after the fateful duel. It is a long and disgraceful story which I need not recall here – a story of court intrigue against the poet, in which his beautiful and frivolous wife, and the Tsar Nicholas, and the head of the police were all involved. From his windows on the first floor, Pushkin could look across the wide square at the Winter Palace. The quays of the Moika, with the old eighteenth- and early-nineteenth-century houses on either side – it was strange to see among them, on the other side, a beautiful Italian-like mansion, of apple-green stucco, with large rounded windows, a white lion over the door, and dancing marble figures in the niches – the quays of the Moika were as deserted as the Neva Embankment. There wasn't a soul around Pushkin's house. All the doors were closed. On the level of the first floor was a memorial marble plate saying the Pushkin had lived and died there. The large porch was also closed, but on its door was nailed a notice: 'A.R.P. The nearest Water Points are on the Moika Embankment. Opposite Houses Nos. 8, 12, 18 and 20.'

We walked on to the point where the Moika and the Catherine Canal join. It was a place of contrasts. On the left a large building had been completely destroyed by a direct hit; instead of a house there was a mountain of rubble, with iron bedsteads emerging from the brick and plaster. In how many countries have I seen these bedsteads, always the same, always the sole survivors protruding from the rubble that was once somebody's home!

On the other side stood resplendent in all its colours the Church of the Resurrection – that modern St. Basil of St. Petersburg, built on the spot where the Tsar Alexander II was assassinated in 1881. The pale-blue and red-and-gold of its onion domes and its mosaics were dazzlingly bright in the sun, and except for a small hole in the entirely golden dome – all the rest of the domes were coloured – it was completely undamaged. This great church, with all its colours reflected in the waters of the narrow canal, was the brightest patch of colour in the whole of Leningrad – unnaturally bright perhaps, yet it had become in the course of years a familiar part of the urban landscape.

Behind us, on the left, was the vast Champ de Mars, with the low granite monument to the people killed in the February Revolution, in the middle. It had been a dusty parade ground in the past; then after the Revolution it was turned into a garden, but although twenty-five years had elapsed the trees had not developed in this wind-swept spot, and it had remained the same open space as before, but covered with lawns and flowerbeds and gravel paths. The idea of making the Champ de Mars a continuation of the Summer Garden had not materialised. Now it was like one vast cabbage field, nearly half a mile long and quarter of a mile wide, right in the centre of Leningrad. But several parts were separated from the rest by barbed wire, and soldiers could be seen somewhere around the mass grave of the people killed in the Revolution. Probably they were in charge of anti-aircraft guns.

Everywhere, there were only a very few people about – outside the Summer Garden, and in the blitzed drabness of the Panteleimon Street. Some canine instinct had taken me back to the old Mokhovaya, and my companions had followed; they were mildly amused to find themselves again on this 'pilgrimage.' Now I realised more fully than the first time how serious the damage was in this blitzed area; an enormous bomb must have fallen on the six-storey building on the corner of the Panteleimon Street and the Mokhovaya – at this corner there had once been one of the finest flower shops in town. Now there was nothing but one wall dangerously standing on its edge, and high up, on the fifth floor, inside the wall, was still a wardrobe, with two overcoats and a woman's garment suspended on coat-hangers above the void. In the house opposite had been a big fruiterer's shop; the house was badly blasted, and the windows of the former fruiterer's shop were boarded up; but above them one could still faintly read the owner's name, written in the old spelling. Who, I wondered, had occupied these premises for the last twenty-five years without properly erasing the old owner's name – Sherepennikov, Fruiterer? He used to have a grand display of oranges and tangerines and pears and apples, and even pineapples and bananas. I remember once going in with my father, and the man at the cash-desk said, 'Would you like the change of your hundred roubles in notes or gold, sir?' And I was impressed by the little stream of golden five- and ten-rouble pieces that flowed on to the counter. It remained one of those more trivial childhood memories which we all have.

Except for a crowd of soldiers who were going somewhere, and a morose-looking old woman standing outside a gate, there was nobody in the Mokhovaya. We passed the old house and looked into the yard, but the children were not there. A few houses down was the former Tenishev School with its small but famous concert hall. It used to be Rachmaninov's favourite concert hall, and I remember the mad scramble for tickets there used to be whenever a Rachmaninov recital was announced. I had gone there to dozens of piano recitals, good, bad and indifferent, in those middle teens when I almost seriously thought of taking up music as a profession. The Revolution, thank heaven, killed that ambition.

What was happening in the Tenishev Hall now? It had been turned into a children's theatre, and behind the glass of the locked front door was the latest theatre bill:

The Young Spectators' Theatre

Programme for November 24th to 30th, 1941.
All the performances begin at 1.30 p.m.

The plays performed on alternate days were *Puss in Boots* and Gogol's *Revisor.* And then, after November 30th, 1941, at the height of the famine, there was nothing more. The theatre closed down. Only the old theatre bill remained to show at which point everything had stopped. But before that the shows must have gone on even after a large part of the Mokhovaya had been destroyed.

Further down the street, several more buildings had been completely destroyed by direct hits from large H.E.s; but hardly anywhere did I see any destructions caused by fire. The fire-watching in Leningrad had been almost foolproof. Only at the end of the Mokhovaya, outside the old Simeon Church built in the reign of the Empress Anna Ioannovna, and now looking in a miserably dilapidated condition – it had clearly not served as a church for many years (there were now, as somebody told me, only ten or twelve churches open in Leningrad) – did we see a crowd of people. On the steps of the church a crowd of young girls and lads, most of them wearing red ties, were doing first aid and stretcher practice.

We turned right, crossed the bridge on the Fontanka, with the great Ciniselli Circus on the right – it was now called 'Goscirque' – or State Circus – then turned into the narrow Karavannya Street and reached the Nevsky. Suddenly the whole scene changed. The great avenue was alive – as no other street of Leningrad was. There were crowds on both sides of the street and a great deal of traffic. There was no shelling that morning, and everybody was quite at ease; one just had to take a chance with the 'first one.' There were crowds of people outside several large cinemas, and crowds inside the great Eliseyev foodshop with the enormous plate-glass windows. On their ration cards they were receiving meat and tinned food, and sausage and butter and even caviare; and the cheeses and barrels of caviare and the tins – some of them American – were impressively piled up, several feet high. There was even a counter with blocks of chocolate and chocolate boxes. And people received their provisions without much waiting, and almost no queueing.

It is hard to describe the Leningrad crowd in the Nevsky that morning. As in Moscow, so in Leningrad, the crowd looks non-committal. About half the people were soldiers; but there were also many young girls, some in military uniform, others smartly dressed, with rouge and lipstick carefully applied; here and there one also came across an old lady, but most of the old ladies looked rather down-at-heel. Everybody seemed to have a quiet, business like air; there was no laughter, little loud talking or gesticulation; one felt a kind of inner solemnity in all these people – even when they were standing outside a cinema, or buying patriotic postcards and postage stamps at the two or three little open-air stalls in the Nevsky. Physically, most of the people looked fairly well and some looked very well, and I did not see any faces that looked positively ill or undernourished. But one could see a certain strain in their eyes. As distinct from Moscow, I did not see a single beggar anywhere, or even anyone looking obviously down and out.

It all made me wonder whether there wasn't some truth in the theory that hunger worked on the 'kill or cure' principle. Unfortunately, it had killed far more people than it had cured, but I had heard several people tell me that some sick people had definitely been cured of almost incurable diseases by going through the famine – particularly people with duodenal ulcers.

There were not many shops open in the Nevsky, and those that were open were not very exciting, except the little scent shop near the old Catholic church. Two girls behind the glass counter, below which was a good display of their various wares, were selling to an eager crowd of customers boxes of face-powder, eau-de-cologne, little lipsticks and bottles of scent, all made in Leningrad. 'You're from Moscow, I suppose,' said one of the girls, 'no wonder you've come here. Everybody coming from Moscow comes here first thing!'

It was an amusing moment. It was like the old capital speaking a trifle condescendingly to provincial Moscow! Leningrad had something that Moscow didn't have – a shop where scent was freely sold to anyone. The scent was in dainty little bottles with golden labels, and was called 'Boyevyie Podrugi' – a difficult phrase to translate. It does not mean 'Soldier's Sweetheart' – though that is, perhaps, the person for whom it is primarily intended; it means literally 'Women Comrades in Battle,' or perhaps 'Girlfriend in Arms' – though that sounds a little ambiguous. Anyway, it was a pleasant enough smell, though not quite on a level with Guerlain or even Coty. A small bottle cost 150 roubles, or over £3, but the Russian customers, who have little to spend their money on anyway these days, all seemed to think it very good value.

So we wandered about the Nevsky, and walked down the Catherine Canal where we crossed the beautiful little foot-bridge with its large golden-winged dragons, and down various other streets, till it was time to go back to the Astoria for dinner. After dinner the car came for us, and we drove to the now celebrated Writers' Bookshop in the Nevsky, near the Anichkov Bridge. It was enough to drive any booklover crazy with joy. Mr. Rachlin, the manager, might well, like the girl in the scent shop, have laughed at us Muscovites, but he didn't. He must have had a fairly long experience by now of people from Moscow walking away with enormous parcels and with happy grins on their faces. For two years Moscow has been very short of books, both new and second-hand, and what second-hand books do appear in the shops for a brief moment are – if of any interest – extremely expensive. Sets of the Russian classics are almost unobtainable in Moscow. Here, in the Writers' Bookshop in Leningrad, there was everything – many old books about St. Petersburg, several of which I greedily snatched up; sets of Gorki and Chekhov and Dostoievsky, and anyone one could think of; not just one set of each, but several; flimsy and rare little volumes of poetry printed in the last forty years; whole sets of historical works, and several sets of Shakespeare in Russian, and what not. Also an impressive display of new books of prose and verse newly published in Leningrad, though few of the most famous ones, such as Inber's *Pulkovo Meridian* which, as I wrote before, had sold out in two days. And the second-hand books which Dangulov and Studyonov and I bought – by the time we were finished we had five enormous parcels – were of a kind you could not buy in Moscow at all, or for which, with luck, you would have to pay three or four times as much. The manager, a lively little man who was quite a Leningrad character and a great pal of all the literary celebrities of the town, offered to show me the section of second-hand foreign books which, he said, was very remarkable, but I refused to be led into temptation, especially as the colonel kept reminding us that there was a limit to the luggage we could take on the plane. I rather regret it now.

At heart we knew what all this wealth meant; but it was no use brooding over it. These books came from the libraries of people who had been evacuated, or killed in the war, or who had died during the famine. 'You just cannot imagine the kind of books that came our way during the winter of 1941, and to some extent, ever since,' said the manager. 'First editions of Pushkin, first editions of Lermontov, some inscribed by the author, valuable French first editions, manuscripts by great writers, the very existence of which was unknown. We made a point of putting the most valuable things aside – for the State Library. The State Library is going to gain tremendously from what has happened.' He added that the other second-hand bookshops in Leningrad had pursued the same policy. Also that Leningrad was now exporting a lot of books to the whole Red Army.

We drove back to the hotel with our haul of five parcels, and then, for lack of anything better to do, we drove again to the Dramatic Theatre, where we saw an amusing American play about a dashing American reporter who eloped by mistake with a millionaire's daughter. It was called *The Road to New York*, and was a stage adaptation of the film scenario called *It Happened One Night*. It was a play full of movement, and good fun, with its detectives and gangsters, all dressed like 'real' Americans, in the brightest light-blue and purple suits. There was also the irate but fundamentally decent millionaire papa, in his nickel-tubed office on top of the skyscraper, and with half a dozen telephones on his enormous desk. The play was full of slightly 'risky' situations, with the hero and heroine sleeping in the same boarding-house room with only a curtain between them; there was also the comic landlady who claimed that the room in question had been slept in by Jack London. At the bright moments the band played the *Lambeth Walk*, and at the sentimental moments *Sonny Boy*. The Leningrad audience greatly enjoyed it all.

In the first interval, as we stood smoking on the pavement outside the theatre with a crowd of officers and sailors, I had my last sight of Leningrad in daylight – the battered buildings and almost deserted quay on the other side of the Fontanka river.

After supper, Likharev said goodbye, while the others went and had a few hours' sleep. I stayed up, trying to sort out my notes and thoughts. I had seen something that was very great, very moving and very tragic. I had seen human greatness before. I had seen it in Spain, and in the London blitz; I had seen it in that grim Arctic convoy that brought me to Russia in May 1942; I had seen the generals and the men who had won the battle of Stalingrad; I had seen Russian peasant girls in the devastated country round Voronezh tilling their fields again, with nothing more than shovels to work with; but the greatness of Leningrad had a quality of its own. It was hard to define; words like 'solidarity' or 'patriotism' or 'self-sacrifice' or 'spirit of defence' are only words; I felt that the spirit of Leningrad was a blend of all these, and of much else besides. I decided right then that only a detailed account of all I had seen could, by the cumulative effect of all the details, explain the substance of the Leningrad epic. Five days are not much to spend in a city; nor had I seen as many people as I might have seen in more normal circumstances, and in a place which was not a military zone, and where my movements would not have been limited by military rules. Yet I had every reason to be grateful and no cause for complaint. Moreover I had never felt lost; I knew Leningrad; it was, after all, my native city, though I often found it difficult to think of it in those terms. It meant to me both less and more. Finally, I had had over two years' experience of the war in Russia; I could compare, and could observe things with reference to that experience.

We said a fond goodbye to Anna Andreievna, and left at three in the morning. Through the complete blackout we drove to some airfield, a long way out of town. The streets were empty and silent. Major Lozak, sitting next to the driver, kept humming *Sonny Boy* and tunes from *The Princess of the Circus.* It was very chilly when we arrived at the airfield. We had an hour to wait, and rather than wait in the car, Major Lozak took us to a wooden building among the pine trees, and knocked on the door for some time. An elderly woman, looking very sleepy, finally opened the door, and thereupon led us in with a show of genuine cordiality. It was the officers' club. She made us hot tea, and Studyonov and Lozak played a game of billiards, while Dangulov and I played a less strenuous game of draughts. I was tired and lost every time.

At last we were called out, and a few minutes later the plane took off.

A sort of physical and nervous exhaustion then came over me. Once or twice I imagined that we were crashing and I started up with a feeling of acute fear. But it was nothing. The sun had risen, and below us were miles of dark-green forests, with the yellow fluffy patches of the birch trees among them, and I fell back into a restless slumber. This time we were flying non-stop to Moscow. Even before the usual breakfast time, I was back in my room at the Metropole.

17

Leningrad's Liberation: The Second Visit

After that I continued to watch the rather scanty news from Leningrad in the Russian press with even more than the usual eagerness. Immense events were occurring in the south. The Red Army was overrunning the Ukraine and pushing the Germans beyond the Dnieper. Melitopol was captured, and Zaporozh, and Dniepropetrovsk, and finally Kiev, and there seemed no limit to the Russian advance. The Moscow Conference was an enormous success; and later came the conference at Teheran. But still there was little news from Leningrad or the Leningrad front.

Then, one day in December, while I was on a short visit to Egypt, I saw in a local paper, dated December 7th:

Significant Declaration

Referring to the Leningrad sector, yesterday's Soviet communiqué made the following significant declaration:

'German and Finnish barbarians are destroying the habitations and non-military objectives in Leningrad.

'The artillery of the German and Finnish invaders placed at the approaches to Leningrad has during many months been systematically destroying the habitations in the city.

'During the past three weeks the shelling has been considerably increased. There are no military objectives in Leningrad at present.

'The Finnish and German Governments think that if Finnish and German troops destroy Leningrad, the question of Leningrad's security will not arise for the Soviet Union.

'The German and Finnish invaders have, however, undoubtedly committed a grave mistake. The Soviet people and the Red Army have sufficient strength to defend Leningrad, to guarantee the future safety of the city, and to force the German and Finnish invaders to bear full responsibility for the crimes committed.'

It sounded very grim, especially in the light of what I read a few days later:

Rocket Shells on Leningrad

Stockholm, Sunday. – The *Svenska Dagbladet* today quotes travellers from Berlin as saying that the Germans recently used a new secret weapon to bombard Leningrad. They were unable to give details but said the weapon might be the rocket shell gun with which the Germans are now said to be experimenting.

A few days later still, a New York message told a lurid and, to all appearances, improbable story of a German rocket shell weighing fifteen tons, and with a range of 150 kilometres – not quite far enough to reach London. It added, however, that the Germans had already been using it against Leningrad.

Actually, this secret weapon story turned out to be just as unfounded as the numerous other secret weapon stories that Nazi propagandists had been hawking about the various neutral and semi-neutral capitals. I returned to Moscow at the beginning of January, and what I discovered from several people who had just come from Leningrad was this. It was quite true that Leningrad had been having, and was still having, a very difficult time. During the last two months shelling had increased in intensity, larger shells – including some 16-inch shells – were being used, and now shelling was going on not only during daytime as before but also during the night, with the result that physical and nervous strain on the people of Leningrad was correspondingly greater. On some days the Germans concentrated on the city with particular fury – those were the days when Hitler had received a great licking somewhere else. He was taking it out of Leningrad. Every great Russian victory in the Ukraine, or say the sinking of the *Scharnhorst,* was followed in Leningrad by a day of intensive shelling.

But then, when to the outside world the outlook in Leningrad seemed grimmer than it had been for a long time, the hour of revenge suddenly struck. Soldiers in Leningrad itself had known for some time that it was coming, but no one outside (except the Supreme Command) knew it – least of all the Germans. They, on the contrary, had been preparing to strike a blow at that very Oranienbaum bridgehead from which the Russians launched the attack on January 14th. The German plan was not only to eliminate this bridgehead, but perhaps even, ice conditions permitting, to strike at Kronstadt and perhaps at Leningrad itself across the ice of the Gulf of Finland. As General Gvozdkov declared some time later, two S.S. divisions, the Nordland and Niederland, had been concentrated against the Oranienbaum bridgehead shortly before the Russians attacked from there towards the east and south-east, thus forestalling the German attack. One of the most amazing episodes in this war is how the Russians managed to concentrate sufficiently large forces on the extremely precarious Oranienbaum bridgehead, to launch from there the attack which was to play such a decisive part in the liberation of Leningrad.

One of the disturbing factors in this winter of 1943–4 was the weather. There was very little snow, and throughout December the temperature had hovered round freezing point. Even in Leningrad, days of hard frost had been few – and January was no better. There was only a thin and uncontinuous crust of ice on the Gulf of Finland – just sufficient to allow infantry to walk carefully across it from Kronstadt and places on the north side of the Gulf. As for heavy equipment, there could be no question of taking it across the ice. Ships took guns, tanks and ammunition to Oranienbaum with the help of ice-breakers when necessary, and all this was done during the night under the very noses of the Germans and their Peterhof and Strelna batteries, which were busy at that time shelling Leningrad. Not a single Russian was lost in this extraordinary operation.

Oranienbaum struck out on the 14th. Leningrad struck out next morning – and how! One of the biggest artillery barrages of this war was set loose against the German positions at Ligovo, right on Leningrad's south-west doorstep, and on a hill called Finskoye Koirovo, slightly west of Pulkovo. These two areas were what the Germans called 'Leningrad's padlock.' Both represented a continuous labyrinth of trenches interlarded with minefields and barbed wire, the latter constituting, moreover, a complicated mechanism of booby-traps. To cut the wire was as dangerous as not to cut it. The trenches and underground passages connected hundreds of concrete pillboxes or, rather, 'wells,' from which in almost complete safety the Germans could use almost any kind of gun and machine gun. The barrage was intended to 'plough up' these two fortified zones which the Germans considered impregnable. Smashing the concrete wells with either bombing or shelling was almost impossible. There were only two solutions, since frontal attack was necessary and encirclement was impossible – so solid were these German defence lines. One was to 'drive the Germans crazy' inside the wells, with the intensity of the barrage demolishing everything around them. But that took time. The other was to attack the wells individually. Men had to be found who, after some hours of general shelling, would undertake the almost suicidal job of crawling up to the wells and hurling hand grenades into them. And such was the frenzy of Leningrad troops to finish with the blockade and the shelling once and for all that several of the wells were put out of action in precisely this way. That morning of January 15th was the most exciting moment in Leningrad's life. The whole city shook with excitement and anticipation and the barrage of one thousand guns. These were front-line guns – just like those near the Putilov works I had seen that morning in September and smaller field guns still nearer the front line, and the powerful naval guns firing from the warships on the Neva right in the centre of Leningrad. And the same thought was in everybody's mind: 'No, they must not, they cannot fail this time.'

It was a damp muggy day that 15th of January, and it wasn't until midday that the weather somewhat cleared up. It was then that hundreds of Russian planes roared over the city from airfields in the north to drop their bomb-loads on the Germans.

For about two days this battle went on. There were moments, as a young officer who had taken part in it later told me, when even the bravest were beginning to wonder and the troops were showing signs of nervousness. After the barrage had ploughed up everything around the German pillboxes, and guns had specially blasted passages in the minefields for the Russian tanks, the tanks went forward followed by infantry. 'What, across the minefields?' I asked. 'Yes,' said the officer, 'the shells had ploughed up the terrain to such an extent that most of the mines had been buried deep underground or blown up. Of course, it was very dangerous, nevertheless. However, once we captured Ligovo and Finskoye Koirovo and the road was relatively clear to Krasnoye Selo, things became easier. From now on frontal attacks on this scale were no longer necessary. We could apply our well-tested envelopment tactics, and it was by envelopment that we liberated Pushkino and Krasnoye and Gatchina. The Germans, seized with panic at the thought of what had happened to their pals in the Ligovo–Strelna salient (the fierceness of the fighting was such that we didn't take many prisoners), pulled out as fast as they could. Our job was to pursue them, and I will bet you that not very many of Hitler's Leningrad troops got away to the Estonian border.'

It was on January 19th, five days after the launching of the Oranienbaum offensive and four days after the 'great Leningrad barrage,' that the two armies joined at Ropsha – a place until then known in history only for the assassination there of Catherine's husband, the Prussomaniac and dipsomaniac Tsar Peter the Third.

With the breaking of the 'padlock' the whole German chain of fortifications crumbled. One by one Pushkino (Tsarskoye Selo), Pavlovsk, Mga in the east and Gatchina in the south fell. Further east still Novgorod had been taken by troops of the Volkhov front. By February 14th practically the whole of Leningrad Province had been cleared of the Germans – except for probably 60,000 or 75,000 new German corpses left behind in the last month.

How many hundred thousand dead the senseless Leningrad adventure cost Germany since 1941 we shall perhaps never know. On February 14th the Russians had already recaptured Luga and the whole east bank of Lake Peipus. There were not many German prisoners who boasted they would ever come near Leningrad again. Meantime in the north the Finns were shaking in their shoes, especially since the big Russian air raid of February 6th on Helsinki. They would now have to pay for the 'glorious adventure' of having been Hitler's accomplices for so many years.

I revisited Leningrad at the beginning of February. Externally it had changed less than I had feared after reading all those 'secret weapon' stories in the Cairo papers. People were happy and, though physically tired, full of energy and plans for the future. 200 soldiers were helping in the rebuilding of the Mariinsky Theatre, which had been shattered by a half-ton bomb back in 1941, and by shells since that – the Mariinsky Theatre where Pavlova and Nijinsky had danced and Chaliapin sung. Soldiers – yes, because there weren't enough civilians available for this kind of work. Baranov, the chief architect of Leningrad's Town Council, remarked, 'It shouldn't take more than two – perhaps three – years fully to restore Leningrad. But it's a question of labour. How soon will the war end? How many demobilised soldiers will be available for municipal reconstruction work? Anyway, it's part of the general economic reconstruction of the country. We shall need glass for millions of windows, and several train-loads of plate glass for the Winter Palace alone.'

And the reconstruction of Leningrad is nothing compared with that of other towns in the Soviet Union which have been almost or completely obliterated. One of the most tragic sights of all is the country round Leningrad. The city now stands in the middle of a desert. There is nothing left of thousands of country houses round Leningrad; Peterhof is wiped out, and little more than a heap of ruins is left of Tsarskoye Selo, Pavlovsk and Gatchina. Of all the neighbourhood of Leningrad, the historically uninteresting and artistically non-existent north-east is more or less intact. But the famous Imperial Palaces and their beautiful parks – all those towns where every inch of ground is full of historical and literary associations – have practically disappeared.

I was with several other correspondents on this second trip to Leningrad, and I inevitably saw less and talked less. We went there by train. After following the Moscow–Leningrad main line it branched off somewhere to the east, and later we crossed the Volkhov and passed through Schlusselburg. It took thirty-six hours to reach Leningrad, but shortly the direct line will be restored and the famous Red Arrow express will run again between the two capitals. By the way, speaking of capitals, there were many Leningraders who believed that shortly Leningrad would be made the capital of the R.S.F.S.R., that is, Russia proper, as distinct from Moscow, which would remain the capital of the Soviet Union as a whole. Though I didn't see very much of Leningrad on this second visit, I spent two days in the wasteland around it – in those places which in September I'd only been able to see from that observation tower near the Narva Gate. Snow had fallen since the great battles of January, and had modestly covered up the earth. Even with the snow covering it the terrain was irregular – ploughed up by that fantastic Russian barrage. And here and there a leg or a head was still protruding from under the snow. All around Ligovo and Pulkovo, where the main battle had been fought, there was nothing but a strange white lunar landscape with a few fantastically shaped fragments of brick walls standing (I identified one of them as Ligovo station). But already the trains were running among the ruins, running westwards towards Estonia. Here and there also a tree stood raising its bare shattered arms helplessly into the winter sky. Such was the immediate neighbourhood of Leningrad. Verdun – worse than Verdun after the last war. At Strelna, among what had once been cosy-looking little country houses (many of these were still standing, for there hadn't been much shelling here) stood monstrous German siege guns inside concrete blockhouses eight inches thick. The Germans had certainly put in a lot of time and trouble to shell Leningrad. Beyond that was Peterhof with the pathetic remains of the great Rastrelli Palace, and a canal denuded of all its statues and fountains to show where the centre of Peterhof had been. The town of Peterhof had disappeared with the exception of a shattered church and a few other buildings. Tragic in a different way were the numerous villages, with their high-gabled huts, in the snowy plain between Peterhof and Tsarskoye Selo and Gatchina. They looked normal and intact. Yet there wasn't a soul to be seen anywhere. Everybody had been driven away into the rear by the Germans. Gatchina was the first place where 'native' population could be found – a couple of thousand people who had lived through two and a half years of the usual Nazi terror – with the concentration camp, still with barbed wire round it, occupying one of the main buildings of the town. From Gatchina the Germans had left in a great hurry. Mr. Glinka, who was curator of Gatchina Palace – that beautiful Palace, with its English landscape garden, built by Catherine for her favourite Gregory Orlov and later the summer residence of Tsar Paul the First – told me how he arrived at Gatchina four hours after the Germans had been driven out. Firing was still going on at the aerodrome, where the remaining Germans were being finished off, German bodies were being piled up outside the Palace gates, half-demented local inhabitants were rushing around telling soldiers what they'd lived through, and great clouds of black smoke were rising from the Palace. In their fury the Huns had set fire to it before leaving. Fury – yes. But not only fury. There was method in all this destruction.

'Why?' Glinka said, 'Why, I ask you. Wasn't it enough to have looted the Palace of all its art treasures? Wasn't it enough to have its top floor turned into an officers' brothel?' And he added sadly that this was probably his last trip to Gatchina. The architects, he said, could no doubt patch up the solidly built Palace, but for the curator of its art treasures there was nothing more to do.

The quiet charm of Pavlovsk and the splendour of Tsarskoye Selo, with its beautiful baroque Palace built for Catherine by Rastrelli and the classical colonnade built by Cameron, the Scottish architect, and all the rest of that wonderful ensemble of eighteenth-century art – all was now in ruins. True, part of the Catherine Palace had escaped complete destruction. That was only because some German sappers had been caught and had been ordered to remove immediately eleven delayed-action mines they had placed under the Palace. However, everything inside had been looted. Pavlovsk Palace had been set on fire the day the Germans left. Most of the trees in those poetic parks of Tsarskoye and Pavlovsk which had been sung by Catherine's Poet Laureate, the great Derzhavin, by the young Pushkin and much later by Innokenti Annensky, the great symbolist poet, who was headmaster of Tsarskoye Selo high school and who in 1909 collapsed and died while wandering through the park – most of the trees had been cut down by the Germans. Most of this damage will never be repaired. The destruction of these palaces and parks has aroused among the Russians as great a fury as the worst German atrocities against human beings. Many people in Leningrad have told me: 'People who deliberately destroy works of art have no right to own any. They cannot have any real love of art. Why, then, should the Huns own the European art treasures of Dresden, Munich, and Berlin? The least thing we can expect is that as compensation our people receive the contents of some of the German art galleries. We shall rebuild the walls of our palaces. Perhaps it is the most we can do. But at least we shall have something valuable to put into them.'

I did not mean to touch on wider political issues in this book, which deals simply with a great human story. But I should like to say just this. When I see all the destruction that has been caused by this war in Russia and try to imagine the immense work of reconstruction lying ahead and all the labour that will be required to carry out this reconstruction – not to mention the equally great task of completing the pre-war plans of economic prosperity – when I see and imagine all this, I find it hard to take much notice of any talk about 'Russian Imperialism.' Clearly what Russia requires is many years of peace and security, without which there can be no real reconstruction and no real prosperity. Whether we like it or not Russia will insist on obtaining the maximum security even though in the process there may be moments of unpleasantness between her Allies and herself.

One of Russia's postwar aims is to have once again a secure and prosperous Leningrad – that one and only European capital outside London which never suffered the indignity of enemy occupation. Had Leningrad been occupied by the Germans it would have shared the fate of Tsarskoye Selo and Peterhof. The danger was immense and the price of averting it terrible. Today the people of Leningrad feel that a secure and prosperous future is something to which they are entitled. And not only they but still more so the children of those who were killed in battle or died in the Leningrad famine.

Notes

Introduction

1. Alexander Werth, *Russia at War, 1941–1945* (London, Barrie & Rockliff, 1964).
2. Alexander Werth, *The Last Days of Paris: A Journalist's Diary* (London, Hamish Hamilton, 1940).
3. For the Nazi genocidal strategies concerning Leningrad mentioned by Werth in *Russia at War*, cf. the recent work of David Glantz, *The Battle for Leningrad, 1941–1944* (Lawrence, KS, University of Kansas Press, 2002) and of Jorg Ganzenmüller, *Das belagerte Leningrad, 1941–1944: Die Stadt in den Strategien von Angreifern und Verteidigern* (Paderborn, Ferdinand Schöningh, 2005).
4. Among the most ground-breaking studies must be included: John Barber and Andreï Dzeniskevitch (eds), *Life and Death in Besieged Leningrad, 1941–44* (Basingstoke, Palgrave, 2005); Andreï Dzeniskevitch (ed.), *Leningrad v osade: Sbornik dokumentov* (*Leningrad Under Siege*) (St Petersburg, 2006); Nikita Lomagin, *Neizvestnaïa Blokada* (*The Unknown Blockade*), 2 vols (St Petersburg/Moscow, Neva/Olma-Press, 2002); Michael Jones, *Leningrad: State of Siege* (New York, Basic Books, 2008); Svetlana Magayeva and Albert Pleysier, *Surviving the Blockade of Leningrad* (Lanham, MD, University Press of America, 2006); Marina Loskutova (ed.), *Pamiat o blockade: Svidetelstva ochevidtsev i istoricheskoie soznanie obscestva* (*Memory of the Siege: Survivors' Testimony and the Historical Conscience of Society*) (Moscow, Novoie Izdatelstvo, 2006), as well as Richard Bidlack's article, 'Survival Strategies in Leningrad during the First Year of the Soviet–German War', in Robert W. Thurston and Bernd Bonwetsch (eds), *The People's War: Responses to World War II in the Soviet Union* (Urbana, IL, University of Illinois Press, 2000).

5. For a discussion of estimates, cf. the pioneering work of Harrison Salisbury, which, since its publication in 1969, has become a classic on the siege of Leningrad, *The 900 Days: The Siege of Leningrad* (New York, Harper and Row, 1969).
6. Cf. Nadezhda Cherepenina's articles, and those by Svetlana Magaeva and Andreï Dzeniskevitch, in Barber and Dzeniskevitch, *Life and Death.*
7. Cf. Maria Vassilievna Machkova, *V pamiat uchedchix I vo slavu jivuschix* (*In Remembrance of the Dead and to the Glory of the Living*) (St. Petersburg, Rossiiskaia Natsional'naia Biblioteka, 1995), p. 86, and the remarkable selection of diary entries collected by Ales Adamovich and Daniil Granin, *Blokadnaia kniga* (*Book of the Blockade*) (Leningrad, 1984). Finally, two personal journals have been translated into English: Elena Skriabina, *A Leningrad Diary: Survival during World War II* (Edison, NJ, Transaction Publishers, 2000); and Elena Kochina, *Blockade Diary* (Ann Arbor, MI, Ardis, 1990).
8. An expression coined by the Russian historian Elena Osokina, author of a pioneering study of these issues: *Lerarkhia potreblenia* (*The Hierarchy of Consumption*) (Moscow, 2004).
9. Bidlack, 'Survival Strategies'.
10. Salisbury, *The 900 Days.*
11. Lomagin, *Neizvestnaia Blokada* (*The Unknown Blockade*).
12. 9 January 1905 according to the Julian calendar used in Tsarist Russia; 22 January by the Gregorian calendar used in Europe and, from January 1918, in the USSR.
13. Werth, *Russia at War.*
14. Cf. for instance, the work of Andreï Dzeniskevitch, including *Leningrad v osade* (*Leningrad Under Siege*), and specifically his article 'The Social and Political Situation in Leningrad in the First Months of the German Invasion: The Social Psychology of the Workers', in Thurston and Bonwetsch, *The People's War.*

Chapter 3 St. Petersburg – Leningrad

1. By a decree in January 1944, many of the old street names were restored, among them Nevsky, Liteiny, Sadovaya.
2. Actually some of the greatest of Leningrad's buildings were built by pure Russians like Voronikhin, who built the Kazan Cathedral, and Zakharov, who built the Admiralty. Russian art-lovers also emphasise that the great Rastrelli, builder of the Winter Palace, Peterhof Palace and Catherine Palace in Tsarskoye Selo, arrived in Russia as a child of eight.